S0-DSO-424

MENTAL DISORDERS IN URBAN AREAS

RC
445
I 28
F3
1965

MENTAL DISORDERS IN URBAN AREAS

an ecological study of schizophrenia
and other psychoses

copy 1

ROBERT E. L. FARIS
H. WARREN DUNHAM

PHOENIX BOOKS

THE UNIVERSITY OF CHICAGO PRESS

CHICAGO / LONDON

Library of Congress Catalog Card Number: 65–16168

The University of Chicago Press, Chicago & London
The University of Toronto Press, Toronto 5, Canada

© *1939, 1967 by Robert E. L. Faris and H. Warren Dunham. All rights reserved. Published 1939. First Phoenix Edition 1965. Second Impression 1967. Printed in the United States of America*

FOREWORD

The data presented in this book, no matter what interpretation may eventually be given to them, constitute a valuable addition to, and afford a new method of approach in, the study of mental illness. That the environmental setting is an important factor in the etiology of these illnesses has long been recognized; the facts here recorded emphasize the importance and establish for it a statistical validity.

The comments of the authors as to the meaning of their findings are wisely conservative and serve to establish only the complexity of the problem. At first glance it appears as if the significant difference in areal distribution between manic-depressive and schizophrenic psychoses provides confirmation for their clinical separation and suggests that they are different entities. Before accepting this conclusion, however, it is essential to realize that the classification of mental illness at present in use is one of temporary convenience. It is not founded on any unitary criteria. Subdivisions are made according to such varying features as pathologic deviations of structure and the form of the symptoms presented by the patient. While it is sometimes true that symptoms are the direct outcome of structural pathologic conditions, this is by no means always true; many so-called symptoms are descriptive only of the behavior of the patient, and as such depend profoundly on his physiologic constitution, training, experience, and the situations in which he happens to be placed. This is particularly true of the forms of psychosis labeled "schizophrenic" and "manic-depressive."

Viewed from this angle, then, it may well be that the

differences in areal distribution established as prevailing between these psychoses do not depend on differences in the
nature of the illness underlying the psychoses but on differences in personality of the patients who are ill. Such a
view is even suggested by the fact of the areal grouping.
That there are regional differences in the distribution of the
various subgroups of schizophrenic disorders is open to a
similar interpretation. Before it will be possible really to
evaluate the findings reported in this book, it is essential that
the clinician discover some basis for a valid classification of
mental illness.

These comments do not detract from the value of the
study reported; the data presented may even have value in
suggesting lines of cleavage that will point the way to clinical classification. I am glad to have this opportunity to ex-
press my appreciation of the work done and welcome the
advent of the application of the techniques of the sociologist
to the study of mental illness.

H. Douglas Singer, M.D.
Director, Illinois State Psychopathic Institute

INTRODUCTION

This work, *Mental Disorders in Urban Areas*, by Robert E. L. Faris and H. Warren Dunham is a pioneer study in the social aspects of mental disorder. The factual findings are new and many of them are unexpected. They constitute a significant contribution to our knowledge of the mental life of human beings in the large city.

In appraising the contribution of the authors it is important to distinguish between factual findings and interpretations of these findings. This is particularly important in the case of this study, which falls in the borderland between medicine and sociology. As a study in a field between these two disciplines it runs the risk of having unwarranted claims made for it by some readers and all-too-sweeping criticisms by others. The discerning reader will, however, discriminate between the facts presented and the interpretations of those facts. He will, I believe, recognize the value of the factual data as important additions to our knowledge of mental disorder. Those who question the adequacy of the theoretical explanation of the writers may make their own interpretations of the facts in terms congenial to their favorite conceptual systems.

A brief summary of the facts discovered by the authors indicates how definitely and unmistakably the incidence of the chief psychoses are related to the organization of the city.

1. Cases of mental disorders, as plotted by residences of patients previous to admission to public and private hospitals, show a regular decrease from the center to the periph-

ery of the city, a pattern of distribution previously shown for such other kinds of social and economic phenomena as poverty, unemployment, juvenile delinquency, adult crime, suicide, family desertion, infant mortality, communicable disease, and general mortality.

2. Each of the chief types of mental disorder has a characteristic distribution with reference to the differentiated areas found within the large modern city. Each of the following psychoses has its highest rate of incidence in the indicated type of local community: (a) paranoid schizophrenia in the rooming-house districts of the city; (b) catatonic schizophrenia in the neighborhoods of first immigrant settlement which have a high proportion of their population foreign-born or Negro who are the most recent newcomers to the city; (c) manic-depressive psychoses in areas with higher rentals; (d) alcoholic psychoses in rooming-house and in certain immigrant areas; (e) dementia paralytica in lodging and rooming-house districts and Negro communities; (f) senile psychoses and arteriosclerosis in districts with the lowest percentages of home-owners.

3. There is a high degree of association between different types of psychoses as distributed in different urban areas and certain community conditions, as follows: paranoid schizophrenia with percentage of hotel residents and lodgers; catatonic schizophrenia with percentage of foreign-born and Negroes; manic-depressive psychoses with median monthly rentals; alcoholic psychoses with per cent of population on relief; dementia paralytica with distribution of vice resorts and with venereal-disease rates; senile psychoses with percentage of home-ownership; senile psychoses combined with arteriosclerosis with percentage of population on relief and with per cent of population of native-white parentage.

The association of these different types of psychoses with specific types of communities is a discovery of outstanding significance and the authors might well have been content to establish these correlations and to leave their interpretation to further research.

But with the enthusiasm and courage of pioneers in a new field they have proceeded farther and formulated a theoretical explanation for their findings. Particularly with stress upon the concentration of paranoid schizophrenia in rooming-house areas, they suggest the consideration of the hypothesis that communication is essential for normal mental development and that social isolation makes for mental breakdown.

The authors set forth this explanation as a hypothesis rather than as a generalization established by the study. It is a theoretical position congenial to the sociological student and consistent with a great body of sociological theory.

This hypothesis should, however, be confronted with the entire range of facts now available in the field of mental disorder and be orientated within the group of hypotheses suggested by other theoretical viewpoints. Among the chief facts relative to mental disorder that should be taken into consideration by theories and hypotheses are the following:

1. Certain mental disorders are obviously organic in etiology, as dementia paralytica and alcoholic and senile psychoses. Others, in which an organic origin has not been definitely established, have been called functional, of which the schizophrenic and manic-depressive psychoses are the chief types.

2. Nearly all types of psychoses, whether organic or functional, and especially those involving prolonged mental derangement, manifest more or less mental deterioration. The

manic-depressive psychoses, however, are supposed to be followed characteristically by no deterioration.

3. Mental disorders, as reported by Myerson and others, recur in certain families in the same and/or successive generations, but apparently not always with the same type of psychosis.[1]

4. Behavior in the psychoses is generally of a pattern more or less consistent with prepsychotic behavior.

5. Not all chronic alcoholics develop alcoholic psychoses, nor do all syphilitics develop dementia paralytica.

6. Mental disorders appear to be more prevalent where the population is mobile and heterogeneous than where it is stable and homogeneous and where life-conditions are complex and precarious rather than simple and secure.

7. The financial depression beginning in 1929 was accompanied by little or no increase in mental disorders.

8. Insanity rates for different psychoses vary by race, by nationality, by socioeconomic class, and by occupation.

Not all the foregoing facts are conclusively established, but they represent certain points on which there is more or less general consensus. They constitute, therefore, some of our concrete knowledge about mental disorders which must be taken into account in the formulation of a general theory of mental disorder.

The hypotheses which seek to explain behavior in mental disorder may perhaps be classified under three general heads: (1) constitutional, (2) psychological, and (3) sociological.

1. The constitutional descriptions and explanations of mental disorder proceed from hypotheses of the differences,

---

[1] See Abraham Myerson, *The Inheritance of Mental Disease* (Baltimore, 1925).

in comparison with the average, of neural structure, processes, and integrations as basic causative factors. The cause of mental disorders is attributed to congenital or acquired deficiency or disturbance in the neural constitution of the individual.

2. Psychological descriptions and explanations of mental disorder are in terms of hypotheses of psychogenetic disturbances of mental functioning. It is assumed from this standpoint that disturbances in emotional and mental development—i.e., frustrations, regressions, and fixations—are causative factors in mental breakdown.

3. The sociological description and explanation of mental disorders may be concerned with hypotheses upon the role of communication in mental life and upon the effect of isolation upon mental breakdown. This is only one of several sociological explanations that might be formulated. It is the theory, however, that is elaborated by the writers of this study.[2] Mental disorder is interpreted as a phase of personal disorganization arising out of maladjustment in the social relations of the person.

It is at once apparent that the psychological and sociological theories offer no direct explanation of alcoholic psychoses, dementia paralytica, and other organic types of mental disorder. At most, mental and social factors are important only indirectly, as in influencing the formation of habits of alcoholism or in conditioning attitudes and conduct leading to syphilitic infection. Besides indirectly explaining genesis by habits and attitudes, the sociological factors may also be brought into play to explain the evaluations of the person or the group or community of the conduct involved

[2] Cf. chaps. x and xi.

and the corresponding attitudes toward the patient and his role in the community.

The crucial types of mental disorder from the standpoint of theoretical explanation are the so-called "functional" psychoses, i.e., schizophrenia and manic-depressive psychoses. It must be borne in mind that these psychoses may be functional only in the sense that no specific and definite organic basis for them has been established.

There is no doubt that there are both psychogenetic and sociogenetic disturbances in the life-history of persons who later develop a "functional" mental disorder. The crucial question is, however, whether these mental and social disturbances are causal in the mental derangement or only symptomatic of underlying constitutional tendencies. Is the seclusiveness of the precatatonic which appears very early in his life-history a result of the isolation imposed on him in the family circle, or a psychogenetic trait conditioned by an arrest or a regression of the ego in its development leading to isolation, or is it a concomitant of a specific constitutional condition?

Our knowledge at present gives no final answer to this question. Theoretically any one of the three explanations, or some combination of them in varying degrees of significance, may ultimately turn out to be the most satisfactory. The whole evidence is not in. The crucial questions and hypotheses still await the acid test of research.

To many students of mental disorder the recent methods of inducing shock in schizophrenic patients by means of insulin and metrazol give presumptive evidence of the priority in causation to organic factors. At the same time, however, it may be quite possible that a phenomenon may be induced socially and removed organically and vice versa.

The specific relationship between the chemical therapy and the course of the "disease" is as yet too little known. It may even be that they work in the form of shock and that psychological and social equivalents for the chemical "shock" may be found.

This recognition of the greater weight of constitutional factors does not mean the minimizing of the significance of mental and social factors in causation. Even if they play less direct roles, they may nevertheless be essential.

In line with these assumptions the following tentative harmonization of constitutional, psychological, and sociological explanations is offered to take account of the facts as outlined above.

1. A constitutional basis is an essential condition for a "functional" as well as for an organic mental disorder. An organic change as a result either of chemical treatment or of physiological processes is necessary for improvement of the mental condition of the patient. But mental states of anxiety, guilt, and inferiority may exert an effect upon organic processes, and these mental states may in turn be attributed to existing social factors.

2. The particular psychogenetic type of personality determines not the etiology but the symptoms of mental disorder. The classical Kraepelinian description of psychoses is now regarded by many psychiatrists as a classification of complexes of symptoms and not of specific disease entities. It is possible, though not certain, that certain psychogenetic types may be more predisposed to mental breakdown than others.

A distinction needs to be made between neurotics and prepsychotics who later develop psychoses. Persons with neurotic tendencies may become drug addicts, chronic alcoholics, habitual and excessive gamblers, sexual deviates including homosexuals, pathological liars and swindlers, criminals of the compulsive neurosis type, or psychic invalids, but apparently they do not generally become psychotic.

The precatatonic, preparanoid, and premanic-depressive are perhaps variants on a constitutional basis of distinct psychogenetic types widely represented in the general population.

3. Social conditions, while not primary in causation, may be underlying predisposing and precipitating factors. Situations involving stress and strain of adjustment—such as those of isolation, of migration, of love and marriage, and of frustration in a career may, in the cases of persons constitutionally predisposed, make for mental conflict and mental breakdown.

Any attempted integration of the interplay of constitutional, psychological, and sociological factors in mental disorder should be constantly revised to take account of new findings of research. But at any moment such a systematic general theory may be of assistance in utilizing the findings of the different life-sciences both in research and in treatment. Particularly in the study of prepsychotic cases and in the experiments in the prevention of mental disorders, psychological or sociological aspects of mental disorder may be of great importance. For example, there are not as yet, and may never be, organic tests adequate for identifying prepsychotic individuals, but it may perhaps be feasible to make an accurate description of the psychological types of prepsychotics and of specific precipitating social situations leading to breakdown. On the basis of such descriptions social experiments in the prevention of mental breakdown might be undertaken. If social conditions are actually precipitating factors in causation, control of conditions making for stress and strain in industry and society will become a chief objective of a constructive program of mental hygiene.

In such a program of prevention of mental disorders the findings of this study would be of great assistance. For they indicate not only the local communities with the highest rates of mental disorder but also those psychoses which are prevalent in each type of urban neighborhood. Local community programs of mental hygiene can accordingly be directed to dealing with the indirect and precipitating causes of specific types of psychoses, i.e., syphilis, as in the case of dementia paralytica, or lack of social contacts as with the young precatatonic.

The study by Faris and Dunham makes a contribution not only to our understanding of mental disorder but also to our knowledge of the interrelations of personality types and social organization under conditions of modern city life.

Previous urban studies have demonstrated a dynamic association between the spatial pattern of the city and its moral or social order.[3] They define and describe the city as an entity constituted by the interrelations and integration of its component communities, each of which (1) occupies a territorial area, (2) possesses a specialized function, (3) selects a population with characteristic composition by age, sex, occupation, economic class, and nationality and racial stock, and (4) develops a typical cultural and political order. These earlier studies have also shown that marked differences exist in the various types of local communities of the

[3] R. E. Park, "The Spatial Pattern and the Moral Order," *The City* (Chicago, 1925), chap. i.

city in general intelligence,[4] educational status,[5] and social distinction,[6] as well as in the incidence of social problems.

The present study is the first, however, to indicate a striking relationship between community life and mental life. It shows that urban areas characterized by high rates of social disorganization are also those with high rates of mental disorganization. It demonstrates, further, that specific types of psychoses are concentrated in certain types of local communities.

These findings stimulate many interesting speculations. Only two of these will be briefly developed here.

The first one proceeds from the assumption that the syndromes of symptoms that underlie Kraepelin's classifications of mental disorders are not disease entities. The assumption is rather that these symptoms describe the psychogenetic type of personality of the individual who experiences a mental breakdown. If this be the case, then it may be further assumed that in certain of the functional psychoses the incidence of specific mental disorders may be taken as an index of the distribution in the city of its associated psychogenetic type of personality. It may then turn out that human beings in a large city tend to be segregated according to personality types. This hypothesis becomes then a subject for further study.

[4] R. L. Jenkins and A. W. Brown, "The Geographical Distribution of Mental Deficiency in the Chicago Area," *Proceedings of the American Association for the Study of Mental Deficiency* (1935), pp. 40, 291–307.

[5] Richard O. Lang, *The Relation of Educational Status to Economic Status in the City of Chicago by Census Tracts, 1934* (University of Chicago Libraries, 1936).

[6] T. V. Smith and Leonard D. White, *Chicago: An Experiment in Social Science Research* (Chicago, 1929), pp. 8–11, 59–60.

The second speculation is upon the role of movement both in the placing of people within the city and in the concomitant problems of social and mental adjustment. There is evidence in this study that the distribution of types of mental disorder bears some relation to the migration and the movement of population into and within the city. Hobohemia, the area where homeless men concentrate, has a disproportionately large number of cases of paranoid schizophrenia. Studies indicate that a high percentage of hoboes are egocentric.[7] It is highly probable that they are persons who have failed to adjust to conditions of life in other communities and so have drifted downward and collected in Hobohemia.

The distribution of manic-depressives seems to indicate a movement in the opposite direction to that stated for paranoids. Their movement appears to have been into areas of higher economic status and into the better-grade apartment-house and apartment-hotel areas. The assumption is that the person of the psychogenetic type with manic-depressive predisposition puts forth more effort for success than does the average individual and so for a time rises in the economic scale. Those, therefore, who experience a mental breakdown tend to be found in communities of higher economic status.

Even more important than migration itself is the effect of movement upon the social and the mental adjustment of the person. Precipitating factors in mental breakdown may perhaps be found in the difficulties of adjustment to a new situation. In the light of the points suggested by this study, research in migration into and within the city takes on new aspects.

[7] Nels Anderson, *The Hobo* (Chicago, 1923), p. 19.

The significance of a pioneer study lies to a considerable degree in the extent to which it opens up promising and significant problems for future research. Judged by these standards, the present work will achieve a high rating.

ERNEST W. BURGESS

UNIVERSITY OF CHICAGO

AUTHORS' PREFACE

The research method used in the present study is not new. It has a history of development and a record of success in research dealing with other forms of social pathology; but this is the first application of a refined ecological technique to the problem of mental disorder. A preliminary study of the distribution of cases of mental disorder admitted to the Cook County Psychopathic Hospital had been made by Mrs. Clifford R. Shaw in 1928 and had shown the value of further research along this line. In 1930, acting upon a suggestion of Dr. Herbert Blumer of the University of Chicago, Robert Faris continued the study of the distribution of mental disorders as a doctoral dissertation. Two years later H. Warren Dunham began an investigation of certain problems raised by Dr. Faris in his study and also continued to work on certain other related aspects of the ecology of mental disorder, some of the material of which he subsequently used for a Master's thesis. The collaboration commenced in 1933 and has combined the efforts of a large number of persons.

The material presented[1] here falls somewhat naturally

[1] Previously published material based on some of the data included here is contained in the following articles: H. W. Dunham, "Urban Distributions of Schizophrenics," *Collected and Contributed Papers*, Elgin State Hospital (Paramount Press, Inc., Dec., 1932), pp. 134–46; R. E. L. Faris, "Cultural Isolation and the Schizophrenic Personality," *American Journal of Sociology*, XI (September, 1934), 155–69; H. W. Dunham, "The Ecology of the Functional Psychoses in Chicago," *American Sociological Review*, II (August, 1937), 467–79; and R. E. L. Faris, "Demography of Urban Psychotics with Special Reference to Schizophrenia," *American Sociological Review*, III (April, 1938), 203–9.

into the following divisions. The first chapter discusses the growth of the city with its resulting natural ecological organization. The following seven chapters present data showing the distribution patterns of nine major psychoses in Chicago and also the relationships found between these data and selected social phenomena. Chapter ix gives data of a similar nature for Providence, Rhode Island. The final two chapters attempt to present a theoretical point of view by which the facts may be interpreted and also several hypotheses which appear to fit the facts but which can only be substantiated or rejected on the basis of additional research.

It is hoped that this book may be informative to all persons who are dealing with the problem of the disorganized personality. The facts presented in this volume should be of value also to those persons who work with the problem of community reorganization, particularly to those who are interested in community mental hygiene. Of interest both to psychiatrists and sociologists will be the basic statistical data on the relationship between mental disorder and certain aspects of social life.

It is to be emphasized that the facts presented, the generalizations established, and the hypotheses suggested are to be regarded as the sole responsibility of the authors. It is almost needless to emphasize that a study of this character by the very nature of the data and of the methods used cannot, in any sense, be conclusive. The data are not close enough to the phenomena of mental disorder to establish any clear-cut case for the operation of definite causative factors. The method employed only enables one to view the data quantitatively in the community setting in which it occurred. The ecological material and the relationship found between mental disorder and other social phenomena enabled the research worker to raise significant questions and to suggest causal hypotheses for the occurrence of the various types of mental disorders in their particular configurations. The problem of the causal connection of certain types of mental disorder with the social structure, if any, depends on the application of other methods and perhaps the development of new methods which will enable the research worker to analyze the more subtle and intimate aspects of social life.

In the bringing of this study to a successful conclusion, the authors have been aided at all stages by many persons to whom much gratitude is due. Professor Ernest W. Burgess has helped the project in all stages and in a great many ways. His suggestions, encouragement, and labor have been indispensable, and it is impossible to acknowledge the debt to him. Professor Louis Wirth and Professor Herbert Blumer have given valuable suggestions and aid. Professor William F. Ogburn has given advice on the handling of statistical material. Dr. Ruth S. Cavan read the manuscript and made many valuable and helpful suggestions. Mr. Charles Newcomb gave much help in dealing with population and other census material.

Since its inception this study has been sponsored and financially supported jointly by the Social Science Research Committee of the University of Chicago and the Illinois State Department of Public Welfare, first through the Elgin State Hospital with Dr. Charles F. Read, managing officer, and later through the State Psychopathic Institute, directed by Dr. H. Douglas Singer. Dr. Paul Schroeder, director of the Institute for Juvenile Research, gave his valuable cooperation by interesting the state authorities in the proposed study. Dr. Charles F. Read with the co-operation of Mr. Rodney Brandon, former director of the Department of Public Welfare, and Mr. A. L. Bowen, present director, made provision for the collection of the data at the several state hospitals. Dr. Read also contributed numerous critical suggestions during the course of the study. Dr. H. Douglas Singer co-operated in all stages of the research, read the manuscript carefully, and gave suggestions for improvement. Dr. Francis Gerty, superintendent of the Cook County Psychopathic Hospital, generously made available the records at this hospital. Appreciation and thanks are due to Miss Mary Drucker and Miss Eileen Irvine for time given voluntarily in typing various parts of the manuscript. Phyllis I. Dunham was very helpful in reading the proof. The record clerks at the several state hospitals were very helpful on many occasions.

The Works Progress Administration of Illinois provided invaluable aid in setting up a project to analyze some of the statistical material. Miss Ethel Shanas superintended the project, and her assistant, Miss Beatrice Achtenberg, had charge of the statistical analyses. Their co-operation was of much value.

In the part of the study dealing with Providence, Rhode Island, credit is due to Claire G. Faris for gathering data, and to Mr. Thurston Steele for much of the work of analysis. Dr. Seth B. Howes of the Rhode Island State Hospital for Mental Diseases made available the records there.

R. E. L. F.
H. W. D.

TABLE OF CONTENTS

LIST OF ILLUSTRATIONS

MAPS

CHARTS

LIST OF TABLES

xxxii LIST OF TABLES

CHAPTER I

NATURAL AREAS OF THE CITY

A relationship between urbanism and social disorganization has long been recognized and demonstrated. Crude rural-urban comparisons of rates of dependency, crime, divorce and desertion, suicide, and vice have shown these problems to be more severe in the cities, especially the large rapidly expanding industrial cities. But as the study of urban sociology advanced, even more striking comparisons between the different sections of a city were discovered. Some parts were found to be as stable and peaceful as any well-organized rural neighborhood while other parts were found to be in the extreme stages of social disorganization. Extreme disorganization is confined to certain areas and is not characteristic of all sections of the city.

Out of the interaction of social and economic forces that cause city growth a pattern is formed in these large expanding American cities which is the same for all the cities, with local variations due to topographical and other differences. This pattern is not planned or intended, and to a certain extent resists control by planning. The understanding of this order is necessary to the understanding of the social disorganization that characterizes urban life.

THE NATURAL AREAS DEPICTED AS CIRCULAR ZONES

The most striking characteristics of this urban pattern, as described by Professor Burgess,[1] may be represented by

[1] R. E. Park and E. W. Burgess, *The City* (Chicago: University of Chicago Press, 1925).

1

a system of concentric zones, shown in Chart I. Zone I, at the center, is the central business district. The space is occupied by stores, business offices, places of amusement, light industry, and other business establishments. There are few residents in this area, except for transients inhabiting the large hotels, and the homeless men of the "hobohemia" section which is usually located on the fringe of the business district.

Zone II is called the zone in transition. This designation refers to the fact that the expanding industrial region encroaches on the inner edge. Land values are high because of the expectation of sale for industrial purposes, and since residential buildings are not expected to occupy the land permanently, they are not kept in an improved state. Therefore, residential buildings are in a deteriorated state and rents are low. These slums are inhabited largely by unskilled laborers and their families. All the settlements of foreign populations as well as the rooming-house areas are located in this zone.

Zone III, the zone of workingmen's homes, is inhabited by a somewhat more stable population with a higher percentage of skilled laborers and fewer foreign-born and unskilled. It is intermediate in many respects between the slum areas and the residential areas. In it is located the "Deutschlands," or second immigrant settlement colonies, representing the second generation of those families who have migrated from Zone II.

Zones IV and V, the apartment-house and commuters' zones, are inhabited principally by upper-middle-class families. A high percentage own their homes and reside for long periods at the same address. In these areas stability is the rule and social disorganization exceptional or absent.

CHART I

URBAN AREAS

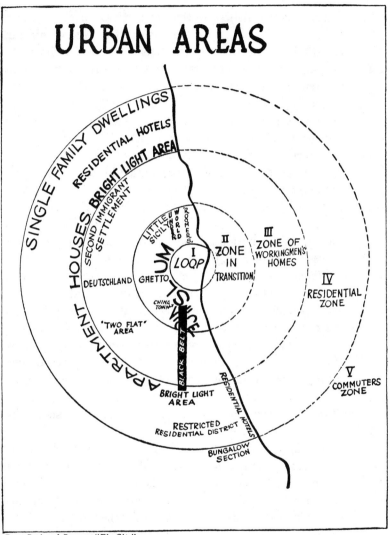

From Park and Burgess, "The City"

NATURAL AREAS AND URBAN ZONES

The characteristics of the populations in these zones appear to be produced by the nature of the life within the zones rather than the reverse. This is shown by the striking fact that the zones retain all their characteristics as different populations flow through them. The large part of the population migration into the city consists of the influx of unskilled labor into the second zone, the zone in transition. These new arrivals displace the populations already there, forcing them to move farther out into the next zone. In general, the flow of population in the city is of this character, from the inner zones toward the outer ones. Each zone, however, retains its characteristics whether its inhabitants be native-born white, foreign-born, or Negro. Also each racial or national group changes its character as it moves from one zone to the next.

Within this system of zones, there is further sifting and sorting of economic and social institutions and of populations. In the competition for land values at the center of the city, each type of business finds the place in which it can survive. The finding of the place is not infrequently by trial and error, those locating in the wrong place failing. There emerge from this competition financial sections, retail department store sections, theater sections, sections for physicians' and dentists' offices, for specialized shops, for light industry, for warehouses, etc.

Similarly, there are specialized regions for homeless men, for rooming-houses, for apartment hotels, and for single homes. The location of each of these is determined ecologically and the characteristics also result from the interaction of unplanned forces. They maintain their characteristics in spite of the flow of various racial and national groups through them and invariably impress their effects on each of these groups. These have been called "natural areas" by Professor Park,[2] because they result from the interaction of natural forces and are not the result of human intentions.

Fortunately, the city of Chicago has been studied somewhat more intensively than most cities of its size. Certain of these areas are significant in relation to social disorganization. It is possible to define and describe these areas with certain kinds of objective data. The major divisions of the city can be seen in Map I. Extending outward from the central business district are the principal industrial and railroad properties. The rooming-house sections extend along three arms radiating from the center to the north, west, and south. The slum areas are roughly defined by the regions containing over 50 per cent foreign-born and native-born of foreign parentage and over 50 per cent Negro. Beyond these areas is the residential section. In the Lake Calumet section at the southeastern corner of the city is another industrial region inhabited by a foreign-born population.

Too small to be shown on this map are the areas of homeless men—the "hobohemia" areas.[3] These are located on three main radial streets and are just outside the central business district. Their inhabitants are the most unstable in the city. The mobility and anonymity of their existence produces a lack of sociability and in many cases deterioration of the personality. Although spending their time in the most crowded parts of the city, these homeless men are actually extremely isolated. For the most part they represent persons unable to obtain an economic foothold in society, and so they maintain themselves by occasional labor,

[2] R. E. Park, "Sociology," in *Research in the Social Sciences*, ed. Wilson Gee (New York: Macmillan Co., 1929), pp. 28–29.

[3] Nels Anderson, *The Hobo* (Chicago: University of Chicago Press, 1923).

MAP I

TYPES OF CULTURAL AND ECONOMIC AREAS

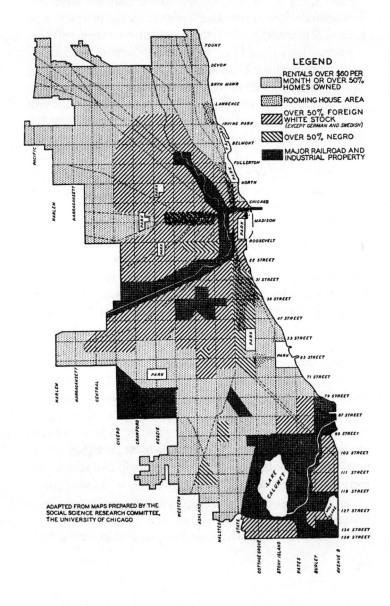

LEGEND

RENTALS OVER $60 PER MONTH OR OVER 50% HOMES OWNED

ROOMING HOUSE AREA

OVER 50% FOREIGN WHITE STOCK *(EXCEPT GERMAN AND SWEDISH)*

OVER 50% NEGRO

MAJOR RAILROAD AND INDUSTRIAL PROPERTY

ADAPTED FROM MAPS PREPARED BY THE SOCIAL SCIENCE RESEARCH COMMITTEE, THE UNIVERSITY OF CHICAGO

by petty thievery, by begging, and by receiving charity. As they have no opportunity for normal married life, their sexual activities are limited to relations with the lowest type of prostitutes and to homosexuals. The rate of venereal infection is high among these men. Chronic alcoholism is also a common characteristic of the members of this group. Their lives are without goal or plan, and they drift aimlessly and alone, always farther from the conventional and normal ways of living.

Another area of importance is the rooming-house area. This is usually located along main arteries of transportation and a little farther from the center of the city. In Chicago there are several rooming-house sections, the three largest consisting of arms radiating to the north, west, and south, just beyond the hobohemia areas, each extending for something over two miles in length and from a half-mile to over a mile in width. The populations of these areas are principally young, unmarried white-collar workers, who are employed in the central business district during the day and live in low-priced rented rooms within walking distance or a short ride from their work.[4] Within the area the population is constantly shifting, turning over entirely about once each four months. Anonymity and isolation also characterize the social relations in this area; no one knows his neighbors and no one cares what they might think or say. Consequently the social control of primary group relations is absent, and the result is a breakdown of standards of personal behavior and a drifting into unconventionality and into dissipations and excesses of various sorts. The rates of venereal diseases and of alcoholism are high in this area,

[4] H. W. Zorbaugh, *The Gold Coast and the Slum* (Chicago: University of Chicago Press, 1929).

and the suicide rate is higher than for any other area of the city.[5]

The foreign-born slum areas occupy a large zone surrounding the central business and industrial area. Within this zone there are a number of segregated ethnic communities, such as the Italian, Polish, Jewish, Russian, and Mexican districts. The newly arrived immigrants of any nationality settle in these communities with their fellow-countrymen. In these groups the language, customs, and many institutions of their former culture are at least partly preserved. In some of the most successfully isolated of these, such as the Russian-Jewish "ghetto," the Old-World cultures are preserved almost intact. Where this is the case, there may be a very successful social control and little social disorganization, especially in the first generation. But as soon as the isolation of these first-settlement communities begins to break down, the disorganization is severe. Extreme poverty is the rule; high rates of juvenile delinquency, family disorganization, and alcoholism reflect the various stresses in the lives of these populations.

Two distinct types of disorganizing factors can be seen in the foreign-born slum areas. The first is the isolation of the older generation, the foreign-born who speak English with difficulty or not at all and who are never quite able to become assimilated to the point of establishing intimate friendships with anyone other than their native countrymen. Within the segregated ethnic communities these persons are well adapted to their surroundings, but as soon as they move away or are deserted by their neighbors, they suffer from social isolation.[6] The second type of disorganizing fac-

[5] R. S. Cavan, *Suicide* (Chicago: University of Chicago Press, 1928).

[6] Louis Wirth, *The Ghetto* (Chicago: University of Chicago Press, 1928).

tor operates among the members of the second and third generations. The very high delinquency rate among the second-generation children has been shown by Shaw.[7] This disorganization can be shown to develop from the nature of the child's social situation. Also growing out of the peculiar social situation of the second generation is the mental conflict of the person who is in process of transition between two cultures—the culture of his ancestors and the culture of the new world in which he lives. As he attends American schools and plays with children of other than his own nationality, the child soon finds himself separated from the world of his parents. He loses respect for their customs and traditions and in many cases becomes ashamed of his own nationality, while at the same time he often fails to gain complete acceptance into the American group of his own generation. This is particularly true if he is distinguished by color or by features which betray his racial or national origin. This person is then a "man without a culture," for though he participates to some extent in two cultures, he rejects the one and is not entirely accepted by the other.[8]

The Negro areas are, in general, similar in character to the foreign-born slum areas. The principal Negro district in Chicago extends for several miles southward from the business district. Two smaller Negro districts are located on the Near West Side, as well as one on the Near North Side. In the larger area on the South Side, the social disorganization is extreme only at the part nearest the busi-

[7] C. R. Shaw *et al.*, *Delinquency Areas* (Chicago: University of Chicago Press, 1929).

[8] Everett Stonequist, *The Marginal Man* (New York: Charles Scribner's Sons, 1937).

ness district.[9] In the parts farther to the south live the Negroes who have resided longer in the city and who have become more successful economically. These communities have much the same character as the nearby apartment-house areas inhabited by native-born whites.

For some miles along the Lake Front in Chicago a long strip of apartment-hotel districts has grown up. These districts occupy a very pleasant and favorable location and attract residents who are able to pay high rentals. The rates of various indices of social disorganization are in general low in these sections.

The outlying residential districts of middle-class and upper-middle-class native-born white population live in apartments, two-flat homes, and single homes. In these districts, and especially the single home areas in which there is a large percentage of homes owned by the inhabitants, the population is stable and there is little or no social disorganization in comparison with those areas near the center of the city.

THE NATURAL AREAS DEFINED IN TERMS OF HOUSING

Not all the differences in the nature of the social life in the various natural areas are known, but it is certain that many phases of life are involved. The life of the slum dweller is different in a great many respects from the life of the suburbanite or of the Gold Coast dweller. It is possible to suggest some of these contrasts in figures. The 120 subcommunities of the city, used as the basis of some of the insanity rates in the following chapters, were divided into eleven areas, each characterized by a predominance of a

[9] E. Franklin Frazier, *The Negro Family in Chicago* (Chicago: University of Chicago Press, 1932).

different type of housing. These areas are designated as follows: (1) Single home (predominating) and two-flat area with rentals of $50 a month and over; (2) single home (predominating) and two-flat area with rentals under $50 a month; (3) two-flat (predominating) and single home area with rentals of $50 a month and over; (4) two-flat (predominating) and single home area with rentals under $50 a month; (5) apartment-house area (native-born white); (6) hotel and apartment-hotel area; (7) apartment-house and two-flat area; (8) apartment-house area (foreign-born); (9) apartment-house area (Negro); (10) tenement and rooming-house area; and (11) rooming-house area. In each of these residential divisions rates have been computed for several indices which show something about the nature of the area.[10] Chart II shows the locations of these areas.

Seven indices were available to describe and delimit these groups of communities or housing areas.[11] The first is the percentage of the population in each group that is foreign-born. The percentage for the whole city is 20.05, and the range in these eleven groups of communities runs from 2.32 to 38.22.

[10] The basic material used to describe these housing areas was provided by the Family Composition Study, a WPA project, supervised by Dr. Ruth Koshuk. In addition, some of the more detailed analyses of the insanity data in the 120 subcommunities and the housing areas was provided by a WPA project, established to study the trend of the different types of mental disease during the depression years. This project was sponsored by the State Psychopathic Institute of the Illinois Department of Public Welfare. Dr. H. D. Singer, director of the Institute, Dr. Louis Wirth, and Dr. E. W. Burgess of the University of Chicago served as advisers for the project. Miss Ethel Shanas, assisted by Miss Beatrice Achtenberg, supervised the project at the University of Chicago. A more extensive acknowledgment of the magnitude of this debt will be found in the Preface.

[11] See Tables 74–80, inclusive, in Appen. B.

CHART II

AREA I
SINGLE HOME AND TWO FLAT AREA
RENTAL OVER $50.00

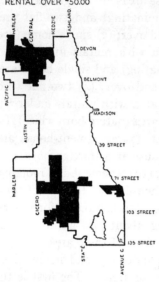

AREA II
SINGLE HOME AND TWO FLAT AREA
RENTAL UNDER $50.00

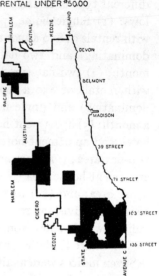

AREA III
TWO FLAT AND SINGLE HOME AREA
RENTAL OVER $50.00

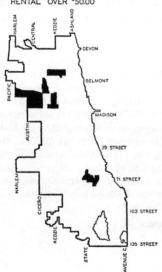

AREA IV
TWO FLAT AND SINGLE HOME AREA
RENTAL UNDER $50.00

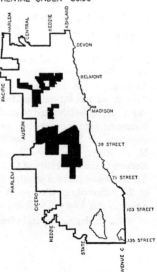

URBAN AREAS BY TYPE OF HOUSING

CHART II—*Continued*

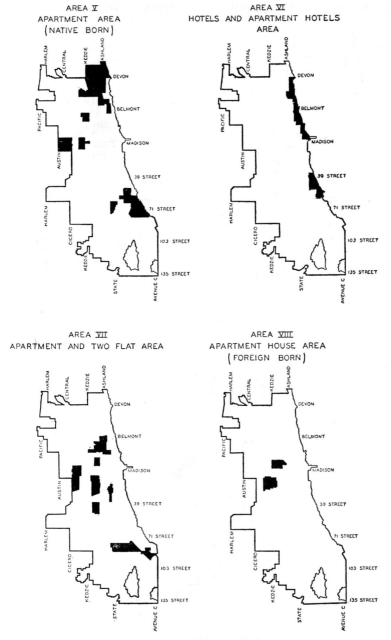

AREA V
APARTMENT AREA
(NATIVE BORN)

AREA VI
HOTELS AND APARTMENT HOTELS
AREA

AREA VII
APARTMENT AND TWO FLAT AREA

AREA VIII
APARTMENT HOUSE AREA
(FOREIGN BORN)

URBAN AREAS BY TYPE OF HOUSING

CHART II—*Continued*

AREA IX
APARTMENT HOUSE AREA (NEGRO)

AREA X
TENEMENT AND ROOMING
HOUSE AREA

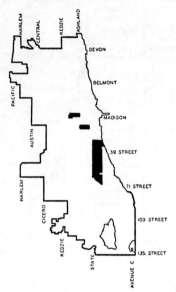
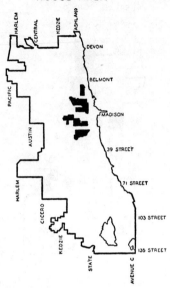

AREA XI
ROOMING HOUSE AREA

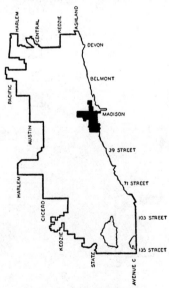

URBAN AREAS BY TYPE OF HOUSING

Rates are also computed for the number of restaurants in each group. A high ratio of restaurants indicates non-family areas and areas of high mobility. In Chicago there are 1.28 restaurants per 1,000 population, and the range in the eleven districts is from 0.54 to 14.56.

Another index used which appeared to bring out differences in areas is the infant-mortality rate. The highest rate is 133.3 and the lowest rate is 38.9 per 1,000 live births. The crude death-rates range from 8.1 to 19.7 per 100,000 population.

Two indices of stability are used. Families living in single homes are less mobile than families or persons living in hotels, apartment houses, and rooming-houses. In Chicago 19.8 per cent of the total dwellings are single homes. The rates for the eleven districts range from 5.02 to 56.18. Another index of stability is home-ownership. The percentage of total dwellings in Chicago owned by the residents is 29.20; the range is from 6.55 to 53.11.

The variation in education is roughly shown by the percentage of the population eighteen years of age and over that completed nine or more grades in school. The percentage for the whole city is 38.84, and the range is from 21.29 to 66.95.

The radio has become a significant means of secondary communication. In Chicago 63 per cent of the families own radio receiving sets. The range in the eleven districts is from 33 to 77 per cent.

Area 1, single home and two-flat area with rentals of $50 and more a month, is one of the most stable of the eleven residential divisions. The foreign-born percentage is only 15.89, much below the city average, and third from the lowest of the eleven areas. It is the lowest in number of restaurants, having only 0.54 per 1,000 population. The infant death-rate is also low—45.8 per 1,000 live births, fourth from the lowest of the eleven areas, and contrasting sharply with the highest rate of 133.3 in the rooming-house area. In the rate of single dwellings this area is second from the highest, with a rate of 47.25. It is also second from the highest in home-ownership with a rate of 49.49. The schooling index is also above the city average and places the area third from the highest in the city, with a rate of 42.49. The area is highest in the city in percentage of families owning radio sets, with a rate of 77.

Area 2, single home and two-flat area with rentals of under $50 a month is also an area of high stability. The foreign-born rate, 22.59, is slightly above the rate for the city as a whole and is fifth from the highest. The restaurant rate is 0.69, next to the lowest. The infant death-rate, 54.7, is fifth from the lowest. In the single homes index, this area is highest with a figure of 56.18 and is also highest in percentage of homes owned, with a figure of 53.11. The educational rate, 30.86, is intermediate and sixth from the highest. The radio-ownership rate is 64, which is fifth from highest and slightly above the average for the city.

Area 3, two-flat and single home area, with rentals of $50 a month and over, also ranks fairly high in stability. It is intermediate in the foreign-born rate, the figure being 19.82, seventh from the highest. The restaurant rate, 0.74, is low, being third from the lowest. In infant mortality, this area has the third lowest rate in the city, 44.5. The single home rate, 23.46, is third from highest, as is the home-ownership rate of 37.62. This area is medium high in the educational index, with a figure of 41.23, fourth from highest. It is third from highest in the radio-ownership, with a percentage of 75.

Area 4, two-flat and single home area, with rentals of under $50 a month, while generally not as stable as the first three areas, still is medium to high in the series. The foreign-born figure is 23.29, fourth from highest. The restaurant rate, 0.81, is low, fourth from lowest. The infant mortality figure is 58.1, which is medium low and sixth from highest. The single home rate is 19.42 and the home-ownership rate is 37.35, both fourth from the highest. The area ranks fairly low in education, with a figure of 25.69, which is next to the lowest, and is medium low in radio-ownership, with a rate of 58, which is sixth from the highest.

Area 5, apartment-house area (native-born white), is located in fairly desirable sections of the city and inhabited by a population which shows little sign of disorganization. The foreign-born rate, 17.20, is low and eighth from the top. The restaurant figure of 1.06 is medium, sixth from the top. The infant-mortality rate is the lowest for all areas with a rate of 38.8. The single home rate, 10.17, is medium low, ranking sixth, and the home-ownership rate of 19.25, is low, ranking eighth. Education, with a rate of 56.41, and radio-ownership, with a rate of 76, are both high and both rank second in the eleven areas.

Area 6, hotel and apartment-hotel area, is occupied by a fairly high economic class, so that although the mobility is somewhat higher than in the residential areas, the population does not show signs of disorganization. In this area the foreign-born rate is next to the lowest in the city, with a rate of 14.61. Infant mortality is low, the figure of 43.7 ranking next to the lowest rate. The single homes rate of 5.02 and the home-ownership rate, 6.55, are both the lowest in the city. The educational rate is highest in the city, the figure being 66.95. Radio-ownership is medium, with a figure of 68, ranking fourth.

Area 7, apartment-house and two-flat area, is on the fringe of the slum areas and is in most respects intermediate between the residential and slum areas. The foreign-born rate is 25.64, which is medium high, and third from highest. The restaurant rate is 1.16, which is medium. The infant-mortality rate is fourth from the highest with a figure of 61.1. The index of single homes is medium low, with a figure of 11.59, and the home-ownership rate, 26.49, is also medium, both ranking fifth from the top. This area has a low educational index of 27.28, which is third from the lowest, and medium low radio-ownership index of 52, which is fourth from lowest.

Area 8, apartment-house (foreign-born), is also on the fringe of the slum areas and shows some signs of the characteristic deterioration as measured by these indices. The foreign-born rate, highest of the areas, is 38.22. The restaurant rate is medium low, seventh from the top, with a figure of .91. The infant-mortality figure, 47.8, is fifth from the lowest. The single home rate is low, next to the lowest, with a figure of 5.3, and home-ownership is medium low, with a figure of 22.05, sixth from the top. The educational rate of 31.24 and the radio-ownership rate of 54 are both medium low, and rank sixth and seventh respectively.

Area 9, apartment-house area (Negro), contains some of the most deteriorated communities of the city. A few more stable regions within this group bring some of the averages up a little, however. The foreign-born rate is lowest in this area, with a figure of 2.32. The restaurant rate, 1.27, is medium, ranking fourth. The infant-mortality rate is next to the highest in the city. The single home rate is low, the figure of 8.34 ranking seventh in the city. Home-ownership is also low, the figure of 11.20 ranking ninth. Education, with a figure of 30.22, is medium low and ranks eighth, and radio-ownership is low, ranking ninth with a rate of 43.

Area 10, tenement and rooming-house area, is one of the most seriously deteriorated communities in the city and is a part of the real slums. The foreign-born rate is next to the highest with a figure of 27.44. The restaurant rate is also high, the figure of 1.82 ranking third. The infant-mortality rate of 68.7 is third highest in the city. The single homes rate ranks eighth with a rate of 7.46. Home-ownership is medium low, ranking seventh with a rate of 19.57. The educational rate is lowest in the city with a figure of 21.29, and the radio-ownership rate is next to the lowest, with a figure of 38.

Area 11, rooming-house area, is in several respects the most unstable and deteriorated in the city. The foreign-born rate, 20.40, is medium, ranking sixth. The restaurant rate is by far the highest in the city, with a figure of 14.56. This, however, is affected by the fact that the central business district is included in this group. The infant-mortality rate is the highest, with a rate of 133.3. Single homes are third from the lowest with a rate of 6.36, and home-ownership is next to lowest with a rate of 7.60. The educational rate of 33.90 is medium and ranks fifth. The radio-ownership rate is 33 and is the lowest in the city. Many persons in this area are apparently denied this channel of secondary communication.

In addition to these differences which are presented for the first time in this publication, much previously printed data show other differences between the various sections of the city. Not only are such statistical facts as population composition, literacy, dependency rates, and disease rates known to vary greatly in the different sections of the city, but also mental life and behavior. In one of the most conclusive of these studies, the study of juvenile delinquency by Clifford R. Shaw and his associates,[12] sufficient control was obtained to establish with reasonable certainty that the high rates of delinquency were products not of the biological inferiority of the population stocks that inhabit the slum areas, nor of any racial or national peculiarity, but rather of the nature of the social life in the areas themselves. The delinquency rates remained constantly high in certain urban areas which were inhabited by as many as six different national groups in succession. Each nationality suffered from the same disorganization in these areas and each nationality alike improved after moving away from the deteriorated areas.

As has been shown, the natural areas which have been defined above can be identified by the use of certain mathematical indices for different types of social phenomena. Such indices as the percentage of foreign-born, the percentage of homes owned, the sex ratio, the median rentals paid, the density of population, the rate of mobility, the educational rate, the percentage of rooming-houses and hotels, and the percentage of condemned buildings, roughly tend to identify these areas and to differentiate between them. These indices might be regarded as ones which measure the extent of social disorganization between the different communities and the natural areas of the city. Other types of objective data, representing such social problems as juvenile delinquency, illegitimacy, suicide, crime, and family dis-

---

[12] C. R. Shaw and H. D. McKay, *Report on the Causes of Crime*, National Commission on Law Observance and Enforcement (Washington, D.C.: U.S. Government Printing Office, 1931).

organization, might be considered as indices representing effects or results of certain types of social processes. As in the research of Clifford Shaw which has been described above, the rates for these different social problems tend to fit rather closely into the ecological structure of the city as described by Park, Burgess, and others. In other words, in all of these social problems there is the concentration of high rates close to the center of the city, with the rates declining in magnitude as one travels in any direction toward the city's periphery. Shaw's study of juvenile delinquency gives one of the most complete pictures of this pattern. The other studies, in general, show the same pattern with certain variations which develop because of the location of certain ethnic groups in certain parts of the city.

The problem of mental disorder has been for the first time approached by the utilizing of this ecological technique. It is the attempt to examine the spatial character of the relations between persons who have different kinds of mental breakdowns. While this type of approach is used in this study, the authors wish to emphasize that they regard it as having definite limitations in understanding the entire problem of mental disorder. It can be looked upon as a purely cultural approach and as such does not tend to conflict with any understanding of this problem which may come from biological, physiological, or psychological approaches. However, in the light of these previous studies of social problems utilizing this method it does seem particularly desirable to study the distribution of the different types of mental disorders.

It might be pointed out that there have been several early attempts appearing in the literature to study mental disorder by this method.[13] These attempts were limited, however, during the nineteenth century, because of the tremendous problem presented by classification.[14] In view of the definite relationship which appears to exist between other social problems and the areas of social disorganization in the modern city, the question may be raised as to whether mental disorder will tend to follow this typical pattern. If it does tend to follow the ecological pattern of other social problems, will the different types of mental disorders also follow this same configuration? It is these questions which this study will attempt to answer in the following chapters.

[13] See *Journal of the Statistical Society of London*, 1851, pp. 49–62; 1852, pp. 250–56; J. F. Sutherland, "Geographical Distribution of Lunacy in Scotland," *British Association for Advancement of Science* (Glasgow, Sept., 1901); W. R. MacDermott, "The Topographical Distribution of Insanity," *British Medical Journal* (London, 1908), p. 950; W. A. White, "Geographic Distribution of Insanity in the United States," *Journal of Nervous and Mental Disease*, XXX (1903), pp. 257–79; A. L. Wright, "The Increase of Insanity," *Conference on Charities and Corrections* (1884), pp. 228–36.

[14] J. C. Bucknill and D. H. Tuke, *A Manual of Psychological Medicine* (Philadelphia: Blanchard & Lea, 1858), pp. 88–100.

CHAPTER II

URBAN DISTRIBUTION OF INSANITY RATES

All cases of mental disorder in Chicago that are cared for in public institutions are first brought to the Cook County Psychopathic Hospital, where they are held for a week or more for examination and a tentative diagnosis. The number of new cases brought here average over 3,000 each year. Some are judged not insane; some cases are mild enough to be allowed to live at home or with relatives. Those needing hospital care are committed to one of several state institutions in the vicinity of Chicago.

DISTRIBUTION OF INSANITY RATES FOR THE PSYCHOPATHIC HOSPITAL

The distribution of the rates for 7,069 first admissions to this hospital for the two years of 1930–31 are shown on Map II. The total number of cases in each of the sixty-eight communities[1] was divided by the 1930 adult popula-

[1] The seventy-five local communities, as worked out by the Local Community Research Council at the University of Chicago, were used as the basis for these rates. Some of the communities, which contained populations too small to be used as a basis for reliable rates, were combined with adjoining areas and three of the largest communities were subdivided. This reduces the total number of communities to sixty-eight. In this manner the city was divided so that each community contains reasonably homogeneous characteristics and yet has a sufficiently large population to make possible reliable rates. A map in the Appendix shows the location of these communities.

Some of the maps for which large numbers of cases were available are based on a more detailed division of the census tracts of the city into 120 subcommunities. The use of these makes possible a somewhat finer discrimination of the differences as found in the various parts of the city. It should

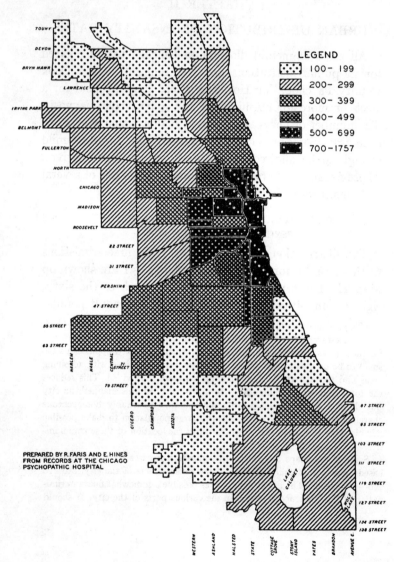

MAP II

INSANITY RATES
IN CHICAGO, 1930–1931
PER 100,000 ADULT POPULATION

1930 POPULATION

LEGEND

	100 – 199
	200 – 299
	300 – 399
	400 – 499
	500 – 699
	700 – 1757

TOUHY
DEVON
BRYN MAWR
LAWRENCE
IRVING PARK
BELMONT
FULLERTON
NORTH
CHICAGO
MADISON
ROOSEVELT
22 STREET
31 STREET
PERSHING
47 STREET
55 STREET
63 STREET
71 STREET
79 STREET
87 STREET
95 STREET
103 STREET
111 STREET
119 STREET
127 STREET
134 STREET
138 STREET

HARLEM
NAGLE
CENTRAL
CICERO
CRAWFORD
KEDZIE
WESTERN
ASHLAND
HALSTED
STATE
COTTAGE GROVE
STONY ISLAND
YATES
BRANDON
AVENUE G.

LAKE CALUMET
WOLF LAKE

PREPARED BY R. FARIS AND E. HINES
FROM RECORDS AT THE CHICAGO
PSYCHOPATHIC HOSPITAL

tion of the community. The adult population was used because of the very small number of persons under twenty-
one years among these cases. The resulting rates range from
a low of 110 per 100,000 adult population in Community
39, a high-class residential area, to a high of 1,757 in Community 32, the central business district. The distribution,
as shown in Map II, shows a very definite pattern. The
highest rates are clustered about the center of the city and
the rates are progressively lower at greater distances from
the center. The slight rise of the rates in the Lake Calumet
region reflects the deteriorated condition of that region,
which, although less severe, is similar to that of the areas
surrounding the central part of the city.

DISTRIBUTION OF RATES FOR STATE HOSPITALS

Map III shows the distribution of 28,763 cases, a much
larger number, and presents the average rates for the more
detailed 120 subcommunities. The cases used are from four
state institutions,[2] and consist of all those committed to
those institutions from Chicago during the years 1922–34.
The distribution resembles closely that shown in the pre-
ceding map.

The heavy concentration of high rates in and around the

---

be noted that the rates on all the maps showing distributions in the 120 subcommunities are average rates as contrasted to total rates in the local communities. The location of these communities is also shown by a map in the
Appendix.

[2] In all the following maps showing rates for the local communities the
distributions are made on the basis of cases admitted to Elgin, Kankakee, and
Chicago State Hospitals. The maps showing distributions in the 120 subcommunities include a minimum number of cases from Chester State Hospital, in which the criminal insane are confined. This explains the label on
the maps that the distribution data are from four state hospitals.

MAP III

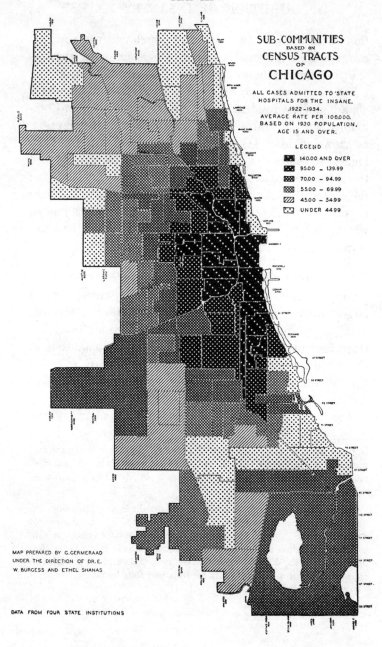

SUB-COMMUNITIES
BASED ON
CENSUS TRACTS
OF
CHICAGO

ALL CASES ADMITTED TO STATE
HOSPITALS FOR THE INSANE.
1922-1934.
AVERAGE RATE PER 100,000,
BASED ON 1930 POPULATION,
AGE 15 AND OVER.

LEGEND

140.00 AND OVER
95.00 — 139.99
70.00 — 94.99
55.00 — 69.99
45.00 — 54.99
UNDER 44.99

MAP PREPARED BY G.GERMERAAD
UNDER THE DIRECTION OF DR.E.
W. BURGESS AND ETHEL SHANAS

DATA FROM FOUR STATE INSTITUTIONS

central business district represents a real concentration of cases as can be seen in Table 1.

This table shows that the high-rate communities in the two upper quartiles have 70 per cent of the cases but only 49 per cent of the population. It is significant to note that while each quartile contains approximately the same percentage of population, the percentage of cases within each

TABLE 1

PERCENTAGE OF ALL CASES OF MENTAL DISORDER ADMIT-
TED TO STATE HOSPITALS AND PERCENTAGE OF THE
POPULATION IN EACH FOURTH OF THE 120 SUBCOMMU-
NITIES GROUPED ON THE BASIS OF THE MAGNITUDE OF
THE RATES

Quartile Grouping	Percentage of Cases in Each Quartile	Percentage of Population in Each Quartile
Fourth or upper............	45.6	23.1
Third....................	24.7	26.0
Second..................	16.7	24.4
First....................	13.0	26.5
Total................	100.0	100.0

quartile shows significant variations and decreases consistently from the upper quartile to the lowest or first quartile.

The state hospital records do not include all psychotic persons in the city of Chicago. Because of the possibility that these cases may represent a selection of the poorer classes in the population, it seemed necessary to compare the distribution of private hospital cases with those from state hospitals. It is an obvious possibility that the concentration of high rates of mental disorder in the central parts of the city might mean no real concentration at all, but merely a concentration of those patients whose families are too poor to maintain them in private institutions.

DISTRIBUTION OF RATES FOR PRIVATE HOSPITALS

Map IV shows the distribution of average rates of 6,101 private hospital cases. All the cases for the years 1922–34 from eight of the largest private hospitals in Chicago or vicinity were used in computing these rates. The differences

TABLE 2

RANK ORDER OF PRIVATE HOSPITAL RATES IN THE
TEN HIGHEST SUBCOMMUNITIES WITH
SUBCOMMUNITY DESCRIPTION

Subcommunity	Average Rate	Type of Subcommunity
74	58	Central business district, hotel, hobo area
84	48	Residential-hotel and apartment-hotel area
57	46	Apartment and two-flat area
90	46	Apartment-house area (native-born)
14	45	Hotel and apartment-hotel area
22	40	Hotel and apartment-hotel area
2	39	Apartment-house area (native-born)
67	36	Apartment-house area (foreign-born)
68	36	Apartment-house area (foreign-born)
25	36	Apartment-house area (native-born)

are immediately obvious to the eye. The characteristic pattern of the state hospital cases is a concentration of the highest rates at and near the center, and the lowest rates in the outlying residential areas. On this map the high rates are not in contiguous communities but are much more scattered. The pattern of rates, however, has some definite consistency. The ten highest rates are in the following areas, shown in Table 2.

These high rates are principally in the better-class hotel and apartment-house sections. This is very much in evidence when these rates are correlated with the percentage of apart-

MAP IV

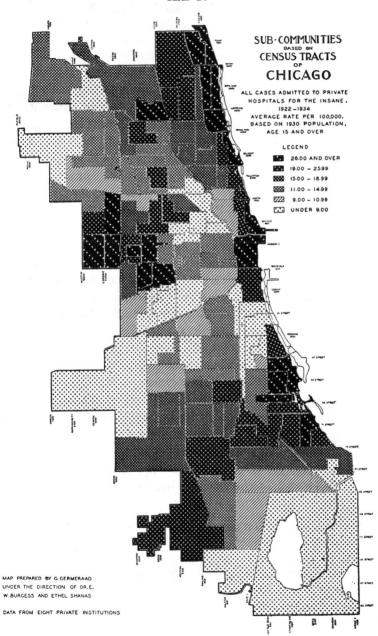

SUB·COMMUNITIES
BASED ON
CENSUS TRACTS
OF
CHICAGO

ALL CASES ADMITTED TO PRIVATE
HOSPITALS FOR THE INSANE.
1922 – 1934
AVERAGE RATE PER 100,000,
BASED ON 1930 POPULATION,
AGE 15 AND OVER.

LEGEND

26.00 AND OVER
19.00 – 25.99
15.00 – 18.99
11.00 – 14.99
9.00 – 10.99
UNDER 9.00

MAP PREPARED BY G. GERMERAAD
UNDER THE DIRECTION OF DR. E.
W. BURGESS AND ETHEL SHANAS

DATA FROM EIGHT PRIVATE INSTITUTIONS

ments and apartment hotels in the subcommunities. The correlation coefficient, in this instance, is .67 ± .05, while the correlation of this index with the state hospital rates is low and negative with a Pearsonian R of − .11 ± .09. While the high rates for private hospital cases are notably in the high-rent apartment and hotel districts, there are certain exceptions to this scheme as seen by the high rates in west and southwest sections of the city. The low rates are in the Negro, the low rental two-flat, and foreign-born subcommunities—a sharp contrast to the pattern of state hospital rates. The chief apparent exception to this consistency of the high rates is in Subcommunity 74, the central business district. However, on examination of the actual cases, it is found that they come from the high-rent transient hotels in the business district. The private hospital population, then, represents a distinct selection, partially, at least, on an economic basis. There are also other significant differences. The average length of residence in the private hospitals is much shorter[3] and the great bulk of mental patients on hospital books are in public hospitals.

It is interesting to note that as far as first admissions are concerned, the public or state hospitals received 82.5 per cent while the private hospitals received only 17.5 per cent of the cases. This corresponds to percentages for the country at large.[4] It can readily be seen that this low percentage of private hospital cases can have no effect on the pattern in the city formed by the total insanity rates. The next most

[3] See John Maurice Grimes, *Institutional Care of Mental Patients in the United States* (published and distributed by the author, 1816 N. Clark St., Chicago, 1934).

[4] *Mental Patients in State Hospitals, 1928* (Washington, D.C.: U.S. Department of Commerce, Bureau of the Census, 1928), p. 5.

significant point in relation to differences between state and private hospital cases is that approximately 50 per cent of the cases in the manic-depressive series were admitted to private hospitals and 50 per cent were admitted to the state hospitals. A very high percentage with a psychoneurotic diagnosis is also reported from the private as compared to the state hospitals.

TABLE 3

PERCENTAGE OF ALL CASES OF MENTAL DISORDER ADMIT-
TED TO PRIVATE HOSPITALS AND THE PERCENTAGE OF
THE POPULATION IN EACH FOURTH OF THE 120 SUBCOM-
MUNITIES GROUPED ON THE BASIS OF THE MAGNITUDE
OF THE RATES

Quartile Grouping	Percentage of Cases in Each Quartile	Percentage of Population in Each Quartile
Fourth or upper...........	46.9	27.1
Third...................	28.1	27.5
Second.................	16.2	23.3
First..................	8.8	22.1
Total...............	100.0	100.0

When the percentage distribution of cases in each main diagnostic category within the state and private hospitals is examined, the facts are similar to those reported in the above paragraph. As usual, the functional psychoses show the greatest percentage discrepancies within the two groups. It is noted that in the private hospitals approximately 20 per cent of the cases are diagnosed manic-depressive while about 23 per cent are diagnosed schizophrenic. In the state hospitals only 4 per cent carry the former diagnosis and 30 per cent the latter. In addition, the percentage diagnosed true paranoia, psychoneuroses, and without psychosis is significantly higher in the private hospital group as compared to the state hospital. In turn, the state hospitals show significantly higher percentages of diagnoses in the organic and toxic psychoses.[5]

There is also a heavy concentration of the private hospital cases in certain communities of the city as shown in Table 3. But, as has already been indicated, the concentration of cases is in very different communities as compared to the concentration of state hospital cases.

DISTRIBUTION OF INSANITY RATES FOR STATE AND PRIVATE HOSPITALS COMBINED

Map V shows the distribution of average rates of state and private hospital cases combined. The rates, also expressed per 100,000 population, age fifteen and over, vary from 48 to 499. The highest ten rates are shown in Table 4.

The concentration of high rates in the rooming-house districts is striking. The Negro areas have high rates and the foreign-born slum areas are almost as high. The low rates are in the outlying residential sections and the lake-front, hotel, and apartment-hotel subcommunities. This is quite similar to the pattern formed by the rates on the first two maps presented.

Although the rates in the Negro area are high, the high incidence of mental disorder does not appear to be due to any racial factor, for within this area there is a considerable variation of rates. The most deteriorated parts near the

---

[5] These facts showing the percentage of cases diagnosed within each of the principal psychoses between state and private hospitals and percentage distribution of cases in each diagnostic category within the state and private hospitals are contained in tables on file with the Department of Sociology, University of Chicago. These differences will be discussed further in the following chapters when each psychosis is considered separately.

MAP V

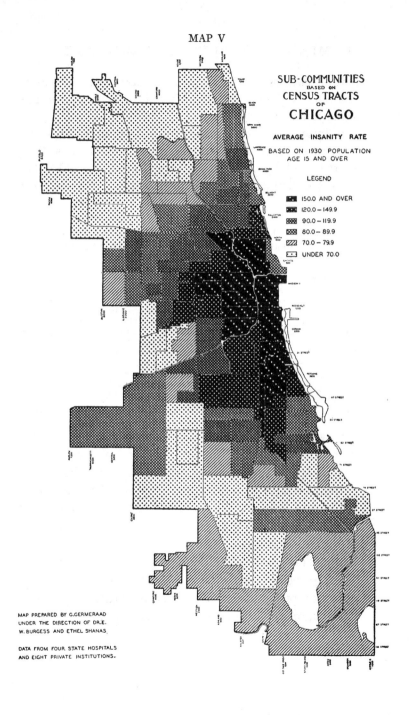

SUB-COMMUNITIES
BASED ON
CENSUS TRACTS
OF
CHICAGO

AVERAGE INSANITY RATE

BASED ON 1930 POPULATION
AGE 15 AND OVER

LEGEND

150.0 AND OVER
120.0 — 149.9
90.0 — 119.9
80.0 — 89.9
70.0 — 79.9
UNDER 70.0

MAP PREPARED BY G. GERMERAAD
UNDER THE DIRECTION OF DR. E.
W. BURGESS AND ETHEL SHANAS.

DATA FROM FOUR STATE HOSPITALS
AND EIGHT PRIVATE INSTITUTIONS.

central business district have the highest rates, the variation ranging from a rate of 322 in Subcommunity 77 to 123 in Subcommunity 83.

In spite of the fact that the private hospital cases are distributed so differently from the state hospital cases, they affect the total pattern very little when they are added, because the numbers are comparatively small. On the same

TABLE 4

RANK ORDER OF COMBINED RATES IN THE TEN HIGHEST
SUBCOMMUNITIES WITH SUBCOMMUNITY DESCRIPTION

Subcommunity	Average Rate	Type of Subcommunity
74	499	Central business district, hotel and hobo area
61	480	Hobo and rooming-house area
75	357	Rooming-house area
77	322	Apartment-house area (Negro)
21	223	Rooming-house area
49	212	Tenement and rooming-house area
65	210	Apartment-house area (Negro)
78	208	Apartment-house area (Negro)
80	202	Apartment-house area (Negro)
62	192	Tenement and rooming-house area

population base, the private hospital rates are very much lower than the state hospital or combined rates. The highest rate in the private hospital group is 58 while in the pattern of rates of private and state hospitals combined the highest is 499. In fact, not one of the private hospital rates is high enough to be out of the lowest class of the rates of both types of cases. Although the correlation of private hospital rates with state hospital rates is a low negative, − .11 ± .09, and with the combined rates, .04 ± .10, the numerical predominance of state hospital cases makes their distribution typical of all cases. The correlation of state hospital rates with the rates of state and private hospitals combined is .99 ± .001.

The concentration of cases and population according to their respective percentage is shown by quartile groupings in Table 5.

While a definite concentration of cases is noted in this distribution which exceeds the percentage of the popula-

TABLE 5

PERCENTAGE OF ALL CASES OF MENTAL DISORDER AND THE PERCENTAGE OF THE POPULATION IN EACH FOURTH OF THE 120 SUBCOMMUNITIES GROUPED ON THE BASIS OF THE MAGNITUDE OF THE RATES

Quartile Grouping	Percentage of Cases in Each Quartile	Percentage of Population in Each Quartile
Fourth or upper...........	40.7	23.5
Third...................	26.2	27.0
Second.................	18.5	24.7
First..................	14.6	24.8
Total................	100.0	100.0

tion in the high-rate communities, the concentration is not as definite as it was when the private hospital cases were excluded. These figures, however, do represent and show a real concentration of cases in the high-rate subcommunities which, as was noted, are in the disorganized parts of the city near the center. High insanity rates appear to cluster in the deteriorated regions in and surrounding the center of the city, no matter what race or nationality inhabits that region.

INSANITY RATES BY URBAN ZONES

A clearer understanding of the actual ecology of insanity in Chicago may be obtained by an examination of the rates

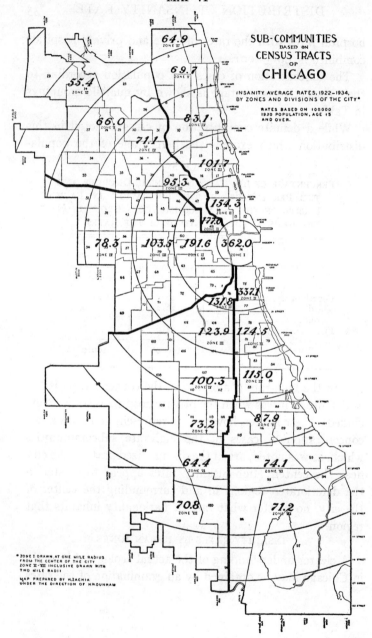

MAP VI

SUB-COMMUNITIES
BASED ON
CENSUS TRACTS
OF
CHICAGO

INSANITY AVERAGE RATES, 1922-1934,
BY ZONES AND DIVISIONS OF THE CITY*

RATES BASED ON 100000
1930 POPULATION, AGE 15
AND OVER.

64.9
ZONE VI

69.7
ZONE V

55.4
ZONE VII

83.1
ZONE IV

66.0
ZONE VI

71.1
ZONE IV

101.7
ZONE III

95.3
ZONE IV

154.3
ZONE II

177.0
ZONE II

78.3
ZONE III

103.5
ZONE III

191.6
ZONE II

362.0
ZONE I

337.1
ZONE II

131.8
ZONE II

123.9
ZONE III

174.5
ZONE III

100.3
ZONE IV

115.0
ZONE III

73.2
ZONE V

87.9
ZONE IV

64.4
ZONE VI

74.1
ZONE VI

70.8
ZONE VII

71.2
ZONE VII

* ZONE I DRAWN AT ONE MILE RADIUS
FROM THE CENTER OF THE CITY
ZONE II - VII INCLUSIVE DRAWN WITH
TWO MILE RADII

MAP PREPARED BY H.ZACHIA
UNDER THE DIRECTION OF H.W.DUNHAM

by zones shown in Map VI. This merely portrays the fore-going material by another method. On this map the city is divided into five sections, each containing four or more zones within a two-mile radius of each other, with the exception of Zone I, the central business district, constructed on a one-mile radius. On examination of Map VI it is clearly shown that by far the highest rate for insanity in the city occurs in the central business district or Zone I. In every zone, in every section of the city, with the exception of the southwest side, there is a steady decline in rates as one travels from the center of the city to the periphery. On the southwest side there is a slight rise in Zone VII.

This presentation definitely establishes the fact that insanity, like other social problems, fits into the ecological structure of the city. As such the distribution of insanity appears to be a function of the city's growth and expansion, and more specifically of certain undetermined types of social processes. With this fact well established the question immediately arises whether the different psychoses are distributed in the same manner throughout the city. In the following chapters the various psychoses will be examined to see whether they fit into the configuration which has been established for all types of mental disorder.

CHAPTER III

THE TYPICAL PATTERN IN THE DISTRIBUTION OF SCHIZOPHRENIA

The symptomatology of schizophrenia is varied but certain symptoms appear to be somewhat common to all forms. The textbooks of psychiatry generally include the following symptoms: apathy and indifference, lack of contact with reality, disharmony between mood and thought, stereotyped attitudes, ideas of reference, delusions, illusions, hallucinations, impaired judgment, lack of attention, generally intact memory, lack of insight, defects of interest, seclusive makeup, hypochondriacal notions, negativism, and autistic thinking. These are some of the chief mental symptoms upon which there is more or less agreement. There are numerous physical symptoms listed also upon which there is much less agreement.[1] The hypothesis has been made and is still held by numerous psychiatrists that these different expressions of abnormality are caused by some single basic condition. Though the concept "schizophrenia," or the older one "dementia praecox," is used to designate that basic condition, there is little agreement as to its nature and causes.

[1] See D. K. Henderson and R. D. Gillespie, *A Textbook of Psychiatry* (Cambridge: Oxford University Press, 1927), pp. 194–201; William A. White, *Outlines of Psychiatry* (Washington, D.C.: Nervous and Mental Disease Publishing Co., 1918), pp. 142–49; F. M. Barnes, *An Introduction to the Study of Mental Disorders* (St. Louis: C. V. Mosby Co., 1923), pp. 237–39; E. A. Strecker and F. G. Ebaugh, *Clinical Psychiatry* (4th ed.; Philadelphia: P. Blakiston's Son & Co., 1935), pp. 356–74; A. Rosanoff, *Manual of Psychiatry* (6th ed.; New York: John Wiley & Sons, 1927), pp. 103–96.

This psychosis constitutes between 25 and 40 per cent of the first admissions to hospitals for mental disorders in the United States.[2] Between 1922 and 1931, 7,253 persons admitted to the state hospitals from Chicago for the first

TABLE 6

PERCENTAGE DISTRIBUTION OF 7,253 SCHIZOPHRENICS BY SEX
ACCORDING TO AGE AT COMMITMENT WITH COMPARABLE
DATA FROM THE CHICAGO POPULATION IN 1930

AGE	MALE		FEMALE		TOTAL		POPULATION 1930
	No.	Per Cent	No.	Per Cent	No.	Per Cent	Per Cent
15–19.........	292	7.5	187	5.6	479	6.6	11.4
20–24.........	698	17.8	401	12.0	1,099	15.2	12.7
25–29.........	826	21.1	591	17.7	1,417	19.5	12.9
30–34.........	738	18.8	606	18.2	1,344	18.5	12.2
35–39.........	595	15.2	572	17.1	1,167	16.0	12.4
40–44.........	357	9.1	417	12.5	774	10.7	10.4
45–49.........	219	5.6	291	8.7	510	7.1	8.3
50–54.........	121	3.1	156	4.7	277	3.8	6.3
55–59.........	52	1.3	70	2.1	122	1.7	4.6
Over 60.......	15	.4	43	1.3	58	.8	8.8
Unknown.....	3	.1	3	.1	6	.1	.0
Total.....	3,916	100.0	3,337	100.0	7,253	100.0	100.0

time were given a diagnosis of schizophrenia. The number of cases and percentages in each five-year age period for the series is shown in Table 6.

From this table it can be seen that the female cases have a somewhat older average age than do the male cases. The bulk of the schizophrenic cases in both sexes apparently fall

[2] *Mental Patients in State Hospitals, 1928*, Washington, D.C.: U.S. Department of Commerce, Bureau of the Census.

in the middle years of life, a fact indicated by other age analyses of schizophrenic cases.[3]

COMMUNITY RATES FOR SCHIZOPHRENIA

The rates of schizophrenia per 100,000 of the adult population[4] show a great variation for the different local communities in the city. The extremes are in Community 1, a high-rental apartment-house district with a rate of 111, and in Community 32, the hobo and central business district, with a rate of 1,195. The average rate of 289 and the median rate of 322 indicate that the bulk of the community rates cluster at the low end of a skewed frequency distribution.

The distribution of rates shown in Map VII follows the same general pattern as the rates for the general insanity series. The high rates are in and near the center of the city

[3] Kraepelin, who described and separated this psychosis from the other diagnostic categories, was the first to point out the significance of the factor of age. See his *Dementia Praecox and Paraphrenia*, trans. R. Mary Barclay (Edinburgh: E. and S. Livingstone, 1919), p. 226. Also see Rosanoff, *op. cit.*, p. 121; H. M. Pollock, "Frequency of Schizophrenia in Relation to Age, Environment, Nativity and Race"; *Schizophrenia—An Investigation of Most Recent Advances* (New York: The Association for Research in Nervous and Mental Diseases; Paul B. Hoeber & Co., 1928), V, 48–51, Ellen B. Winston, *A Statistical Study of Mental Disease* (Doctor's dissertation, Department of Sociology, University of Chicago, 1930), p. 31.

[4] For the population base of the rates for the various psychoses distributed in the local communities the estimated adult population of each community in 1927, the middle year, is used. This is not exactly the mid-point in this period because of the different dates on which the 1920 and 1930 census were reported. However, the adjustment appears adequate for the present purpose. In addition, the use of the adult population is not a perfect adjustment for age, but, since there are few persons under twenty-one years of age in any of the psychotic series studied, the adjustment still appeared to be adequate. It should be noted that in those maps showing the distribution of cases in the 120 subcommunities of the city there has been a closer refinement for age in the respective psychoses.

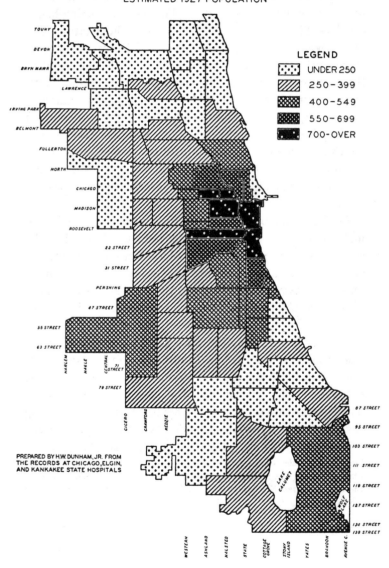

MAP VII

SCHIZOPHRENIA RATES
(ALL TYPES)
IN CHICAGO, 1922–1931
PER 100,000 ADULT POPULATION

ESTIMATED 1927 POPULATION

LEGEND

- ⠿ UNDER 250
- ▨ 250–399
- ▩ 400–549
- ▦ 550–699
- ■ 700–OVER

PREPARED BY H.W. DUNHAM, JR. FROM
THE RECORDS AT CHICAGO, ELGIN,
AND KANKAKEE STATE HOSPITALS

and the low rates consistently occur at the city's periphery. The characteristic rise in the Lake Calumet region in South Chicago is also shown. The highest rates occur in the hobohemia communities, 28a and 32. The central rooming-house districts, 8b, 28b, and 36 also have very high rates. The rates above the average are also found in first-settlement immigrant communities near the center of the city and in the deteriorated parts of the Negro area immediately south of the central business district. The three Negro communities, 35, 38, and 40, in the column extending to the south of the loop have rates of 662, 470, and 410, respectively. Since all three communities are populated almost entirely by Negroes, the gradation of rates would require an explanation in terms of some other factor or factors than racial tendency toward this psychosis.

In this series of cases of schizophrenia, the number of males is slightly higher than the number of females, the ratio being 117 to 100.[5] This would indicate that the factor of sex has some significance in connection with schizophrenia. However, in a study of the male and female cases separately, there appears to be no radical deviation in the pattern. Of the 7,253 schizophrenic cases, 3,916 are males. The rates based upon these male cases vary from 79 in Community 1, to 1,416 in Community 32. It should be noted that these are the same communities which form the extremes in the distribution of all cases of schizophrenia. The average rate is 396 and the median rate is 325, showing that the majority of the community rates are at the low

[5] The sex ratio in the estimated adult population used as a basis for the rates is 105 males to 100 females. There is, then, a real excess of schizophrenics among the males, a fact which is also true of the total number in the United States. See *Mental Patients in State Hospitals, 1928*, p. 12. Also see Pollock, *op. cit.*

end of the skewed distribution. The distribution of these rates, shown in Map VIII, is very similar to the pattern of total schizophrenic rates. The similarity is strikingly shown by the fact that the communities in the upper quartile of each series are identical.

The female rates, Map IX, based on 3,337 cases, also have a wide range. The lowest rate, 130, is in the Gold Coast, Community 8a, and the highest, 932, in a hobohemia community, 28a. The average rate is 367 and the median rate is 312, and so a similar skewed frequency distribution is in evidence.

The pattern of the female schizophrenic rates is quite similar to that of the male schizophrenic rates, with three exceptions: communities 17, 32, and 56+.[6] Community 32, the central business district with its near-by hobo area, has a low rate, although it has the highest rate in the male series. The ninety-eight schizophrenic males from this area came almost exclusively from the cheap hotels and flophouses on State Street and Wabash Avenue. There are practically no women residing in this hobo area. The three female cases which came from Community 32 were as follows: a maid at an expensive club on Michigan Boulevard, a resident of a first-class loop hotel, and a resident of a cheap hotel of a disorderly character on Wabash Avenue. The other two communities had higher rates than might be expected. In contrast to Community 32, Community 17 has a very marked predominance of females, seventeen females to five males. Both communities 17 and 56+ have a low population base for each sex and so a slight rise in the number of cases affects the rates markedly and raises a question

[6] Community 56+ refers to the fact that communities 56, 57, 62, 64, and 65 were combined to form one community.

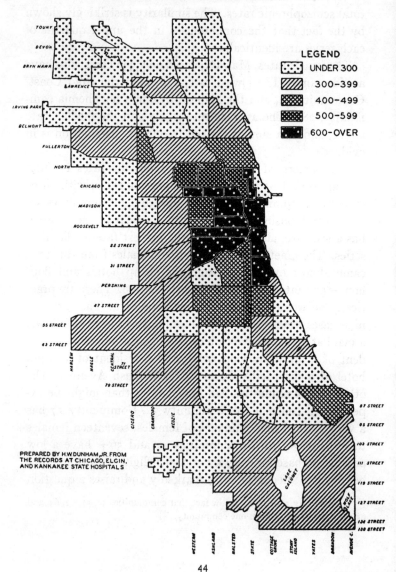

MAP VIII

SCHIZOPHRENIA RATES FOR MALES
IN CHICAGO, 1922–1931
PER 100,000 ADULT POPULATION

ESTIMATED 1927 MALE POPULATION

LEGEND

UNDER 300
300–399
400–499
500–599
600–OVER

PREPARED BY H.W.DUNHAM,JR.FROM
THE RECORDS AT CHICAGO, ELGIN,
AND KANKAKEE STATE HOSPITALS

MAP IX

SCHIZOPHRENIA RATES FOR FEMALES
IN CHICAGO, 1922−1931
PER 100,000 ADULT POPULATION

ESTIMATED 1927 FEMALE POPULATION

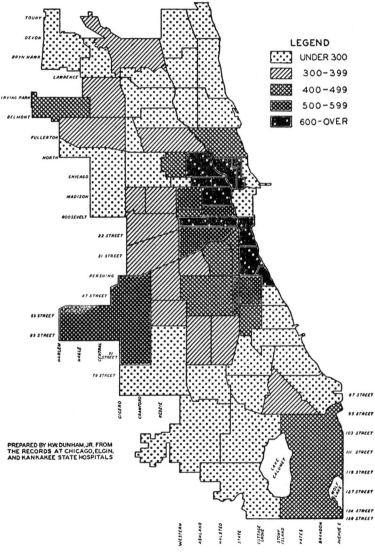

LEGEND

UNDER 300

300−399

400−499

500−599

600−OVER

PREPARED BY H.W.DUNHAM,JR. FROM
THE RECORDS AT CHICAGO,ELGIN,
AND KANKAKEE STATE HOSPITALS

45

as to their statistical validity. The correlation coefficient between the male and female schizophrenia rates is .59 $\pm$ .07 and is lower than might be expected because of the unusual position of these three communities.

It is interesting that the sex ratio with a slight excess of males holds true for the high-rate areas as well as for the entire city. In the thirteen communities whose rates are in the upper quartile of both the male and female series, the sex ratio in the population is 130 males to 100 females. In the schizophrenic cases from these communities the males exceed in a ratio of 143 to 100.

In addition to the distribution of these schizophrenic rates by local communities these case data for 1922–31 with the addition of three more years have been distributed in the 120 subcommunities of Chicago. The distribution of the average yearly rates based on a total of 10,575 schizophrenic cases is shown in Map X.[7] The range of rates of this larger series of cases is from 14 in Subcommunity 92, an apartment and two-flat area, to 150 in Subcommunity 74, the central business district, with a median rate of 30.1 and an average rate of 34.6. The same skewed frequency distribution as was noted in the previous distribution of schizophrenic rates is also in evidence. As can be seen on comparing this distribution with Map VII, the same concentration of rates is

---

[7] In these maps showing rates by the 120 subcommunities, it should be noted that the cases included are from both public and private hospitals. In the schizophrenic distribution the private hospital cases are negligible, amounting in all to 13.7 per cent of the total, while in the manic-depressive distribution (chap. iv), the private hospital cases amount to 50 per cent of the total, a large enough percentage to affect the distribution of the pattern. See chap. ii. However, while there is a difference in the distribution of the manic-depressive rates when the cases from the state and private hospitals are distributed separately (Pearsonian R, $-.06 \pm .10$), this does not affect the generalizations relative to the distribution of these two functional psychoses.

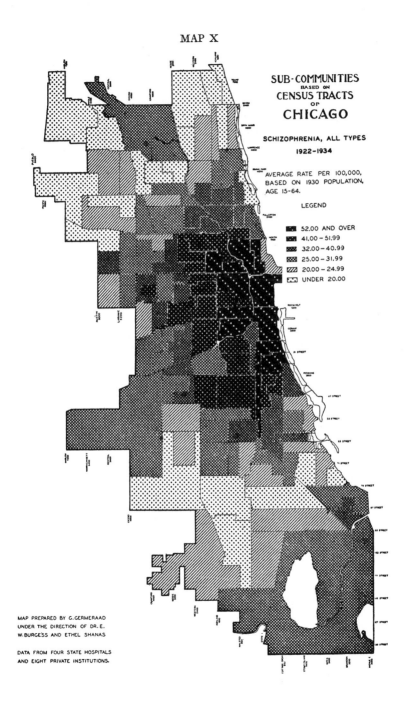

MAP X

SUB-COMMUNITIES
BASED ON
CENSUS TRACTS
OF
CHICAGO

SCHIZOPHRENIA, ALL TYPES
1922-1934

AVERAGE RATE PER 100,000,
BASED ON 1930 POPULATION,
AGE 15-64.

LEGEND

52.00 AND OVER
41.00 – 51.99
32.00 – 40.99
25.00 – 31.99
20.00 – 24.99
UNDER 20.00

MAP PREPARED BY G. GERMERAAD
UNDER THE DIRECTION OF DR. E.
W. BURGESS AND ETHEL SHANAS

DATA FROM FOUR STATE HOSPITALS
AND EIGHT PRIVATE INSTITUTIONS.

noticed, with the high average rates falling at or near the center of the city and the low rates on the periphery. There is hardly any deviation from this regular pattern. As in Map VII, the high rates are to be found in the hobohemia, rooming-house, foreign-born, and Negro communities.

The extent of concentration of cases in comparison to the population in each quartile in this schizophrenic series is shown in Table 7.

TABLE 7

THE PERCENTAGE OF SCHIZOPHRENICS AND PERCENTAGE OF THE POPULATION IN EACH FOURTH OF THE 120 SUB-COMMUNITIES GROUPED ON THE BASIS OF THE MAGNI-TUDE OF THE RATES

Quartile Grouping	Percentage of Cases in Each Quartile	Percentage of Population in Each Quartile
Fourth or upper..............	39.6	23.8
Third.......................	27.3	26.1
Second.....................	19.0	24.5
First.......................	14.1	25.6
Total...................	100.0	100.0

The table indicates practically the same concentration of cases in the upper quartile as was found in the series of all types of mental disorders. The bulk of the schizophrenic cases, a total of 67 per cent, is concentrated in the two upper quartiles, while these quartiles contain only 50 per cent of the population.

From the pattern of rates it appears possible that much of the variation might be explained on the basis of the varying proportions of the foreign-born in the different parts of the city. A useful test of this possibility is found in the following foreign-born rates. These are computed on the basis of the eleven groupings of subcommunities based on housing, presented in chapter i, and are formed by dividing the number of foreign-born cases of schizophrenia in each housing area by the foreign-born population of the area. Table 8 shows the rates and the range of variability.[8]

The high rates in the Negro and the rooming-house areas stand out in contrast to all others. This high rate for the foreign-born in the Negro area indicates that this district contains high rates for other races which, as will be shown, are significantly higher than the rate for Negroes within their own area.[9] The foreign-born have low rates in those areas inhabited by the native-born, although even here the rates are somewhat higher than the rates for the native-born themselves. This variation of rates in the different areas definitely appears to be caused by other factors than the varying proportions of races or nationalities. Table 9 shows that similar results hold for both the male and female foreign-born rates.

ZONE RATES FOR SCHIZOPHRENIA

The closeness with which the configuration of schizophrenia rates follows a typical ecological pattern for Chicago can be seen by an examination of the rates for the different urban zones shown in Map XI. The rates for schizophrenia in the different zones follow very closely the zone rates for all types of mental disorder. In every section of the city with the exception of the Southwest and South sides there

---

[8] The potential range of each rate, shown by the last two figures on the right, shows that the high rates of areas 9 and 11 could not by chance vary low enough to overlap any of the others. The pairs which differ significantly are shown in Tables 81, 82, and 83 in Appen. B.

[9] See Table 10.

TABLE 8

FOREIGN-BORN SCHIZOPHRENIC RATES AND THEIR POTENTIAL VARIABILITY FOR HOUSING AREAS IN CHICAGO 1922–34

Area	Description	Cases	Foreign-born Population as of 1930×13	Rate*	σR	R+3σR	R−3σR
1	Single home and two-flat—over $50	210	997,347	21.06	1.453	25.419	16.701
2	Single home and two-flat—under $50	235	717,691	32.74	2.135	39.145	26.335
3	Two-flat and single home—over $50	189	665,743	28.39	2.065	34.585	22.195
4	Two-flat and single home—under $50	684	1,952,795	35.03	1.339	39.047	31.013
5	Apartment-house (native-born)	356	1,507,441	23.62	1.252	27.376	19.864
6	Hotel and apartment-hotel	134	427,986	31.31	2.704	39.422	23.198
7	Apartment and two-flat	622	1,449,188	42.92	1.720	48.080	37.760
8	Apartment-house (foreign-born)	361	890,474	40.54	2.133	46.939	34.141
9	Apartment-house (Negro)	125	95,732	130.57	11.671	165.583	95.557
10	Tenement and rooming-house	460	711,893	64.62	3.012	73.656	55.584
11	Rooming-house	309	245,427	125.90	7.158	147.374	104.426
City total		3,685	9,661,717	38.14	0.628	40.024	36.256

* Rates computed on the basis of 100,000, 1930 foreign-born population, ages 15–64: total.

TABLE 9

FOREIGN-BORN SCHIZOPHRENIC RATES FOR EACH SEX AND THEIR POTENTIAL VARIABILITY FOR HOUSING AREAS IN CHICAGO 1922-34

Area	Description	Cases	Foreign-born Population as of 1930×13	Rate*	σR	$R+3\sigma R$	$R-3\sigma R$
				MALE			
1	Single home and two-flat—over $50	76	526,656	14.43	1.655	19.395	9.465
2	Single home and two-flat—under $50	110	402,857	27.30	2.603	35.109	19.491
3	Two-flat and single home—over $50	78	353,353	22.07	2.499	29.567	14.573
4	Two-flat and single home—under $50	334	1,052,129	31.75	1.737	36.961	26.539
5	Apartment-house (native-born)	139	789,087	17.62	1.494	22.102	13.138
6	Hotel and apartment-hotel	66	212,758	31.02	3.818	42.474	19.566
7	Apartment and two-flat	323	795,301	40.61	2.259	47.387	33.833
8	Apartment-house (foreign-born)	191	462,020	41.34	2.991	50.313	32.367
9	Apartment-house (Negro)	70	54,717	127.93	15.281	173.773	82.087
10	Tenement and rooming-house	252	407,745	61.80	3.892	73.476	50.124
11	Rooming-house	237	183,521	129.14	8.383	154.289	103.991
City total		1,876	5,240,144	35.80	0.826	38.278	33.322

* Rates computed on the basis of 100,000, 1930 foreign-born population for each sex, ages 15-64.

TABLE 9—Continued

Area	Description	Cases	Foreign-born Population as of 1930×13	FEMALE			
				Rate*	σR	R+3σR	R−3σR
1........	Single home and two-flat—over $50	134	479,691	28.47	2.459	35.847	21.093
2........	Single home and two-flat—under $50	125	314,834	39.70	3.550	50.350	29.050
3........	Two-flat and single home—over $50	111	312,390	35.53	3.372	45.646	25.414
4........	Two-flat and single home—under $50	350	900,666	38.86	2.077	45.091	32.629
5........	Apartment-house (native-born)	217	718,354	30.21	2.051	36.363	24.057
6........	Hotel and apartment-hotel	68	215,228	31.59	3.831	43.083	20.097
7........	Apartment and two-flat	299	653,887	45.73	2.644	53.662	37.798
8........	Apartment-house (foreign-born)	170	428,454	39.68	3.043	48.809	30.551
9........	Apartment-house (Negro)	55	41,015	134.10	18.070	188.310	79.890
10........	Tenement and rooming-house	208	304,148	68.39	4.740	82.610	54.170
11........	Rooming-house	72	61,906	116.31	13.699	157.407	75.213
City total	....	1,809	4,421,573	40.91	0.962	43.796	38.024

52

MAP XI

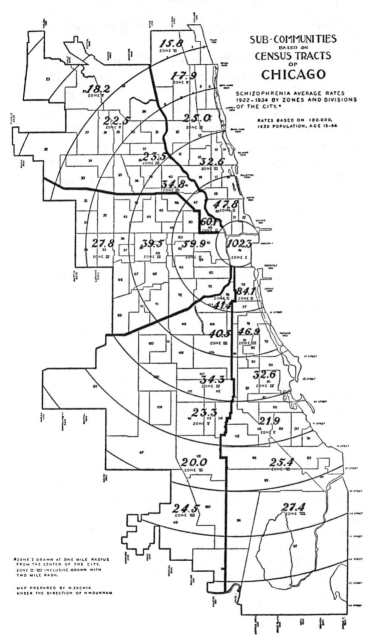

SUB·COMMUNITIES
BASED ON
CENSUS TRACTS
OF
CHICAGO

SCHIZOPHRENIA AVERAGE RATES
1922-1934 BY ZONES AND DIVISIONS
OF THE CITY.*

RATES BASED ON 100,000,
1930 POPULATION, AGE 15-64.

*ZONE I DRAWN AT ONE MILE RADIUS
FROM THE CENTER OF THE CITY.
ZONE II-VII INCLUSIVE DRAWN WITH
TWO MILE RADII.

MAP PREPARED BY H.ZACHIA
UNDER THE DIRECTION OF H.W.DUNHAM

is a steady decline in rates as one travels from the center of the city to its periphery. On the Southwest and South sides there is a slight rise in the rate of Zone VII. The extremely high rate in the central business district, or Zone I, is quite significant in comparison with the much lower rate in Zone II in the various sections of the city. This configuration of schizophrenic rates would appear to indicate that the distribution of this psychosis is a function of the differentiation of urban areas resulting from the growth of the city. The rates reflect the vast differences which are found in the various urban areas.

AREA RATES FOR SCHIZOPHRENIA

In addition to the zone rates for schizophrenia, rates according to the nativity and racial classification were also computed for the eleven housing areas of the city. The number of cases in relation to the population of these various areas is large enough so that practically all the rates are statistically reliable. Table 10 shows the schizophrenic rate for each of these housing areas according to the race and nativity classification.[10]

It is significant that although the rate for the Negroes in Area 9, the apartment-house (Negro) district, is extremely low as compared to the rates for Negroes in the other areas of the city, the rates for the native white of native parentage and the foreign-born white for this area are the highest rates within these classifications as compared to any of the other

---

[10] The rates here presented are based upon the distribution into the 120 subcommunities of total schizophrenic cases, admitted during the period 1922–34 inclusive, and shown in Map X. The rates have been refined by both age and nativity and are expressed per 100,000 of the population of the respective age and nativity group. This also applies to the other tables where rates for the separate psychoses in the different housing areas are shown by nativity and race.

TABLE 10

AREA RATES FOR SCHIZOPHRENIA ACCORDING TO NATIVITY AND RACE, 1922–34

Area	Native White of Native Parentage		Native White of Foreign or Mixed Parentage		Foreign-born White		Total White*		Negro		Other Races		Total (All Classes)	
	No.	Rate	No.	Rate	No.	Rate	No.	Rate	No.	Rate	No.	Rate	No.	Rate
1. Single home $50+	191	18.7	331	19.1	210	21.1	767	20.5	14	35.7	2	60.8	783	20.7
2. Single home $50-	90	24.2	153	19.6	235	32.7	490	26.2	5	37.3	6	37.2	501	26.4
3. Two-flat $50+	137	22.0	242	24.9	189	28.4	605	26.8	2	58.1	1	104.0	608	26.9
4. Two-flat $50-	270	27.1	706	29.4	684	35.0	1,732	32.4	22	37.9	13	49.7	1,767	32.5
5. Apt. (n.-b.)	454	19.8	505	21.8	356	23.6	1,422	23.3	8	67.1	3	27.1	1,433	23.4
6. Hotel, etc.	195	20.4	149	23.5	134	31.3	539	26.7	12	62.0	3	29.9	554	27.1
7. Apt.-two-flat	194	33.2	428	31.1	622	42.9	1,302	38.2	24	68.5	30	37.1	1,356	38.4
8. Apt. (f.-b.)	35	35.6	243	45.1	361	40.5	680	44.5	2	34.0	2	183.2	684	44.6
9. Apt. (Negro)	125	137.4	77	88.2	125	130.6	359	131.0	821	39.4	18	79.1	1,198	50.4
10. Tenement	99	35.1	267	44.6	460	64.6	867	54.5	25	63.8	24	65.2	916	54.9
11. Rooming	202	64.1	157	72.2	309	125.9	697	89.6	38	95.5	40	182.9	775	93.3
City total	1,992	26.1	3,258	28.0	3,685	38.1	9,460	32.7	973	41.4	142	61.4	10,575	33.6

*Includes "White of Unknown Parentage," and this accounts for corrected figures in total cases. The difference between the number of "Total White" and the sum of the three columns to the left equals the number of white of unknown parentage.

areas of the city. It is apparent that the schizophrenic rate is significantly higher for those races residing in areas not primarily populated by members of their own groups. For the entire city the rates, as has been indicated, are highest in the foreign-born and Negro groups. For all classes in the city, Area 11, the rooming-house section, has the highest rate, with the tenement and rooming-house area (10) having the next highest rate and the Negro area (9) following next in order. The highest rates for all classes in these three areas emphasize again the close correspondence and relationship of the high rates of schizophrenia with the disorganized and deteriorated areas of the city. All of the other areas of the city, it should be noted, have rates considerably lower than these three urban areas.

The objective findings in connection with the ecology of schizophrenia can be stated as follows: (1) the high rates for schizophrenia are concentrated in communities of extreme social disorganization in Chicago; (2) the distribution for male and female schizophrenic cases separately shows the same concentration in the disorganized areas of the city; (3) the distribution of rates shows the same pattern and concentration by both local and subcommunities; (4) all distributions of schizophrenic rates show a skewed frequency distribution with the bulk of the communities having low rates and a few of the communities having high rates; (5) the rates of schizophrenia for the foreign-born by total number and by sex in the different housing areas of the city indicate that the variation between rates is due to other factors than the varying proportions of foreign-born; (6) not only are the high rates near the center of the city but the upper quartile of the communities contains 40 per cent of the cases and only 24 per cent of the population; (7)

the rates according to race and nativity in the different housing areas of the city show constant high rates in the extremely disorganized parts of the city; (8) the rate for each white group is the highest in the Negro area, although the rate for Negroes in their own area is low.

COMMUNITY RATES FOR THE UNDIAGNOSED AND "WITHOUT PSYCHOSES" SERIES

In the undiagnosed group[11] there are 814 cases. Since the organic psychoses are generally easier to identify, the undiagnosed cases probably are, for the most part, in the functional group. If this is true, it might be expected that the series would contain more schizophrenic cases than manic-depressive, since the former are more numerous. However, the percentage distribution of ages at the time of commitment (Table 87, Appen. B), resembles the distribution of the manic-depressive cases more than the schizophrenic, though it resembles neither very closely.

The community rates of the undiagnosed psychoses range from zero in Community 11, a single home and two-flat district, to 198 in Community 28a, the West Side hobohemia. This is much greater than the manic-depressive range (see chap. iv), although the number of cases is approximately equal. The median rate is 33 and the average rate is 48. This shows the same skew characteristic of the schizophrenic rates but not of the manic-depressive rates.

The pattern of rates in the city, shown in Map XII, is

[11] This group includes only cases from the Kankakee and Chicago State Hospitals. The decision to include these cases in the study was made while the case data were being collected from the Kankakee State Hospital. At this hospital it was noticed that there was an unusually large percentage of undiagnosed cases. Cases from the Elgin State Hospital, where this group is very small, are not included.

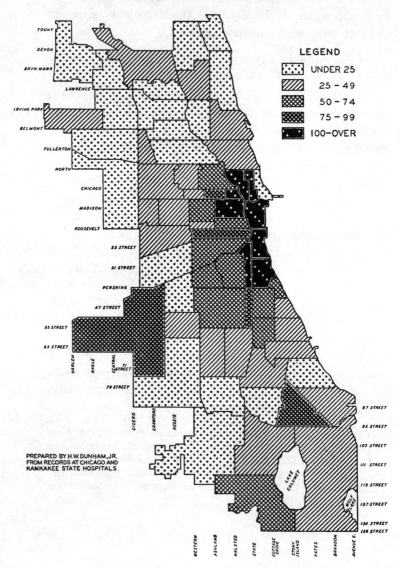

MAP XII

UNDIAGNOSED PSYCHOSIS RATES
IN CHICAGO, 1922–1931
PER 100,000 ADULT POPULATION

ESTIMATED 1927 POPULATION

LEGEND

UNDER 25
25 – 49
50 – 74
75 – 99
100 – OVER

PREPARED BY H.W. DUNHAM, JR.
FROM RECORDS AT CHICAGO AND
KANKAKEE STATE HOSPITALS

similar to that of all types of mental disorder and of the schizophrenic distribution. The highest rates are in the rooming-house and Negro communities near the center of the city. The similarity to the schizophrenic pattern is further shown by the correlation coefficient between the undiagnosed and schizophrenic rates of a .81 ± .04, while the correlation between the undiagnosed and manic-depressive

TABLE 11

PERCENTAGE OF UNDIAGNOSED PSYCHOSES AND THE PER-
CENTAGE OF THE POPULATION IN EACH FOURTH OF THE
SIXTY-EIGHT COMMUNITIES GROUPED ON THE BASIS
OF THE MAGNITUDE OF THE RATES

Quartile Grouping	Percentage of Cases in Each Quartile	Percentage of Population in Each Quartile
Fourth or upper..........	40.7	16.6
Third...................	28.9	24.3
Second.................	21.5	31.9
First..................	8.9	27.2
Total................	100.0	100.0

rates is only .31 ± .11, in both instances by local communities. It can be seen, by employing the test of three times the standard error to this latter figure, that the correlation coefficient is not significant.

The concentration of undiagnosed cases is very marked and quite similar to that which was noted in the case of the schizophrenic cases. This concentration is shown in Table 11.

The rates for persons admitted to institutions and classified as "without psychoses" show a distribution in the city quite similar to that of schizophrenia with the characteristic clustering of high rates in and near the center of the city.

It is most likely that these cases are somewhat like the undiagnosed cases largely composed of mild functional disorders or of persons who have become behavior problems in their respective communities. The distribution of these rates based upon 1,706 cases is seen in Map XIII. The range of rates is fairly large with the lowest rate of 0.56 falling in Subcommunity 23 and with the highest rate of

TABLE 12

PERCENTAGE OF "WITHOUT PSYCHOSES" AND THE PERCENTAGE OF THE POPULATION IN EACH FOURTH OF THE 120 SUBCOMMUNITIES GROUPED ON THE BASIS OF THE MAGNITUDE OF THE RATES

Quartile Grouping	Percentage of Cases in Each Quartile	Percentage of Population in Each Quartile
Fourth or Upper..........	45.6	25.6
Third...................	24.1	23.8
Second.................	19.3	26.3
First..................	11.0	24.3
Total...............	100.0	100.0

39.2 falling in Subcommunity 74. The median rate is 4.6 and the average rate is 5.3. The concentration of cases shown in Table 12 is very marked.

It is apparent from the distributive character of the different schizophrenic series that a majority of persons with this mental disorder are to be found in the disorganized communities at and near the center of the city. Similar to the configuration for all types of mental disorder, the schizophrenic rates decline in every direction as one travels from the center of the city toward its periphery. This analysis indicates that this typical pattern for the rates of schizophrenia is a function of certain underlying social processes

MAP XIII

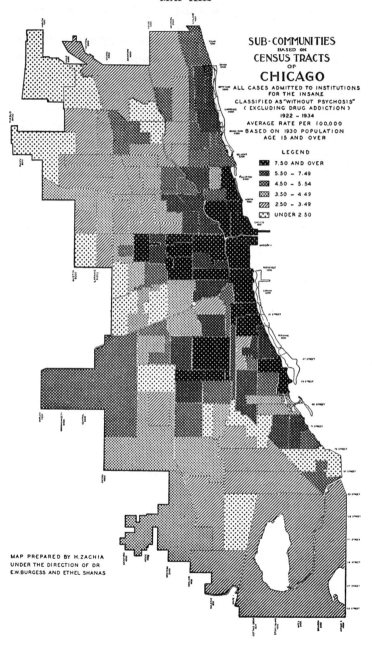

SUB·COMMUNITIES
BASED ON
CENSUS TRACTS
OF
CHICAGO

ALL CASES ADMITTED TO INSTITUTIONS
FOR THE INSANE
CLASSIFIED AS "WITHOUT PSYCHOSIS"
(EXCLUDING DRUG ADDICTION)
1922 - 1934
AVERAGE RATE PER 100,000
BASED ON 1930 POPULATION
AGE 15 AND OVER

LEGEND

7.50 AND OVER
5.50 – 7.49
4.50 – 5.54
3.50 – 4.49
2.50 – 3.49
UNDER 2.50

MAP PREPARED BY H. ZACHIA
UNDER THE DIRECTION OF DR
E.W. BURGESS AND ETHEL SHANAS

affecting city growth. In addition, it is significant to note that those cases included in the undiagnosed and "without psychoses" series follow the pattern set by the schizophrenic rates. It should also be noted that the private hospital cases represent a negligible percentage in both the schizophrenic and the undiagnosed series. However, there does seem to be some tendency toward the classification of "without psychosis" at the private hospitals. This may indicate either that persons who have mild personality disorders go to the private hospitals and are not likely to be admitted to the state hospitals or that persons are more likely to be diagnosed at the private hospitals as "without psychoses." In the next chapter the distribution of the other main functional psychoses will be analyzed and compared with the schizophrenic distributions.

CHAPTER IV

THE RANDOM PATTERN IN THE DISTRIBUTION OF THE MANIC-DEPRESSIVE PSYCHOSES

The distributions of schizophrenic rates attain an additional significance when compared with the other main functional psychosis, manic-depressive. This latter term describes superficially the type of behavior of those persons affected on the one hand by an extremely elated mood, and on the other hand, by an extremely depressed mood. Other forms of this mental disorder have been differentiated and are known as the circular, stuporous, and mixed types. The detection and diagnosis of these forms are of rarer occurrence than is the case for the two main types.

Because the diagnostic problems in the functional disorders[1] are very great, a comparative study of the distribution of the manic-depressive and schizophrenic groups might be significant in indicating whether there is any real distinction between them. The first distribution of rates of the manic-depressive psychosis was based on 734 cases, of which 296 were males and 438 were females. The sex ratio is 68 males to 100 females and is similar to the sex ratio of manic-depressive patients in the United States and very different from the sex ratio of the schizophrenics. Table 13 shows the age and sex distribution of these cases. In each age group under thirty-nine years there is a slightly higher percentage of females than of males.[2] With the exception of

[1] See J. V. May, *Mental Diseases* (Boston: Gorham Press, 1922), p. 45.

[2] In a statistical study of this psychosis, Malzberg makes the same observation. See B. Malzberg, "A Statistical Study of the Factor of Age in the

the age group from fifty to fifty-four years, the percentage of males is higher above the age of forty. This is the reverse of the schizophrenic sex ratios.

TABLE 13

PERCENTAGE DISTRIBUTION OF 734 MANIC-DEPRESSIVE PSYCHOSES BY SEX ACCORDING TO AGE AT COMMITMENT WITH COMPARABLE DATA FROM THE CHICAGO POPULATION IN 1930

AGE	MALE		FEMALE		TOTAL		POPULATION 1930
	No.	Per Cent	No.	Per Cent	No.	Per Cent	Per Cent
15–19.........	4	1.3	20	4.6	24	3.4	11.4
20–24.........	27	9.1	41	9.4	68	9.3	12.7
25–29.........	24	8.1	60	13.7	84	11.4	12.9
30–34.........	47	15.9	73	16.7	120	16.3	12.2
35–39.........	34	11.5	65	14.8	99	13.5	12.4
40–44.........	46	15.5	54	12.3	100	13.6	10.4
45–49.........	42	14.2	42	9.6	84	11.4	8.3
50–54.........	30	10.1	45	10.3	75	10.2	6.3
55–59.........	21	7.1	26	5.9	47	6.4	4.6
Over 60.......	20	6.8	11	2.5	31	4.2	8.8
Unknown.....	1	.4	1	.2	2	.3	....
Total.....	296	100.0	438	100.0	734	100.0	100.0

The distribution of manic-depressive rates is shown in Map XIV. The community rates of manic-depressive psychoses differ in many respects from the rates of all schizophrenic cases, as well as the various types of schizophrenia.[3] The range is low, the rates varying from 8 in Community 59, an area of second-immigrant settlement, to 84, in Com-

---

Manic-Depressive Psychoses," *Psychiatric Quarterly*, III (October, 1929), pp. 590–604.

[3] See chap. v for a discussion of the distribution of the types of schizophrenia.

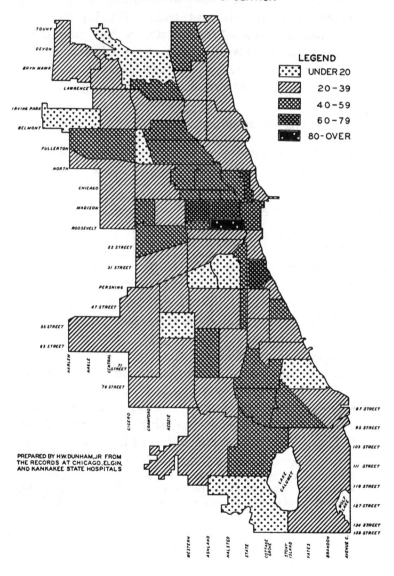

MAP XIV

MANIC DEPRESSIVE RATES
IN CHICAGO, 1922–1931
PER 100,000 ADULT POPULATION

ESTIMATED 1927 POPULATION

LEGEND

UNDER 20
20–39
40–59
60–79
80–OVER

PREPARED BY H.W. DUNHAM, JR FROM
THE RECORDS AT CHICAGO, ELGIN,
AND KANKAKEE STATE HOSPITALS

munity 28c,[4] a foreign-born district. The median rate is 37 and the average rate is also 37, indicating that the characteristic skew of the schizophrenic distribution is lacking in the manic-depressive distribution. The distribution of rates shows no marked concentration of high rates at the center of the city. Though the highest rate is in a community near the center of the city and the next highest in an adjacent community, there is no regular pattern showing.

TABLE 14

PERCENTAGE DISTRIBUTION OF MANIC-DEPRESSIVE PSYCHOSES
WITHIN EACH SEX ACCORDING TO TYPE

	MANIC		DEPRESSED		MIXED		OTHER		TOTAL	
	No.	Per Cent	No.	Per Cent	No.	Per Cent	No.	Per Cent	No.	Per Cent
Male......	158	53.4	113	38.2	18	6.1	7	2.3	296	100.0
Female....	227	51.8	165	37.7	37	8.4	9	2.1	438	100.0
Total..	385	52.4	278	37.9	55	7.5	16	2.2	734	100.0

An analysis of this series of manic-depressive cases by sex according to type of diagnosis is presented in Table 14. It seems significant that the percentage of each sex in the two main types is approximately equal.

Because of the small number of cases in the above distribution of manic-depressive rates, it seemed desirable to secure a series of rates based on a larger number of cases. The distribution of manic-depressive average rates, shown in Map XV, is by subcommunities of Chicago and is based

[4] The female catatonic group, with approximately the same number of cases (711), has a much greater range, varying from zero in Community 32, to 222 in Community 24a. This is pointed out to indicate the very definite concentration of rates in any schizophrenic distribution which is made.

MAP XV

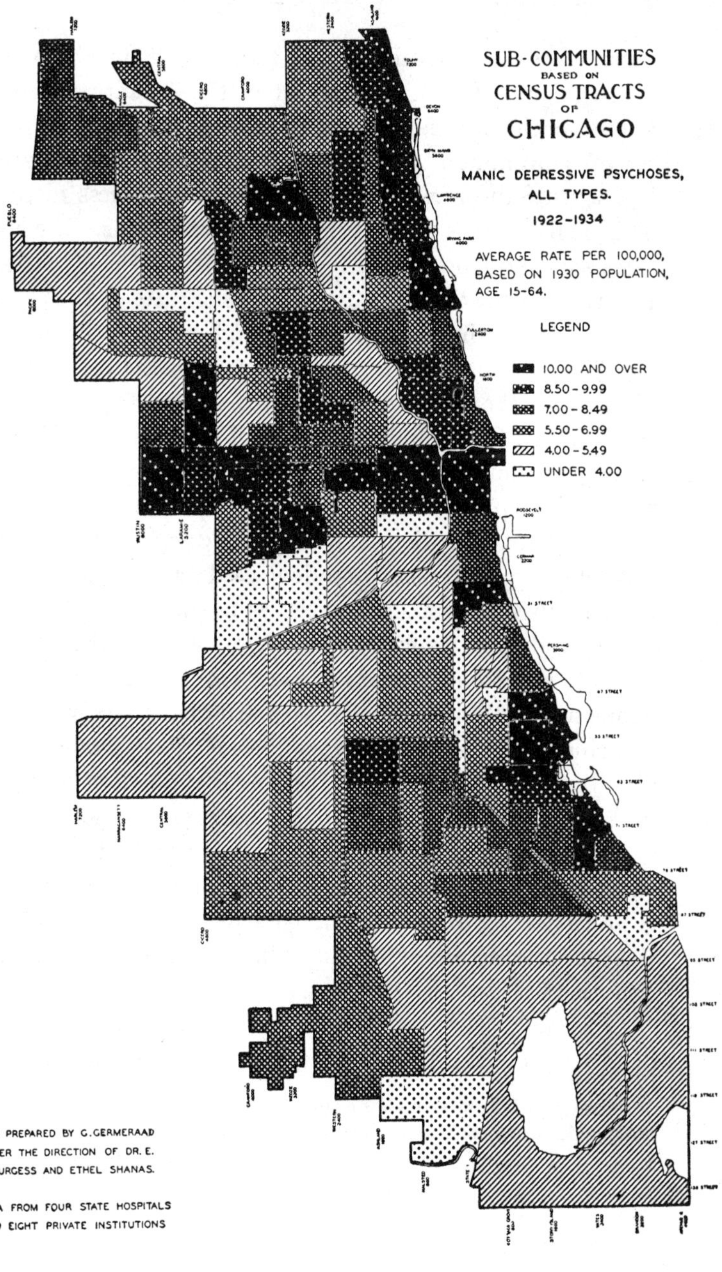

SUB-COMMUNITIES
BASED ON
CENSUS TRACTS
OF
CHICAGO

MANIC DEPRESSIVE PSYCHOSES,
ALL TYPES.

1922-1934

AVERAGE RATE PER 100,000,
BASED ON 1930 POPULATION,
AGE 15-64.

LEGEND

■ 10.00 AND OVER
▨ 8.50 - 9.99
▨ 7.00 - 8.49
▨ 5.50 - 6.99
▨ 4.00 - 5.49
□ UNDER 4.00

MAP PREPARED BY G. GERMERAAD
UNDER THE DIRECTION OF DR. E.
W. BURGESS AND ETHEL SHANAS.

DATA FROM FOUR STATE HOSPITALS
AND EIGHT PRIVATE INSTITUTIONS

upon 2,311 cases. Again there is to be noted the absence of the regular pattern characteristic of the schizophrenic distribution. In this distribution the average rates range from 1.5 in Subcommunity 70, a two-flat and single home area, to 19.3 in Subcommunity 74, the central business district. The median rate is 6.9 and the average rate is 7.2. The high rates show no tendency to form a pattern in their distribution throughout the city. There are high rates at the center of the city and there are also some high rates on the periphery. This is very much at variance from the distribution of any of the schizophrenic rates, where, as has been shown, there is a complete absence of high rates in the outlying communities of the city. Again the lack of skewness in the manic-depressive distribution is to be noted.

When the manic-depressive cases are separated into the two main types of manic and depressed[5] and are distributed in the 120 subcommunities, the same random pattern as formed by the rates for all cases is found. In other words, not only is there no pattern in the total case basis of manic-depressive rates but there is no pattern formed when the two chief types in this group are considered separately. The distribution of manic-depressive, manic type, rates is shown by Map XVI. The rates range from 0.41 in a low-rental, two-flat and single home subcommunity (104) to 10.23 in the Loop (74). The median rate is 2.5 and the average rate is 2.8. These figures indicate a tendency to a skewness which was not characteristic of the other manic-depressive distributions.

In Map XVII is shown the distribution of rates for the manic-depressive, depressed type. The lowest rate is zero

[5] Cases which have been classified according to the other types or where the type is not specified are, of course, not included.

MAP XVI

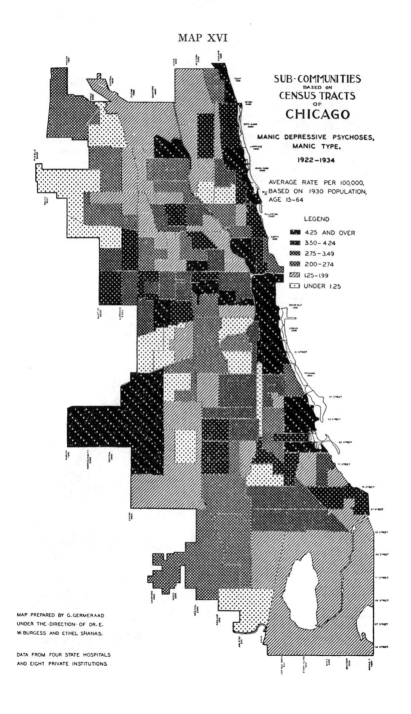

SUB·COMMUNITIES
BASED ON
CENSUS TRACTS
OF
CHICAGO

MANIC DEPRESSIVE PSYCHOSES,
MANIC TYPE.

1922—1934

AVERAGE RATE PER 100,000,
BASED ON 1930 POPULATION,
AGE 15-64

LEGEND

4.25 AND OVER
3.50 - 4.24
2.75 - 3.49
2.00 - 2.74
1.25 - 1.99
UNDER 1.25

MAP PREPARED BY G. GERMERAAD
UNDER THE·DIRECTION· OF DR. E.
W. BURGESS AND ETHEL SHANAS.

DATA FROM FOUR STATE HOSPITALS
AND EIGHT PRIVATE INSTITUTIONS

MAP XVII

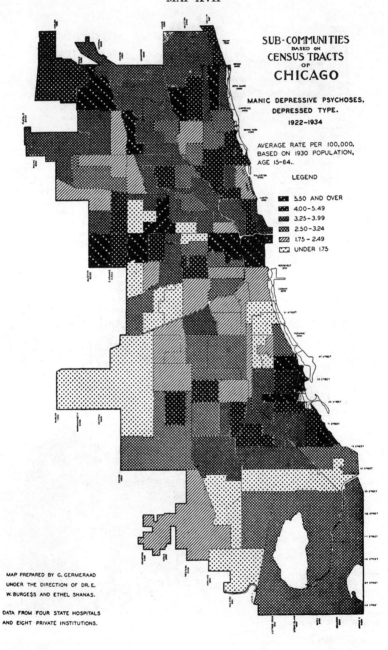

SUB-COMMUNITIES
BASED ON
CENSUS TRACTS
OF
CHICAGO

MANIC DEPRESSIVE PSYCHOSES,
DEPRESSED TYPE.
1922-1934

AVERAGE RATE PER 100,000,
BASED ON 1930 POPULATION,
AGE 15-64.

LEGEND

5.50 AND OVER
4.00 - 5.49
3.25 - 3.99
2.50 - 3.24
1.75 - 2.49
UNDER 1.75

MAP PREPARED BY G. GERMERAAD
UNDER THE DIRECTION OF DR. E.
W. BURGESS AND ETHEL SHANAS.

DATA FROM FOUR STATE HOSPITALS
AND EIGHT PRIVATE INSTITUTIONS.

in Subcommunities 48 and 99 and the highest rate is 7.4 in the West Side hobohemia (61), an extremely low range, although there are more depressed (1,069) than manic (892) cases. The median rate is 3.4 and the average rate is 3.4. In both of these distributions in contrast to the schizophrenic distributions, the random pattern is evident. While there are high rates at the center of the city, there are also high rates in subcommunities on the periphery. It is noted that subcommunities which are similar in character and which fall in the same housing areas have rates for both types which are very much at variance with each other.

ZONE RATES FOR MANIC-DEPRESSIVE PSYCHOSES

In contrast to the schizophrenia series the absence of the typical ecological pattern is also noticeable in the manic-depressive series when the rates are computed for the different zones and the various sections of the city. The zone rates for the various sections of the city are shown in Map XVIII. While the first zone or central business district still has the highest rate in the city, the rates do not decline in magnitude as a function of the distance traveled from the center of the city. In all the other zones of the city the difference between rates is so small that they have hardly any statistical significance. On the North, Northwest, West, and Southwest sides it appears significant to note the low rates in Zones II and III, the inner zones, as contrasted to the higher rates in the outer zones in these sections of the city. Again, the difference in comparison with the schizophrenic series is observed with the absence of a rise in Zone VII on the South and Southwest sides of the city.

AREA RATES FOR MANIC-DEPRESSIVE PSYCHOSES

Again in contrast to the schizophrenic series the rates for the manic-depressive psychoses by housing areas show a

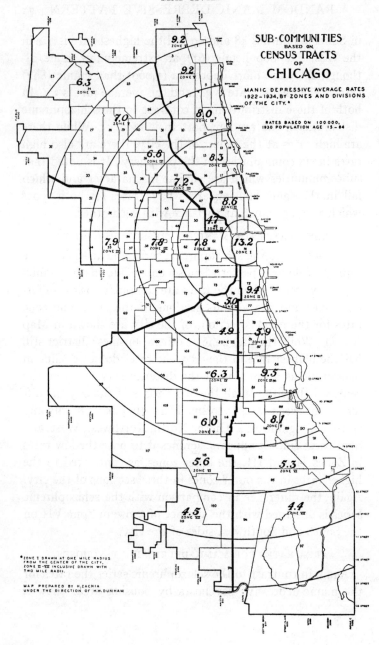

MAP XVIII

SUB-COMMUNITIES
BASED ON
CENSUS TRACTS
OF
CHICAGO

MANIC DEPRESSIVE AVERAGE RATES
1922-1934, BY ZONES AND DIVISIONS
OF THE CITY.*

RATES BASED ON 100,000,
1930 POPULATION AGE 15-64

*ZONE I DRAWN AT ONE MILE RADIUS
FROM THE CENTER OF THE CITY,
ZONE II-VIII INCLUSIVE DRAWN WITH
TWO MILE RADII.

MAP PREPARED BY H.ZACHIA
UNDER THE DIRECTION OF H.W. DUNHAM

lack of consistency as well as a lack of pattern. The lack of pattern is clearly seen by an examination of Table 15 which presents these rates according to nativity and race by housing areas. It is true that the rates in Area 6, the hotel and apartment-hotel district, and Area 11, the rooming-house section, are significantly higher than the rates in the other areas. However, no significant difference is found between these two areas. The reverse was the case with the schizophrenic series. It is to be noted that while the rate for native white of native parentage within Area 8, the foreign-born district, is extremely high, the rate for native white of foreign or mixed parentage is extremely low. In fact, the rate is as low as the rate in better organized communities of the city. While the rate for foreign-born within this area is also extremely low, it is not statistically significant as compared with the rates in the better organized areas of the city. It is to be noted that the rate for Negroes is also extremely low.[6] This absence of consistency in the rates by nativity and race for the different areas of the city tends to reinforce the generalization of the random character of the pattern of manic-depressive rates.

CONCENTRATION OF MANIC-DEPRESSIVE CASES

The concentration of manic-depressive cases is shown in Table 16. The concentration of the cases in each quartile is quite comparable to the concentration of the schizophrenic cases, although, as has been shown, in different communities. In the two upper quartiles there are found 66 per cent of the cases, while these quartiles contain 52 per cent of the population. The concentration might be unduly weighted

[6] It is to be noted that the number of Negroes found in all the areas of the city except Area 9 are too few to compute statistically reliable rates.

TABLE 15

AREA RATES FOR MANIC-DEPRESSIVE PSYCHOSES ACCORDING TO NATIVITY AND RACE, 1922–34

AREA	NATIVE WHITE OF NATIVE PARENTAGE		NATIVE WHITE OF FOREIGN OR MIXED PARENTAGE		FOREIGN-BORN WHITE		TOTAL WHITE*		NEGRO		OTHER RACES		TOTAL (ALL CLASSES)	
	No.	Rate	No.	Rate	No.	Rate	No.	Rate	No.	Rate	No.	Rate	No.	Rate
1. Single home $50+	66	6.5	86	5.0	57	5.7	223	6.0	...	...			223	5.9
2. Single home $50−	22	5.9	32	4.1	32	4.5	89	4.8	1	7.5	1	6.2	91	4.8
3. Two-flat $50+	56	5.0	45	4.6	45	6.8	157	7.0	1	29.0			158	7.0
4. Two-flat $50−	72	7.2	97	4.0	114	5.8	314	5.9	2	1.7			315	5.8
5. Apt. (n.-b.)	210	9.2	166	7.2	147	9.8	569	9.3		16.8			571	9.3
6. Hotel, etc.	86	9.0	53	8.3	34	7.9	209	10.4			2	20.0	211	10.3
7. Apt.-two-flat	58	9.9	62	4.5	101	7.0	243	7.1	3	8.6	2	2.5	248	7.0
8. Apt. (f.-b.)	20	20.4	30	5.6	69	7.8	140	9.2					140	9.1
9. Apt. (Negro)	17	18.7	23	26.4	19	19.9	71	25.9	65	3.1	2	8.8	138	5.8
10. Tenement	32	11.4	18	3.0	60	8.4	121	7.6	2	5.1	1		123	7.4
11. Rooming	35	11.1	16	7.4	33	13.5	91	11.7	1	2.5	1	4.6	93	11.1
City total	674	8.8	628	5.4	711	7.4	2,227	7.7	76	3.2	8	3.5	2,311	7.3

*Includes "White of Unknown Parentage," and this accounts for corrected figures in total cases.

by the high percentage of cases from private hospitals in the manic-depressive group. But even then the concentration of cases is practically the same in the state and private hospitals as in the total group. However, when the respective types of manic and depressed are considered separately, it appears that the percentage of cases is approximately the

TABLE 16

THE PERCENTAGE OF MANIC-DEPRESSIVE PSYCHOSES AND
THE PERCENTAGE OF THE POPULATION IN EACH
FOURTH OF THE 120 SUBCOMMUNITIES GROUPED ON
THE BASIS OF THE MAGNITUDE OF THE RATES

Quartile Grouping	Percentage of Cases in Each Quartile	Percentage of Population in Each Quartile
Fourth or upper...........	40.5	27.8
Third...................	25.5	24.3
Second.................	21.9	25.8
First...................	12.1	22.1
Total................	100.0	100.0

same in each quartile.[7] Apparently the "other" and "unclassified" types account for the concentration of cases observed in the series containing the total cases.

The objective findings in connection with the ecology of the manic-depressive psychosis can be stated as follows: (1) The pattern formed by the states is a random one. Neither high nor low rates are distributed in any systematic fashion throughout the city. (2) The distribution for male and female manic-depressive cases separately show the same typical random and unsystematic distribution.[8] (3)

[7] See Tables 89 and 90 in Appen. B.

[8] The maps showing the distribution of manic-depressive rates for each sex are not shown here, but the rates may be found in the Appendix.

The distribution of rates for private and state hospitals exhibits the same random pattern for both local communities and subcommunities. (4) The rates for the separate types, both manic and depressed, are also extremely random in their distribution. This is expressed by the low coefficient of correlation found when the respective rates are correlated together. This figure is .104 ± .09. (5) Both distributions of manic-depressive rates show an absence of skewness in their frequency distributions, with approximately the same number of communities having high rates as have low rates.[9] (6) The percentages of cases in each quartile is approximately the same for each of the two main types of the manic-depressive psychoses. This indicates the absence of any definite concentration of cases. However, the percentages of cases in each quartile for the complete series is similar to the concentration of schizophrenic cases. (7) The rates for nativity and race by housing areas show the same lack of consistency and absence of pattern.

The absence of similarity between the distribution of rates for the schizophrenic and manic-depressive psychoses is finally to be seen when they are correlated together. In the first set of rates showing the distribution of rates in the 68 local communities of Chicago, the correlation figure is .37 ± .10. When the second series of schizophrenic and manic-depressive rates is correlated together, the coefficient

---

[9] While it is emphasized that the manic-depressive rates form a random pattern in contrast to the "typical" pattern formed by the schizophrenic rates, this is not to imply that the manic-depressive distribution may not be significant in relation to other social factors or in relation to the urban process itself. Rather does it mean that the significance of this pattern is difficult to interpret in terms of social factors. Other implications of this contrast in pattern between these two major functional psychoses are discussed in chap. xi.

of correlation is .24 ± .08. There then appears from this evidence a marked lack of similarity in the pattern formed by the distribution of rates of these two functional disorders. In other words, when any sample of schizophrenic cases is distributed, a definite pattern appears which follows the ecological structure of the city; when any sample of manic-depressive cases is distributed, there is no pattern formed which fits into this ecological scheme of the city.

In several other ways, the manic-depressive group shows striking differences when compared with the schizophrenic group. Both manic and depressed types have larger numbers of married than of single for both sexes, while all three main types of schizophrenia have a larger number of single than married men, although more married than single women.[10] No striking racial differences in the manic-depressive rates show up, except for the low percentage of Negroes with the depressed type of manic-depressive psychoses.[11]

Further evidence on this difference between the two series can be seen when the rates of these two mental disorders are correlated with certain indices of social life. In the second series of distributions of these two functional disorders, a correlation was computed between the respective rates and the housing index for the subcommunities. For this index the percentage of hotels, apartments, and apartment-hotels of the total kind of dwellings in the subcommunities was used. The manic-depressive distribution of rates correlated with this index .50 ± .07. When the manic-depressive cases from private hospitals are eliminated, and this index is correlated with the rates based upon a dis-

[10] See Tables 84 and 85 in Appen. B.

[11] See Table 92 in Appen. B.

tribution of only manic-depressive state hospital cases, the correlation figure drops to .08 ± .10. The distribution of schizophrenic rates in the subcommunities of the city correlates with this housing index −.12 ± .09.

Other indices tend to bring out the differences in the distribution of these two functional psychoses. If one takes as an index of cultural level the median school grade reached by the population in the subcommunities and correlates it with the manic-depressive rates, the resulting coefficient is .44 ± .07. When this index is correlated with the schizophrenic rates, the resulting figure is −.47 ± .07. This would seem to indicate a tendency for the manic-depressive cases to come from those urban areas with a fairly high cultural level. The negative correlation in connection with schizophrenia indicates exactly the opposite, namely, that where one finds a low cultural level in the city one finds, in general, high rates of schizophrenia. This same phenomenon is noted when correlating these rates with an index of economic level in the subcommunities. For such an index the median monthly rental for housing paid by families in each subcommunity was taken. This index correlates with the manic-depressive rates .41 ± .08, and with the schizophrenic rates −.51 ± .07.

It was pointed out in chapter ii that in the second sample of manic-depressive cases exactly 50 per cent of the cases were admitted to public hospitals and 50 per cent were admitted to private hospitals. This high percentage of private hospital cases in the manic-depressive group stands in sharp contrast to the low percentage of schizophrenic cases admitted to private hospitals. This high percentage of private hospital cases in the former group might be explained by either one of two conditions. First, there is a tendency for the private hospital to give the more hopeful diagnosis, which of course means, according to traditional psychiatry, a manic-depressive diagnosis; second, it is possible that there may be a real selection of manic-depressive cases by the private hospitals. Some psychiatrists in the Chicago area feel that the former condition is the true one. However, there is some evidence in this study to indicate that the second condition is more than a remote possibility.

While the pattern of manic-depressive rates in any distribution of such cases does appear to be extremely random, the correlation coefficients with certain selective indices indicate the tendency of the manic-depressive cases to come from a higher social and economic level in contrast to the schizophrenic cases. Some additional evidence on this point similar to that presented above is obtained in contrasting the manic-depressive patients with the schizophrenic patients in terms of median rental paid in the subcommunities.

Over half of all the manic-depressive cases corrected for the population factor come from communities in the city where the median rental paid is $61.68, while half of the schizophrenic total number of cases corrected for the population factor come from communities which pay a median rental of $33.45 or above. There is no doubt that the excessive numbers of private hospital'cases in the manic-depressive group tend to increase markedly this median rental figure. When the private hospital cases are eliminated, however, it is found that the remaining manic-depressive cases, which are now entirely state hospital cases, come from areas where the median rental is $43.44 or above. This rental figure is still considerably higher than that for one-half of the schizophrenic cases where the private hospital cases were not eliminated. This does indicate a definite tendency for the manic-depressive cases to be drawn from higher economic and social levels in the city[12] in contrast to the schizophrenic cases.

From the comparative analysis of the distribution of the schizophrenic and manic-depressive psychoses and their relation to certain indices of social life, the following conclusions might be briefly stated: (1) A comparison of the distribution of the rates of the schizophrenic and manic-depressive psychoses shows them to be unlike each other in almost every respect. (2) The schizophrenic rates show the typical ecological pattern and are concentrated in the disorganized areas of the city, while the manic-depressive psychoses do not show a typical pattern nor any definite concentration in the disorganized and poverty-stricken areas of the city. (3) There is a tendency, although not clearly defined, for the manic-depressive cases to come from a higher cultural and economic level than the schizophrenic cases. (4) The manic-depressive rates according to race and nativity within the different housing areas of the city show a lack of consistency and pattern while the schizophrenic rates tend to show that a rate for a given nativity group increases in areas not primarily populated by members of that group.

From this ecological and statistical evidence it appears that there is some real distinction in the distribution of these two functional disorders in Chicago. How far this will hold true in other American cities is problematical. Every psychiatrist realizes that the diagnostic problems in the functional disorders are great, and the question can be raised as to whether anything is gained by making distributions of

---

[12] Table 86 in Appen. B shows the median rental for the cases corrected for the population factor in all the principal psychoses reported on in this study.

cases falling in these two categories when the percentage of diagnostic error is so high.[13] If this pattern will stand the test of further research, it would seem highly tenable that the evidence here presented indicates that some valid distinction has been made in the classification of these functional disorders.[14] The next chapter will examine the distribution of the different types of schizophrenia to discover whether or not they follow the typical pattern found for the total schizophrenic series.

[13] The difficulty in making the differential diagnosis between the manic-depressive psychosis and schizophrenia, especially the catatonic type, has often been noted in the various textbooks. Certain psychiatrists have estimated that the present data probably contain an error of 30 to 40 per cent in diagnosis. Even with this high percentage of error the number of cases is large enough in each series to claim that the pattern of rates for each of these psychoses is a fairly reliable one.

[14] In connection with the manic-depressive distribution it is of interest to note that a distribution was made of all cases which were diagnosed as psychoneurosis at both private and state hospitals. However, because the total number (977) represented such a small percentage of the estimated total of psychoneurotic cases in the population, it did not appear advisable to present this map. In addition, of the total number of cases in this series, 67 per cent were from private hospitals. This merely seemed to indicate that psychoneurotic persons of some financial means were taken into the private hospitals, while other psychoneurotic persons of less financial security were excluded from the state hospitals, especially because the space would be needed for the more severe cases of mental disorder. The distribution appeared to be somewhat similar to that of the manic-depressive pattern as indicated by a coefficient of correlation between the two distributions of .69 ± .05.

CHAPTER V

THE DIFFERENTIAL DISTRIBUTION OF THE TYPES OF SCHIZOPHRENIA

The symptomatology which, in general, characterizes schizophrenia has already been described. In this major diagnostic category certain subtypes, it is believed, have been clinically differentiated.[1] The hospitals included in this study did attempt to differentiate and diagnose the various subtypes of schizophrenia, which made possible a comparative study of their distribution by urban areas.

The schizophrenic cases in this study are classified, therefore, into the paranoid, hebephrenic, catatonic, simple, and unclassified types. Because of the different conceptions held as to the nature of schizophrenia itself, it is practically impossible to find agreement as to the characteristics of the various types.[2]

[1] Not all institutions even attempt to classify this category of mental disorder into subgroups. Statistical and ecological study of the different types of schizophrenia is made even more difficult than in the major diagnostic groups because of the confusion and inaccuracy of diagnosis. Table 88, in Appen. B, which shows the rate for the paranoid and hebephrenic types of schizophrenia by race and nativity for each sex and in three different periods, gives evidence of this confusion by showing the unreasonably large fluctuations of these diagnoses over periods of a few years.

[2] The authors of the various textbooks are by no means in agreement as to the symptoms of these various subtypes. The descriptions of these types as given here are brief and to some extent represent textbook pictures. One should bear in mind that these pictures of the various types may not correspond to the particular conceptions of these types as held by the psychiatrists who diagnosed the cases used in this study. In fact, it was found that there was considerable variation in the diagnosis of these types in the three

The paranoid type is usually described as having a gradual onset developing on the basis of a stubborn and insensitive nature. The psychosis itself is generally characterized by a relatively fixed system of delusions of persecution and grandeur. Hallucinations are often present and, in general, center around the sense of hearing. A certain apathy and indifference to surroundings are also found, and it is generally held that in the course of time mental stagnation and deterioration take place.

In the hebephrenic type hallucinations and delusions are both present but center around no organized system of ideas. The hebephrenic's behavior is often silly, manneristic, and untidy; absurd and bizarre ideas are usually present, and indifference to environment often makes him appear stupid. As with the paranoid, the onset is supposed to be gradual and the later stages are characterized by a lowered intellectual capacity and mental deterioration.

The catatonic type is usually regarded as developing suddenly and is characterized by one of two states, either excitement or stupor. In the excited state the patient is disturbed and given to impulsive acts, many actions are repeated, and mental confusion often appears marked. His actions apparently have no sense or purpose but are often very stereotyped. The boundaries between the excited and stuporous states are not very well defined and the former often appears to fuse with the latter. In the stuporous state the patient appears listless, is untidy, mute, and shows signs of catalepsy. In this type delusions are often present but hallucinations are rare. It is generally held that recovery

state hospitals from which the data were secured. This was particularly marked in the attempt to make the differential diagnosis between paranoid and hebephrenic schizophrenia.

occurs more often in this type than in the others, but some psychiatrists hold that the recovery is on a lower emotional and intellectual level and is often not permanent.

The simple type is characterized by a gradual falling-off of interest in the external world. There is present a sense of lowered mental ability. The patient is generally moody, irritable, indolent, and indifferent. He appears to lack ambition and is quite content to do the simplest of routine tasks. Delusions and hallucinations are generally never present. The unclassified type is self-explanatory and in it are placed those patients for whom it appears impossible to make the differential subtype diagnosis.

These, in general, represent the textbook descriptions of the types of schizophrenia. As indicated in chapter iii, there are many symptoms which apparently characterize all the types. Of the first three types, there were sufficient numbers available to make it possible to compute rates for local communities. Even though much confusion does exist as to the characteristics of these types, certain differences do appear in the distribution of the rates as indicated by the tables and maps which follow.

COMMUNITY RATES FOR PARANOID SCHIZOPHRENIA

Of the 7,253 cases of schizophrenia, covering the period 1922–31, 2,154 were diagnosed as falling in the paranoid group. The sex and age distribution of these cases is shown in Table 17.

A negligible percentage of paranoid cases are under twenty years of age. Only 26 per cent of the paranoid males and 14 per cent of the females are under thirty years of age, while 28 per cent of the males and 52 per cent of the females are over forty years old. The paranoid series contains by far a much older age group than any of the other types. The preponderance of males is higher than in total schizophrenia, the ratio being 134 males to 100 females.

Map XIX shows the distribution of the paranoid schizophrenic rates in Chicago.[3] The range of rates extends from

TABLE 17

PERCENTAGE DISTRIBUTION OF 2,154 PARANOID
SCHIZOPHRENICS BY SEX ACCORDING TO AGE
AT COMMITMENT

AGE	MALE		FEMALE		TOTAL	
	No.	Per Cent	No.	Per Cent	No.	Per Cent
15–19.........	15	1.3	7	.7	22	1.0
20–24.........	90	7.4	34	3.6	124	5.8
25–29.........	209	17.2	89	9.4	298	13.8
30–34.........	313	25.8	147	15.6	460	21.4
35–39.........	250	20.6	176	18.8	426	19.8
40–44.........	151	12.4	155	16.5	306	14.2
45–49.........	96	7.9	156	16.6	252	11.7
50–54.........	53	4.3	94	10.0	147	6.8
55–59.........	31	2.6	46	4.9	77	3.6
Over 60.......	6	.5	33	3.6	39	1.8
Unknown......	....	....	3	.3	3	.1
Total......	1,214	100.0	940	100.0	2,154	100.0

22 per 100,000 adult population in Community 8*a*, the Gold Coast, directly north of the center of the city, to 532 in Community 32, the central business district and hobo area. The median rate is 93 and the average rate is 115, and these figures indicate a skewness similar to the total schizophrenic series.

[3] The class intervals in the legend are not equal. Ordinarily this is considered an undesirable method of presentation. In this study, however, the intervals are deliberately chosen to reveal contrasts most clearly. All maps should be read with some caution and all legends should be examined.

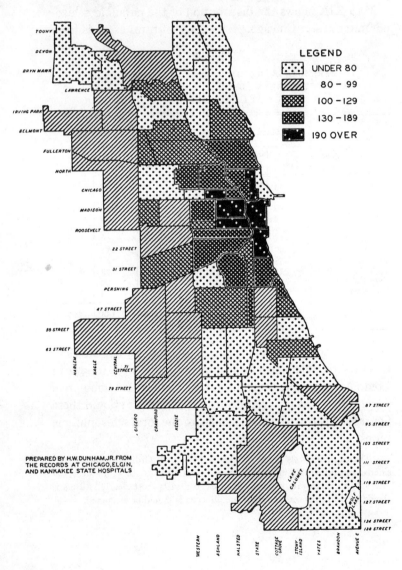

MAP XIX

PARANOID SCHIZOPHRENIA RATES
IN CHICAGO, 1922–1931
PER 100,000 ADULT POPULATION

ESTIMATED 1927 POPULATION

LEGEND

UNDER 80
80 – 99
100 – 129
130 – 189
190 OVER

PREPARED BY H.W.DUNHAM,JR. FROM
THE RECORDS AT CHICAGO,ELGIN,
AND KANKAKEE STATE HOSPITALS

The pattern of rates is much like that of total schizophrenia. The high rates cluster near the center of the city and the low rates are on the periphery. The Negro areas show the characteristic variation of rates from a high rate of 206 in Community 33 south of the business district, a socially deteriorated area, to a low rate of 91 in Community 40, a more stable area. Even in the outlying districts, the rooming-house areas have higher rates than the adjacent residential areas. Community 42, for example, cut in half by Sixty-third Street, an important retail shopping center, is in process of becoming a rooming-house district. The paranoid schizophrenic rate in this area is 101. The adjacent residential apartment-house community on the north, Community 41, has a rate of 58, and the same type of community on the southern side has a rate of 63. This higher rate for the rooming-house district is found also when the rates are computed for each sex separately.

The distributions of paranoid rates for each sex (not shown on maps) are similar to each other but with two exceptional communities. Community 32, which has the highest male rate, is one of the lowest in the female series. Community 17 has an exceptionally high female rate and a low male rate. The position of these exceptional communities has been discussed in connection with the total schizophrenic series. The coefficient of correlation between the rates for the sexes is .46 ± .09.

To indicate more definitely the concentration of cases, the sixty-eight communities were divided into four quartiles on the basis of the magnitude of rates. Table 18 indicates the percentage of the total number of cases and the percentage of the population in the communities of each quartile. The communities in the upper quartiles, although they contain only 48 per cent of the population of the city, contain 65 per cent of the cases.

COMMUNITY RATES FOR HEBEPHRENIC SCHIZOPHRENIA

Of the 3,447 cases diagnosed as the hebephrenic type of schizophrenia, 1,905 are males and 1,542 are females. This ratio, 124 males to 100 females, is lower than the sex ratio of paranoid cases. The average age of the hebephrenic group

TABLE 18

PERCENTAGE OF PARANOID SCHIZOPHRENICS AND THE PERCENTAGE OF THE POPULATION IN EACH FOURTH OF THE SIXTY-EIGHT COMMUNITIES GROUPED ON THE BASIS OF THE MAGNITUDE OF THE RATES

Quartile Grouping	Percentage of Cases in Each Quartile	Percentage of Population in Each Quartile
Fourth or upper...........	38.5	22.0
Third....................	26.5	26.3
Second..................	22.0	28.9
First....................	13.0	22.8
Total...............	100.0	100.0

is lower, 52 per cent of the males and 38 per cent of the females being under thirty years of age. The majority of cases are between the ages of twenty and thirty-five. In each age group over thirty the females have a higher percentage of cases than the males. The percentage distribution by age and sex is shown in Table 19.

The rates vary from 36 in an apartment-house community (1) at the northeast end of the city to 568 in the Loop (32). The median rate is 160 and the average rate is 190. The pattern of distribution, shown in Map XX, is similar to the paranoid distribution. The highest rates are in the same area on both maps and cluster near the center. All of the communities in the upper quartile of the hebephrenic and paranoid groups are the same, with four exceptions. These four communities in the paranoid upper quartile that do not fall in the hebephrenic upper quartile fall close by in the third quartile. The same is true of the four communities

TABLE 19

PERCENTAGE DISTRIBUTION OF 3,447 HEBEPHRENIC
SCHIZOPHRENICS BY SEX ACCORDING TO
AGE AT COMMITMENT

AGE	MALE		FEMALE		TOTAL	
	No.	Per Cent	No.	Per Cent	No.	Per Cent
15–19.........	169	8.9	78	5.0	247	7.2
20–24.........	385	20.2	203	13.2	588	17.1
25–29.........	439	23.1	303	19.6	742	21.5
30–34.........	306	16.1	315	20.4	621	18.0
35–39.........	263	13.8	276	17.9	539	15.7
40–44.........	158	8.3	188	12.3	346	10.0
45–49.........	100	5.3	99	6.4	199	5.8
50–54.........	57	2.9	50	3.2	107	3.0
55–59.........	17	.9	22	1.4	39	1.1
Over 60........	9	.4	8	.6	17	.5
Unknown.......	2	.1	....	....	2	.1
Total........	1,905	100.0	1,542	100.0	3,447	100.0

in the hebephrenic upper quartile that are not in the paranoid upper quartile. All eight communities are near the center of the city.

The hebephrenic rates in the Negro areas show the same gradation as the paranoid rates, with high rates near the center and lower rates to the south. The high rates are in the central business district and nearby hobo areas, in the slums and in the rooming-house districts. None of the communities in the lowest quartile are near the center of the city, except the Gold Coast residential-hotel district (8a).

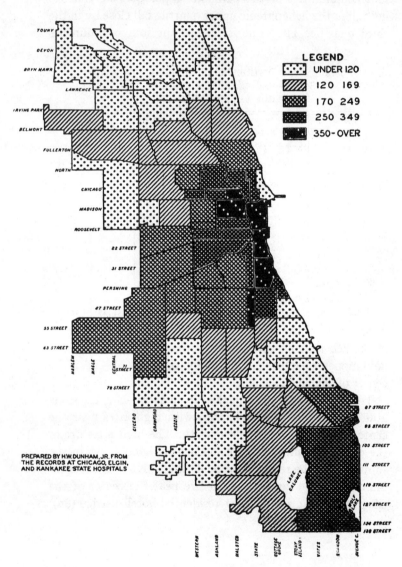

MAP XX

HEBEPHRENIC SCHIZOPHRENIA RATES
IN CHICAGO, 1922–1931
PER 100,000 ADULT POPULATION

ESTIMATED 1927 POPULATION

LEGEND

⣿	UNDER 120
▨	120 169
▦	170 249
▨	250 349
■	350- OVER

PREPARED BY H.W.DUNHAM, JR. FROM
THE RECORDS AT CHICAGO, ELGIN,
AND KANKAKEE STATE HOSPITALS

Community 42, the district which includes Sixty-third Street and a rooming-house area, has a higher rate than the residential communities (41 and 43) on either side, but this difference is not as marked as in the paranoid rates. The similarity of distribution of these types is further shown by the high coefficient of correlation between the hebephrenic and paranoid rates, .75 with a standard error of .05. The

TABLE 20

PERCENTAGE OF HEBEPHRENIC SCHIZOPHRENICS AND THE PERCENTAGE OF THE POPULATION IN EACH FOURTH OF THE SIXTY-EIGHT COMMUNITIES GROUPED ON THE BASIS OF THE MAGNITUDE OF THE RATES

Quartile Grouping	Percentage of Cases in Each Quartile	Percentage of Population in Each Quartile
Fourth or upper...........	35.5	18.4
Third....................	29.5	25.8
Second..................	21.9	28.3
First....................	13.1	27.5
Total...............	100.0	100.0

male hebephrenic rates correlate with the male paranoid rates, .73 ±.05. The female rates of these two types, however, correlate somewhat less, with a coefficient of .49 and a standard error of .09. The lower figure is largely due to four communities which have high hebephrenic rates but low paranoid rates.

The correlation between male and female hebephrenic rates is .50 with an error of .09. This is similar to the correlation between the sex rates for the paranoid series. As in the paranoid correlation, the two communities with unusual positions are 17 and 32. The concentration of cases and population in each quartile is shown in Table 20. The communities of the upper two quartiles contain 65 per cent of the cases but only 44 per cent of the population.

COMMUNITY RATES FOR CATATONIC SCHIZOPHRENIA

Of the 1,360 cases diagnosed as catatonic schizophrenia, 611 are male and 749 are female, a ratio of 82 males to 100 females. This ratio contrasts sharply with the sex ratios of the paranoid and hebephrenic types. The ages of the catatonics average younger than the ages of the other types. The age groups under thirty years contain 67 per cent of the males and 57 per cent of the females. Only 9 per cent of the males and 12 per cent of the females are over forty. There are no cases over sixty years of age in this sample. This age and sex distribution is shown in Table 21.

The catatonic rates[4] range from 10 in an apartment-house community (39) to 177 in a foreign-born community (28e). The median rate is 62 and the average rate is 69. The distribution, shown in Map XXI, is strikingly different from the paranoid and hebephrenic distributions. The rates in the central hobo areas are in the lowest class interval. The high rates are in the immigrant areas but not consistently in those closest to the center. The Negro areas show a gradation that reverses the paranoid and hebephrenic rates. In the Negro belt the catatonic rates are low near the center and successively higher in each community to the south. Community 8b, the rooming-house district north of the

---

[4] The rates presented here were computed on the base of the adult population. A second set of rates was computed using the population of the ages 15–44 years as a base. This latter adjustment, while theoretically a better adjustment for age, actually made very little change in the general pattern of distribution. The second set of rates is shown in Table 96, in Appen. C. The correlation between these two sets of catatonic rates is $+.94\pm.01$.

Loop and west of the Gold Coast district, has a very low catatonic rate although it has a very high paranoid rate.

An examination of the communities 8a, 8b, and 8c, all directly north of the business district, yields some interesting comparisons. In these three areas there are very sharp con-

TABLE 21

PERCENTAGE DISTRIBUTION OF 1,360 CATATONIC SCHIZOPHRENICS BY SEX ACCORDING TO AGE AT COMMITMENT

AGE	MALE		FEMALE		TOTAL	
	No.	Per Cent	No.	Per Cent	No.	Per Cent
15–19	97	15.9	97	13.0	194	14.3
20–24	177	29.0	150	20.0	327	24.0
25–29	132	21.6	180	24.0	312	23.0
30–34	92	15.1	123	16.4	215	15.8
35–39	59	9.7	107	14.3	166	12.2
40–44	34	5.6	62	8.3	96	7.1
45–49	13	2.1	22	2.9	35	2.6
50–54	5	.8	7	1.0	12	.8
55–59	1	.1	1	.1	2	.1
Over 60	....	....	....	....	....	....
Unknown	1	.1	....	....	1	.1
Total	611	100.0	749	100.0	1,360	100.0

trasts in the nature of the social life which are reflected in the high rates of the three types of schizophrenia. Community 8a, the Gold Coast on the lake front, is an area settled by large hotels and high-priced apartment buildings and inhabited primarily by the wealthy. The lack of serious social problems in this area is reflected in the low rate for all types of psychoses.[5] Community 8b is a hobo and room-

[5] The criticism has been made that the wealthy persons in this area use other means than hospitalization to cope with the problem of mental disorder in the family. It may, however, be pointed out that case data on persons admitted to the private hospitals in the Chicago region were included in

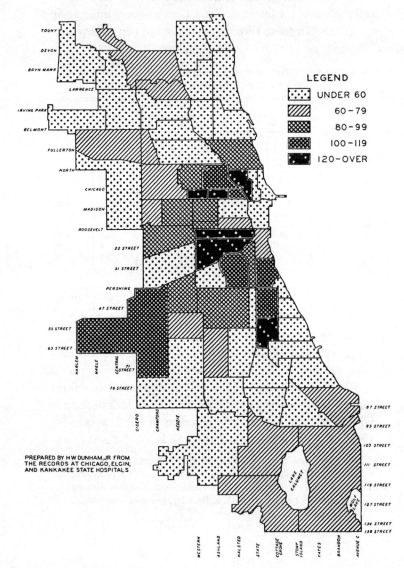

MAP XXI

CATATONIC SCHIZOPHRENIA RATES
IN CHICAGO, 1922–1931
PER 100,000 ADULT POPULATION

ESTIMATED 1927 POPULATION

LEGEND

- UNDER 60
- 60–79
- 80–99
- 100–119
- 120–OVER

PREPARED BY H.W.DUNHAM,JR FROM
THE RECORDS AT CHICAGO, ELGIN,
AND KANKAKEE STATE HOSPITALS

ing-house area, inhabited by a drifting population. There is little family and neighborhood life. For the most part the individuals have few friends and acquaintances. This community has a very high rate of both paranoid and hebephrenic schizophrenia, but a very low catatonic rate. Community 8c, known as "Little Sicily," is a slum area, inhabited primarily by recent immigrants from Italy, although the Negroes have been moving into the community for some time and now have a fair-sized settlement contiguous to the Italian neighborhood. Social disorganization, though somewhat different in type from that of the rooming-house district, is marked. The paranoid and hebephrenic rates are high in this area but not as high as in the rooming-house district. The catatonic rate, however, is much higher than in the other two districts.

Table 22 shows the contrast in each of these three communities of the paranoid, hebephrenic, and catatonic schizophrenic rates. The striking difference in the distribution of rates occurs in the rates for each sex separately as well as for the total cases.

Further evidence of the difference between the pattern of the catatonic rates and the patterns of rates of the paranoid and hebephrenic types are the low coefficients of correlation presented in Table 23.

––––––––

this study. Then, also, a great number of cases which come from this area did not actually live in the Gold Coast proper but in the cheap rooming-houses and hotels on the side streets adjoining this wealthy community. Approximately 50 per cent of the cases in this community were admitted to private hospitals. If it is assumed that these cases are more likely to be from the Gold Coast itself, it would be necessary to have six times the number of cases to equal the rate of the community (8b) adjacent to it, twelve times the number of cases to equal the rate in the hobohemia community (28a) and thirteen times the number of cases to surpass the highest rate in the Loop (32).

Although the community rates for males and females in the catatonic group vary from the corresponding rates of

TABLE 22

COMPARISON OF RATES BY SEX FOR TYPE OF SCHIZOPHRENIA
IN THREE COMMUNITIES

COMMUNITY	PARANOID			HEBEPHRENIC			CATATONIC		
	Male	Female	Total	Male	Female	Total	Male	Female	Total
8a. Gold Coast...	17	26	22	70	78	74	17	13	15
8b. Rooming-house	292	308	299	303	316	309	39	42	40
8c. "Little Sicily".	141	144	142	228	287	255	173	144	160

TABLE 23

RELATIONSHIPS BETWEEN CATATONIC RATES
AND THE PARANOID AND HEBEPHRENIC
RATES BY SEX AND TOTAL

Series	Pearson R	Standard Error
Catatonic with paranoid............	.11	±.12
Catatonic with hebephrenic.........	.39	±.11
Male catatonic with male paranoid ..	.03	±.12
Female catatonic with female paranoid	.25	±.11
Male catatonic with male hebephrenic	.21	±.11
Female catatonic with female hebephrenic.......................	.39	±.11

the paranoid and hebephrenic types, their relationship to each other is similar to that found for the other types. The correlation between male and female catatonic rates is .52 with an error of .09.

The concentration of the catatonic cases, shown in Table 24, is as great as in the other types, although in different areas. It will be noted that 67 per cent of the cases are in the communities of the upper two quartiles, although these communities contain only 48 per cent of the population of the city.

TABLE 24

PERCENTAGE OF CATATONIC SCHIZOPHRENICS AND THE PERCENTAGE OF THE POPULATION IN EACH FOURTH OF THE SIXTY-EIGHT COMMUNITIES GROUPED ON THE BASIS OF THE MAGNITUDE OF THE RATES

Quartile Grouping	Percentage of Cases in Each Quartile	Percentage of Population in Each Quartile
Fourth or upper............	38.9	22.7
Third.....................	28.3	25.5
Second...................	21.3	27.9
First.....................	11.5	23.9
Total...............	100.0	100.0

SIMPLE AND UNCLASSIFIED TYPES OF SCHIZOPHRENIA

Apart from the three types of schizophrenia studied above, there remain 292 cases, of which 230 are classified as simple type, and 62 are unclassified as to type. Of these 292 cases, 186 are males and 106 females. The age distribution is similar to that of the hebephrenic group, i.e., the age group under thirty years contains 55 per cent of the males and 36 per cent of the females. The age and sex distribution is shown in Table 25.

Because of the small number of cases no rates are computed for these cases. Map XXII shows the residence at the time of hospitalization of each of the cases. As in the

other distributions of schizophrenic types a definite clustering of cases in communities near the center of the city
is noted.

TABLE 25

PERCENTAGE DISTRIBUTION OF 292 SIMPLE AND UNCLASSIFIED
SCHIZOPHRENICS BY SEX ACCORDING TO
AGE AT COMMITMENT

AGE	MALE		FEMALE		TOTAL	
	No.	Per Cent	No.	Per Cent	No.	Per Cent
15–19.........	11	5.9	5	4.7	16	5.5
20–24.........	46	24.7	14	13.2	60	20.5
25–29.........	46	24.7	19	17.8	65	22.3
30–34.........	27	14.5	21	19.8	48	16.4
35–39.........	23	12.4	13	12.3	36	12.3
40–44.........	14	7.6	12	11.3	26	9.0
45–49.........	10	5.4	14	13.2	24	8.2
50–54.........	6	3.2	5	4.7	11	3.7
55–59.........	3	1.6	1	1.0	4	1.4
Over 60.......	....	....	2	2.0	2	.7
Total......	186	100.0	106	100.0	292	100.0

TYPES OF SCHIZOPHRENIA RELATED TO INDICES OF
SOCIAL DISORGANIZATION

The distributions of rates of the paranoid, hebephrenic,
and catatonic types of schizophrenia appear to indicate
that both high paranoid and high hebephrenic rates occur in
communities in which the populations are highly mobile.
The catatonic cases, however, do not come from the same
areas but principally from the foreign-born slum areas. In
order to bring out these differences more clearly, correlations are presented showing the relationship of each type
of schizophrenia to certain indices of social disorganization.

MAP XXII

DISTRIBUTION OF 292 CASES OF SCHIZOPHRENIA, SIMPLE AND UNCLASSIFIED TYPES IN CHICAGO, 1922–1931

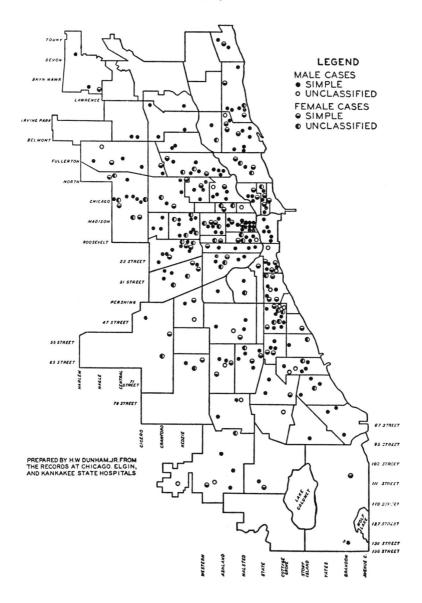

LEGEND

MALE CASES
● SIMPLE
○ UNCLASSIFIED

FEMALE CASES
◐ SIMPLE
◑ UNCLASSIFIED

PREPARED BY H.W DUNHAM,JR. FROM
THE RECORDS AT CHICAGO. ELGIN,
AND KANKAKEE STATE HOSPITALS

INDICES OF STABILITY AND MOBILITY

The percentage of home-ownership is a good index of stability, since high mobility makes home-ownership more difficult and home-ownership inhibits moving. In this study home-ownership rates for each of the sixty-eight communities are computed, based on census data for 1930. The percentages of home-ownership range from 1.2 in Community

TABLE 26

RELATIONSHIPS BETWEEN THE PERCENTAGE OF
HOME-OWNERSHIP AND SOME FUNCTIONAL
PSYCHOSES BY COMMUNITIES

Percentage of Homes Owned with:	Pearson R	Standard Error
Schizophrenic rates (total)*	−.49	±.09
Catatonic rates..........	−.17	±.11
Manic-depressive rates...	−.33	±.10
Undiagnosed rates.......	−.42	±.09

* The similarity of the paranoid and hebephrenic series to the total schizophrenic series accounts for the fact that these series were not correlated with the percentage of home-ownership, although the paranoid and hebephrenic rates are used with the other indices.

32 to 82.6 in Community 17. Coefficients of correlation, shown in Table 26, show the relationships between the home-ownership rates and the rates for the functional psychoses studied. The catatonic rates show a much lower negative relationship to home-ownership than do the rates for the paranoid and hebephrenic types as well as total schizophrenia. These figures more definitely show the relationship between areas of mobility and the high paranoid and hebephrenic rates.

A possible index of mobility is the percentage of total residents and lodgers in each community. From the 1930 census data the computed rates range from zero in several communities on the periphery of the city to 80.9 in Community 32. Table 27 shows the coefficients of correlation of these rates with the rates for the main functional psychoses. The differences between the three types of schizophrenia show up very clearly; the paranoid rates correlate high with mobility, the hebephrenic correlation is somewhat lower, and the catatonic correlation is low and negative.

TABLE 27

RELATIONSHIPS BETWEEN PERCENTAGE OF HOTEL
AND LODGING-HOUSE RESIDENTS AND SOME
FUNCTIONAL PSYCHOSES BY COMMUNITIES

Percentage of Hotel Residents and Lodgers with:	Pearson R	Standard Error
Paranoid rates..........	.82	± .04
Hebephrenic rates.......	.57	± .08
Catatonic rates..........	− .29	± .11
Undiagnosed rates.......	.51	± .08
Manic-depressive rates...	.18	± .11

The distribution of rates in the city and the correlations with the indices of mobility indicate that the catatonic rates have little relationship with the areas of high mobility. The maps do show, however, that the high catatonic rates are found in foreign-born areas and in the Negro areas. In order to test this relationship, correlation coefficients are computed for each functional psychosis to show the relationship between the psychosis and an index of foreign-born and Negro population.[6] The rates range from

[6] The percentage of foreign-born and 50 per cent of the Negro population were used as the base of the rate. The reason for using 50 per cent of the Negro population rather than the entire population is that the children of

20.4 in Community 1 to 70.6 in Community 24a. Table 28 shows the relationships. The differences as compared to the mobility relationships are significant. The catatonic rates show a high relationship to the index of foreign-born and Negro population, while the hebephrenic relationship is much lower, and the paranoid relationship is almost zero.

TABLE 28

RELATIONSHIPS BETWEEN THE PERCENTAGE OF
FOREIGN-BORN PLUS NEGROES AND SOME
FUNCTIONAL PSYCHOSES BY COMMUNITIES

Percentage of Foreign-born and Negroes with:	Pearson R	Standard Error
Paranoid rates............	.11	±.12
Hebephrenic rates........	.40	±.10
Catatonic rates..........	.86	±.03
Undiagnosed rates........	.25	±.11
Manic-depressive rates...	.14	±.11

In a further effort to establish the facts showing the differences between the catatonic rates and the rates for the other schizophrenic types, all the cases of each of the three types of schizophrenia admitted during 1922–34 were sorted into the different nativity and racial classifications. Table 29 shows the percentages. An unexpected fact, apparently inconsistent with the above findings, emerges. The paranoid series has a higher percentage of foreign-born cases than does the catatonic series, and, although the excess of cases is very slight, it is rather interesting to note that the percentage of cases for each type of schizophrenia is approxi-

---

the foreign-born are not themselves foreign-born and are not counted in this class. It is therefore necessary to make the adjustment to prevent the Negro figures from outweighing the foreign-born. The source of these figures is the 1930 census.

TABLE 29

Percentage Distribution of Schizophrenics by Nativity and Race Within Each Type, 1922–34.

Type of Schizophrenia	Native White of Native Parentage		Native White of Foreign or Mixed Parentage		Foreign-born White		Negro		Other Races		White of Unknown Parentage		Total (All Classes)	
	No.	Per Cent	No.	Per Cent	No.	Per Cent	No.	Per Cent	No.	Per Cent	No.	Per Cent	No.	Per Cent
Paranoid.........	511	18.1	891	31.6	1,086	38.5	171	6.1	28	1.0	133	4.7	2,820	100.0
Catatonic........	290	14.9	618	31.7	659	33.8	266	13.6	31	1.6	87	4.5	1,951	100.0
Hebephrenic.....	866	18.7	1,395	30.1	1,714	36.9	496	10.7	75	1.6	94	2.0	4,640	100.0
Other and unclassified......	325	27.9	354	30.4	226	19.4	40	3.4	8	.7	211	18.1	1,164	100.0
Total schizophrenia (all types).	1,992	18.8	3,258	30.8	3,685	34.9	973	9.2	142	1.3	525	5.0	10,575	100.0

mately the same for the native white of foreign or mixed parentage. The lower percentage of foreign-born cases within the catatonic group, however, is made up by the high percentage within the Negro group. The paranoids within this group have a very low percentage of cases.

A similar fact is shown in Table 30. Although the percentage of foreign-born cases in the catatonic group is higher than the percentage of foreign-born persons in the population of the same areas, the percentages of foreign-born cases in the hebephrenic and paranoid group are even higher. The percentage of Negro cases in the catatonic group, however, is higher than the percentage in the hebephrenic and paranoid groups and is also higher than the percentage of Negroes in the population.

The apparent inconsistency between the high correlation of catatonic and foreign-born rates and the lower percentage, even though very slight, of foreign-born cases in the catatonic series as contrasted with the other schizophrenic types is probably to be explained by the age difference between the catatonic cases and the other types. The high catatonic rates in foreign-born and Negro areas, then, are not merely reflections of the different proportions of these groups in the population but apparently result from the operation of other social factors. The catatonic population is similar to the paranoid and hebephrenic population in nationality and racial composition, but of somewhat younger ages and in a very different type of community. The high Negro catatonic rate is the only exception. Negroes, if they show schizophrenic tendencies, are apparently much more likely to develop a catatonic than a paranoid or hebephrenic reaction. The low percentage of paranoids among Negroes may be connected with their culturally impoverished backgrounds as compared to the whites, for it is necessary to have some sort of educational heritage and experience in order

TABLE 30

PERCENTAGE DISTRIBUTION OF SCHIZOPHRENICS BY TYPE ACCORD-
ING TO COUNTRY OF BIRTH AND RACE, IN SELECTED COM-
MUNITIES,* WITH COMPARABLE DATA FROM THE 1930 POPU-
LATION

COUNTRY OF BIRTH AND RACE	PARANOID		HEBE-PHRENIC		CATATONIC		POPULATION—1930	
	No.	Per Cent	No.	Per Cent	No.	Per Cent	No.	Per Cent
Poland...........	82	16.7	199	22.1	67	18.4	61,386	11.1
Italy.............	44	9.4	71	7.9	32	8.8	35,603	6.5
Russia...........	39	8.4	53	5.9	16	4.4	12,792	2.3
Czechoslovakia.....	25	5.3	37	4.1	20	5.5	18,472	3.3
Austria...........	20	4.3	37	4.1	11	3.0	5,369	1.0
Hungary..........	11	2.4	17	1.9	4	1.1	2,300	.4
Lithuania.........	16	3.4	31	3.4	17	4.7	11,960	2.2
Rumania..........	1	.2	5	.5	2	.5	1,274	.2
Greece...........	9	2.4	7	.8	3	.8	2,956	.5
Scandinavia†.......	10	2.1	11	1.2	1	.3	4,310	.8
Ireland...........	3	.6	14	1.6	5	1.9	6,430	1.2
Germany..........	10	2.1	14	1.6	5	1.3	10,400	1.9
England, Scotland, and Wales.......	1	.2	4	.4	1	.3	2,396	.4
Other races........	8	1.7	25	2.7	14	3.8	12,555	2.3
All others.........	9	2.4	13	1.4	7	1.9	6,746	1.2
Total foreign-born..	288	61.6	538	59.6	207	56.8	194,959	35.3
Native-born........	151	32.3	303	33.7	134	36.8	332,189	60.3
Negro............	19	3.7	51	5.7	23	6.4	24,295	4.4
Unknown..........	9	2.4	8	1.0	....	....	....	....
Totals........	467	100.0	900	100.0	364	100.0	551,433	100.0
Total cases.....	2,154	21.7	3,447	26.1	1,360	26.8	3,376,438	16.3

* Communities selected include 8c, 24a, 24b, 28c, 28d, 28e, 31, 34, 37, 60, 61.
† Includes Denmark, Norway, and Sweden.

to construct the elaborate mental system which characterizes the paranoid reaction.

The mobility which appears to be of significance in the paranoid, and perhaps to a less extent in the hebephrenic group, does not appear to be related to the catatonic rates. A further measure of this fact may be found in the relationships of each type of schizophrenia and the ratio of married to single persons for each community, as shown in Table 31. It is assumed that stability is related to a high marriage

TABLE 31

RELATIONSHIPS BETWEEN THE RATES OF EACH TYPE OF SCHIZOPHRENIA AND THE RATIO OF MARRIED TO SINGLE PERSONS BY COMMUNITIES

Marriage Ratio with:	Pearson R	Standard Error
Paranoid rates	− .66	± .06
Hebephrenic rates	− .52	± .08
Catatonic rates..........	− .00	± .12
Schizophrenic rates (total)	− .57	± .08

rate and that mobility and disorganization is related to a low marriage rate. In this table the paranoid and hebephrenic rates show a fairly high negative relationship and the catatonic rates show no relationship at all.[7]

The schizophrenic rates according to nativity and race have already been presented for the eleven housing areas of the city in chapter III. While rates for these nativity groupings for the different types of schizophrenia are not presented here, they tend to follow the same scheme as was noted for the total group. The breaking-up of the total

[7] It should be remembered that these are correlations of rates of marriage and the type of schizophrenia and that they do not indicate the percentage of each type of schizophrenic that is married or single. Table 85 in Appen. B shows these data.

series for the presentation of the nativity rates for the three types of schizophrenia raises some question as to the reliability of such rates because of the small number of cases. However, the rates for the paranoid, catatonic, and hebephrenic types of schizophrenia are shown separately for the different housing areas of the city. These rates are shown in Table 32.

TABLE 32

AREA RATES FOR PARANOID, HEBEPHRENIC, AND
CATATONIC TYPES OF SCHIZOPHRENIA, 1922–34

AREAS	PARANOID		HEBEPHRENIC		CATATONIC	
	No.	Rate	No.	Rate	No.	Rate
1. Single home $50+..	218	5.8	308	8.1	158	5.4
2. Single home $50−..	128	6.7	231	12.2	104	7.1
3. Two-flat $50+.....	164	7.2	243	10.7	116	6.9
4. Two-flat $50−.....	412	7.6	823	15.2	346	8.2
5. Apt. (n.-b.)........	435	7.1	542	8.8	217	4.8
6. Hotel, etc.........	183	8.9	204	10.0	75	5.0
7. Apt.–two-flat......	352	10.0	607	17.2	271	9.9
8. Apt. (f.-b.)........	141	9.2	321	20.9	142	12.0
9. Apt. (Negro).......	238	10.0	584	24.6	305	16.0
10. Tenement.........	265	15.9	418	25.1	164	13.0
11. Rooming..........	284	33.8	359	42.7	53	9.4
City total.........	2,820	9.0	4,640	14.7	1,951	8.2

The first significant fact that stands out in this table is the unusually high paranoid rate in Area 11, the rooming-house district, and the extremely low catatonic rate in this area. The highest catatonic rate is found in Area 9, the Negro apartment-house area. The paranoid rate is considerably lower in this area than is the rate in Areas 10 and 11. The paranoid rate is also considerably lower than the catatonic rate in the foreign-born apartment-house area (8).

This difference between the paranoid and the catatonic rates, as shown by this table, only tends to emphasize the differences found by the examination of the respective maps. The hebephrenic rates follow very closely the rise and fall of the paranoid rates in the different areas, with the possible exception of Area 8, where a low paranoid rate is in evidence but a significant, high hebephrenic rate.

Much of the ecological and statistical evidence presented in this chapter tends to show that the paranoid type of schizophrenia, as compared to the catatonic type, is related to a different type of urban area. The paranoid type of schizophrenia apparently finds its highest incidence in the rooming-house areas of the city and the catatonic type finds its highest incidence in the foreign-born and Negro areas of the city. This distinction might be more clear cut if it were not for the confusion in making the diagnosis in these subtypes of schizophrenia. As the ecological material indicates that the psychiatrists have made a kind of differentiating classification between schizophrenia and manic-depressive psychosis, so would it appear that they have also roughly defined either certain types within the schizophrenic grouping or separate mental disorders in themselves. The hebephrenic grouping appears to be the most uncertain classification of the subtypes and, while in some instances in this statistical material it shows relationships to the paranoid rates, it also shows other median relationships to the catatonic rates. The hebephrenic group possibly represents a poorly defined category within the schizophrenic classification. It is further significant to note that the high rates of all types of schizophrenia are concentrated in the deteriorated sections of the city, although there is a difference in the patterns of these types within the deteriorated areas.

Certain wide differences in the distribution of the various functional psychoses have been shown, even though there still is considerable confusion in the problem of diagnosis. In the following chapters the distribution of psychoses with toxic and organic bases will be examined to see if there are any differences in ecological pattern which occur within these groups as well as in comparison with the patterns for the functional disorders.

CHAPTER VI

THE CONCENTRATION OF THE ALCOHOLIC PSYCHOSES AND DRUG ADDICTS IN THE ZONE OF TRANSITION

There is a wide range of difference in psychiatric opinion upon the etiology of the so-called alcoholic psychoses.[1] Early writers as Kraepelin and Féré stressed hereditary factors in the use of alcohol. Later writers such as Noyes[2] emphasize a homosexual basis. Myerson[3] recognizes social factors but at the same time lays a great deal of emphasis on what he terms individual peculiarity. Henry[4] finds in various degrees of personality stability an index of the amount of alcohol which a person might take without harm to himself. Other writers feel that the use of alcohol is merely the symptom of underlying psychosis and does not in itself provide the etiological basis for a psychosis. Schneider and Pot-

[1] It is, of course, well recognized that within this group of psychoses there are several different reaction types with distinctive enough symptoms for clinical differentiation. A distribution of a sample of alcoholic pcychoses indicating the different types, made at the beginning of this study, showed an absence of differential distribution as to type. The following types were included in this distribution: delirium tremens, Korsakow's psychosis, acute and chronic hallucinosis, acute and chronic paranoid trend, alcoholic deterioration, and other reaction types.

[2] A. P. Noyes, *A Textbook of Psychiatry* (New York: Macmillan & Co., 1928), p. 244.

[3] A. Myerson, *The Inheritance of Mental Disease* (Baltimore: Williams & Wilkins Co., 1925), p. 35.

[4] G. W. Henry, *Essentials of Psychiatry* (Baltimore: Williams & Wilkins Co., 1925), p. 70.

lisch on the basis of their research and clinical experience lean toward this view.[5] DeFursac, while he accepts in a small degree hereditary factors, emphasizes that they are of slight importance as compared to the social factors.[6] Henderson and Gillespie attempt to summarize much of this prevailing opinion as to the consequences of the use of alcohol.

The role of alcohol is responsible for only a comparatively small proportion of certifiable cases of mental disorder. . . . . There is a considerable number of minor mental conditions either of a transient or permanent nature, due to alcohol, which do not reach mental hospitals, but are responsible for much of the homicidal and sexual crimes, and for a considerable portion of the suicides. Alcohol is more commonly a symptom than a cause of mental disorder of a serious and long standing kind.[7]

These statements, in brief, constitute a sample of the prevailing opinion as to the factors behind the alcoholic disorders. If, as some psychiatrists believe, social factors are significant in these psychoses, it might be expected that some insight as to their nature could be gained through a study of the distribution of persons diagnosed as having an alcoholic psychosis.

COMMUNITY RATES FOR ALCOHOLIC PSYCHOSES

During the period of 1922–31, 1,930 patients were admitted to the state hospitals from Chicago and given a diagnosis of alcoholic psychosis. Of these cases 1,652 were males and 278 were females. This extreme preponderance

[5] Quoted from W. A. White, *Outlines of Psychiatry* (Washington, D.C.: Nervous and Mental Disease Publishing Co., 1918), p. 283.

[6] See A. J. Rosanoff, *Manual of Psychiatry* (6th ed.; New York: John Wiley & Sons, 1927), p. 220.

[7] D. K. Henderson and R. D. Gillespie, *A Text Book of Psychiatry* (Cambridge: Oxford University Press, 1927), p. 46.

of males is typical of the sex ratio in the United States for these psychoses.[8] The community rates for the alcoholic psychoses per 100,000 adult population range from zero in Communities 9 and 10, a high-rental residential area, to 554 in Community 28a, a hobohemia and rooming-house district. The median rate is 71 and the average rate is 116, indicating a definite skewness in the distribution of rates.

The configuration formed by the rates is shown in Map XXIII and is similar to that of the total insanity and the schizophrenic series.[9] The high rates are clustered in and near the central parts of the city and the low rates are in the outlying residential districts. A slight rise in the South Chicago region, similar to the schizophrenic configuration, is also noticeable. The foreign-born and central rooming-house areas appear to have the highest rates.

The cases of alcoholic psychoses are mostly between the ages of thirty-five and sixty-four years, the peak age being forty-five to fifty-four years. They come from a low-income group as measured by monthly rentals. In fact, over half of the cases corrected for the population factor come from communities where the median monthly rental is $23.41 or

[8] See *Mental Patients in State Hospitals* (Washington, D.C.: Bureau of the Census, 1928), p. 12.

[9] It is interesting to note that the correlation by local communities between the schizophrenic rates and the alcoholic psychoses rates is .86 ± .03. There is, however, no intention to claim that this similarity of distribution indicates that the alcoholic psychoses are related to schizophrenia, but only that the high rates for these psychoses and schizophrenia occur fairly consistently in the same communities. In this respect, it might be significant to note that both of these disorders are often spoken of as "escapes" from reality. From unpublished studies of alcoholism in Chicago (in the possession of the Department of Sociology at the University of Chicago) it is known that it is in these areas that the high incidence of chronic alcoholism is found. A spot map showing residence of cases of deaths due to alcoholism shows this similiar distribution.

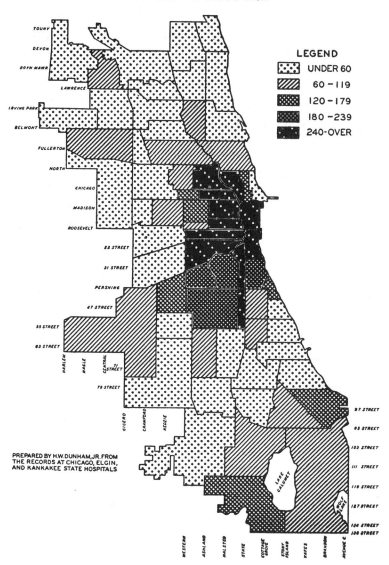

MAP XXIII

ALCOHOLIC PSYCHOSIS RATES
IN CHICAGO, 1922–1931
PER 100,000 ADULT POPULATION

ESTIMATED 1927 POPULATION

LEGEND

UNDER 60
60 – 119
120 – 179
180 – 239
240 - OVER

PREPARED BY H.W.DUNHAM,JR.FROM
THE RECORDS AT CHICAGO, ELGIN,
AND KANKAKEE STATE HOSPITALS

less. The alcoholic psychoses come from the communities with the lowest monthly rentals as compared to any of the principal psychoses.[10]

The effect of group customs on these rates is shown by the position of two communities which include many Russian Jews in their population. These two communities, 24e and 29, have much lower positions in the rank order of rates for this series than in the schizophrenic rank order of rates. The Russian Jews contribute their quota of cases to the schizophrenic rates but not to the alcoholic rates, nor, as will be seen in the following chapter, to the general paralysis rates. In Community 24e only one of the thirty patients with alcoholic psychoses is Jewish and in Community 29 only one of the thirty-seven is Jewish.[11]

Additional evidence concerning the distribution of these psychoses as well as their relationship to nativity can be seen in Table 33, which gives the data by nativity and race as distributed in the eleven housing areas. The rates by sex according to nativity are not presented in this table because the small number of female cases makes such rates extremely unreliable. It is significant to point out, however, that the rates for the two sexes follow a similar pattern and distribution in the different housing areas.

From an examination of the distribution of these rates by areas within the different nativity and racial groups, it can easily be seen that the high rates consistently occur in the rooming-house and Negro areas in the zone of transition at the center of the city. It is significant to note that the rates

[10] See Table 86 in Appen. B.

[11] For further evidence of this lack of alcoholism among the Jews see Henderson and Gillespie, *op. cit.*, p. 45; also Rosanoff, *op. cit.*, p. 14, and B. Malzberg, "The Prevalence of Mental Disease among Jews," *Mental Hygiene*, XIV (October, 1930), 926–46.

TABLE 33

AREA RATES FOR ALCOHOLIC PSYCHOSES ACCORDING TO NATIVITY AND RACE, 1922–34

AREA	NATIVE WHITE OF NATIVE PARENTAGE		NATIVE WHITE OF FOREIGN OR MIXED PARENTAGE		FOREIGN-BORN WHITE		TOTAL WHITE*		NEGRO		OTHER RACES		TOTAL (ALL CLASSES)	
	No.	Rate	No.	Rate	No.	Rate	No.	Rate	No.	Rate	No.	Rate	No.	Rate
1. Single home $50+	16	2.3	31	2.5	58	5.5	110	3.7	3	9.6	....	....	113	3.7
2. Single home $50−	16	6.6	21	4.6	105	14.4	144	10.1	3	27.8	....	....	147	10.1
3. Two-flat $50+	13	3.0	28	3.9	31	4.4	77	4.1	..	....	....	....	77	4.1
4. Two-flat $50−	41	6.7	120	8.3	290	14.3	462	11.3	8	17.5	1	5.6	471	11.3
5. Apt. (n.-b.)	40	2.3	59	3.2	70	4.4	179	3.5	6	60.4	....	....	185	3.6
6. Hotel, etc.	35	4.5	16	2.9	25	5.9	81	4.6	3	18.2	....	....	84	4.8
7. Apt.-two-flat	29	7.4	111	14.5	314	21.5	460	17.6	7	26.1	6	19.2	473	17.5
8. Apt. (f.-b.)	4	6.7	24	11.6	40	4.8	69	6.3	3	68.5	1	130.4	73	6.6
9. Apt. (Negro)	22	30.5	14	23.6	49	47.9	101	43.2	272	16.3	3	17.2	376	19.6
10. Tenement	24	12.1	78	25.4	254	35.4	362	29.6	9	29.5	2	8.0	373	29.2
11. Rooming	79	29.7	72	38.5	104	41.6	267	38.0	19	56.4	4	28.0	290	38.6
City total	319	5.8	574	7.4	1,340	13.5	2,312	10.0	333	17.7	17	10.0	2,662	10.6

* Includes "White of Unknown Parentage," and this accounts for corrected figures in total cases.

for native white of native parentage and for foreign-born white in Area 9, the Negro apartment-house area, are somewhat higher than the rates for these groups in the rooming-house areas (10 and 11). It will be remembered that this fact also stood out in the schizophrenic series. This would seem to imply that persons when living in communities which are populated not primarily by persons of their own nationality or race are more liable to certain forms of mental disorder than when they are living in other communities where the majority of the people are like themselves as to race or nationality. Additional evidence on this point is seen in the Negro rates. The rate for Negroes within their own area (9) is considerably lower than the rates for native white of native parentage, native white of foreign or mixed parentage, and foreign-born white within this area. In fact the Negro rate in this area with one exception is the lowest rate for Negroes as compared to any of the other areas of the city. In addition, it is interesting to note that the rate for foreign-born persons within Area 8, which is primarily populated by other foreign-born persons, is one of the lowest rates for this group. Attention should also be directed to the fairly high rates for the foreign-born white in areas 2 and 4, the single home and two-flat area and the two-flat and single home area, both with rentals under $50. This possibly indicates a certain social and economic striving on the part of the more ambitious foreign-born to push out into the better areas which are inhabited primarily by the native-born. While they may be able to stand the economic strain in these areas, they apparently find it impossible to make a cultural adjustment to the social life about them, and this inability may be reflected in the average high rates for alcoholic psychoses in these areas.

Table 34 shows that the extent of concentration by communities in the distribution of alcoholic psychoses is great. The bulk of the cases are in fact concentrated more heavily at the center of the city than in the schizophrenic series.[12]

Some additional evidence in relation to the type of area with which high rates for alcoholic psychoses are associ-

TABLE 34

PERCENTAGE OF ALCOHOLIC PSYCHOSES AND THE PERCENTAGE OF THE POPULATION IN EACH FOURTH OF THE SIXTY-EIGHT COMMUNITIES GROUPED ON THE BASIS OF THE MAGNITUDE OF THE RATES

Quartile Grouping	Percentage of Cases in Each Quartile	Percentage of Population in Each Quartile
Fourth or upper.....	49.0	17.8
Third.............	28.0	25.3
Second............	15.3	28.3
First.............	7.7	28.6
Total.........	100.0	100.0

ated is shown when these rates are correlated with certain indices of community disorganization. The same indices are used as in the schizophrenic series, and the resulting coefficients of correlation are to be seen in Table 35.

None of these correlation figures are unusually high or low but fall in an intermediate range. High rates for alcoholic psychoses apparently occur equally in communities characterized by mobility as well as those characterized by predominance of foreign-born persons and Negroes. The striking differences found when these indices were corre-

[12] See chap. iii.

lated with the different types of schizophrenia are not in evidence here.

The use of other indices of social life brings out rather strikingly the close identification of these psychoses with the zone of transition. Here it is significant to note that of the total cases of alcoholic psychoses in the period between 1922 and 1934 inclusive, only 4 per cent of the cases were admitted to private hospitals and 96 per cent to state hos-

TABLE 35

RELATIONSHIPS BETWEEN THE RATES FOR ALCO-
HOLIC PSYCHOSES AND CERTAIN SELECTED
SOCIAL INDICES BY COMMUNITIES

Rates for Alcoholic Psychoses with:	Pearson R	Standard Error
Percentage of home-ownership.	−.42	±.09
Percentage of lodging-house and hotel residents.........	.45	±.09
Percentage of foreign-born plus Negroes..................	.48	±.09

pitals. These psychoses, if real mental disorders, evidently affect people almost entirely on the lower income levels. The following additional correlation figures by the 120 sub-communities also attest to this fact. The alcoholic psychoses rate correlates with the percentage of the population on relief .72 ± .04, with median monthly rental and home-valuation −.66 ± .05, with the percentage of the native-born population of German and Scandinavian parentage −.53 ± .07, and with the percentage of the foreign-born German and Scandinavian population −.38 ± .07. The third correlation figure indicates that these psychoses are negatively related to communities with a high percentage of native-born. The German and Scandinavian people represent the oldest nativity groups in the city. The latter correlation figure tends to show that the foreign-born of these two nativity groups live in poorer sections of the city as compared to the native-born and as a result are more closely related to the incidence of alcoholic psychoses.

COMMUNITY RATES FOR DRUG ADDICTION
(WITHOUT PSYCHOSES)

The drug addiction series is in some respects comparable to the alcoholic series. Especially is this true in regard to the sex ratio. Of the 772 cases of drug addiction without psychoses used in this study, the majority are male, the ratio being 308 males to 100 females or actually 583 males and 189 females. Often similar theories are used to explain drug addiction as are used to explain the alcoholic psychoses. When drug addiction is found with a psychotic condition it is possibly a case where the use of drugs is superimposed upon an already existing psychotic base. Unlike the alcoholic psychoses, most of the cases of drug addiction which come to the state hospitals are voluntary admissions,[13] and therefore represent a definite selective group.

The distribution of rates for this series is shown in Map XXIV. The rates range from zero in numerous subcommunities to 68.2 in Community 74, the central business district and hobo area. Because of the relatively small number of cases the chance fluctuation of rates is considerable. The median rate is 0.85 and the average rate is 2.83.

There appears to be a general concentration in and near the center of the city. The highest rates are in the hobo and rooming-house districts although some high rates appear

[13] E. M. Ward, "A Study of Voluntary Commitments," *Collected and Contributed Papers* (Elgin State Hospital; Chicago: Paramount Press, Inc., December, 1932), pp. 156–68.

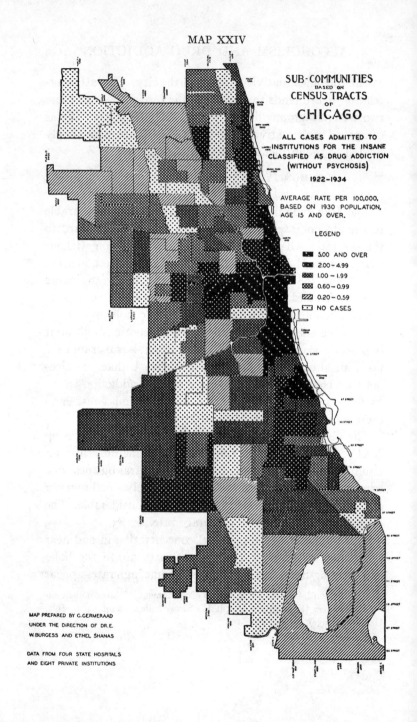

MAP XXIV

SUB-COMMUNITIES
BASED ON
CENSUS TRACTS
OF
CHICAGO

ALL CASES ADMITTED TO
INSTITUTIONS FOR THE INSANE
CLASSIFIED AS DRUG ADDICTION
(WITHOUT PSYCHOSIS)
1922-1934

AVERAGE RATE PER 100,000,
BASED ON 1930 POPULATION,
AGE 15 AND OVER.

LEGEND

5.00 AND OVER
2.00 – 4.99
1.00 – 1.99
0.60 – 0.99
0.20 – 0.59
NO CASES

MAP PREPARED BY G.GERMERAAD
UNDER THE DIRECTION OF DR.E.
W.BURGESS AND ETHEL SHANAS

DATA FROM FOUR STATE HOSPITALS
AND EIGHT PRIVATE INSTITUTIONS

in the apartment and apartment-hotel districts. The age spread of these cases is wide, with a peak age group of thirty-five to forty-four years. There are fewer married cases than single in all nationality groups. The highest rates are among the native-born whites, and the lowest group, the foreign-born white, has rates roughly one-tenth of those

TABLE 36

AREA RATES FOR DRUG ADDICTION (WITHOUT PSYCHOSES) 1922–34

Area	No. of Cases	Rate
1. Single home $50+........	25	.6
2. Single home $50−........	9	.5
3. Two-flat $50+..........	23	1.1
4. Two-flat $50−..........	42	.7
5. Apt. (n.-b.)............	75	1.2
6. Hotel, etc..............	84	3.9
7. Apt.–two-flat...........	41	1.1
8. Apt. (f.-b.).............	17	1.1
9. Apt. (Negro)...........	68	2.8
10. Tenement..............	62	3.5
11. Rooming..............	326	36.4
City total............	772	2.3

of the native-born whites. Negroes and other races are intermediate.

The rates for the different areas of the city are to be seen in Table 36. As can be seen from this table, by far the highest rate occurs in the central rooming-house area. All of the other areas have extremely low rates, although the hotel and apartment-hotel area (6) has the second highest rate which might be expected from the character of the distribution pattern by subcommunities.

It is noted that almost 50 per cent of the cases are in the hobo and rooming-house areas at the center of the city. Like persons with alcoholic psychoses, drug addicts come mainly from the zone of transition where it is, of course, easier to obtain an in-group solidarity and maintain contacts with other addicts and "dope" peddlers. This is

TABLE 37

PERCENTAGE OF DRUG ADDICTS (WITHOUT PSY-
CHOSES) AND THE PERCENTAGE OF THE POPU-
LATION IN EACH FOURTH OF THE 120 SUBCOM-
MUNITIES GROUPED ON THE BASIS OF THE
MAGNITUDE OF THE RATES

Quartile Grouping	Percentage of Cases in Each Quartile	Percentage of Population in Each Quartile
Fourth or upper.............	76.7	24.1
Third.....................	14.5	26.2
Second...................	7.5	26.0
First.....................	1.3	23.7
Total.................	100.0	100.0

attested by a correlation figure of .61 ± .06 by the eleven areas when these two series are taken together. This figure drops to .48 ± .07 when the rates of the two series are correlated by the 120 subcommunities. This low correlation figure is caused by the insufficient number of cases in the drug addiction series for the computation of reliable subcommunity rates.

As might be expected from the area analysis of rates, the concentration of cases in this series is unusually marked. More than three-fourths of all the cases are to be found in the upper quartile. This concentration is shown in Table 37.

This ecological and statistical evidence shows that the alcoholic psychoses have their highest rates in and near the center of the city. In this sense the patterns of their rates are quite similar to those patterns found in the schizophrenic series but unlike the patterns found in the manic-depressive series. In the alcoholic psychoses the rates by housing areas for the different nativity classification indicated that there was some relationship between liability to the psychosis and the fact that the person does not live in a community primarily populated by his own nativity or racial group. The distribution of drug addicts, while representing a definite selection of cases, shows a pattern similar to the alcoholic psychoses. Not only do high rates occur in the zone of transition but also the bulk of the cases are to be found in this zone. The fact that the next highest rate for drug addiction is in the apartment-hotel and hotel area would seem to indicate that drug addicts tend to select the more mobile areas of the city where their habits and activities are less likely to be scrutinized.

CHAPTER VII
THE ASSOCIATION OF GENERAL PARALYSIS
WITH VICE AREAS

Although general paralysis is an organic disease, the result of a syphilitic infection of the brain, it is indirectly but closely connected with certain social conditions making for sexual promiscuity. The cause of this disease has been known for some time but only recently has there been any degree of success in treatment. The final stage of syphilitic infection of the nervous system is often complete dementia because of the damage to the brain tissue caused by the *Spirochaeta pallida*. This end result obviously constitutes a grave problem and medical men have been puzzled as to why it occurs in some cases and not in others.[1]

Out of the total number of cases of general paralysis in our series for the period of 1922–34 inclusive, 94 per cent were admitted to the state hospitals and only 6 per cent of the cases were cared for in the private hospitals. It is also found that of all the diagnoses during this period, general paralysis accounted for 14 per cent in the state hospitals and for 5 per cent in the private hospitals. Therefore, a higher proportion of persons on the lower-income levels develop general paralysis. The possibility, however, must be considered that persons with syphilis eventually lose their earning power, find it impossible to compete successfully with other members of their respective occupational groups, and consequently tend to drift into the low-income groups.

[1] A. Rosanoff, *Manual of Psychiatry* (New York: John Wiley & Sons), pp. 270–75.

This disorder does not constitute so great a percentage of admissions to mental hospitals as is popularly believed, varying, as it does, between 9 and 20 per cent in the hospitals throughout the United States.[2] There is a much higher rate of admissions in urban areas than in rural areas. During the period 1922–31, 3,106 persons from Chicago were admitted to the state hospitals and given a diagnosis of general paralysis. Of this total, 2,459 were males and 647 were females.

The distribution of these rates by local communities is shown in Map XXV. The rates per 100,000 adult population range from 27 in an apartment-house community (2) to 628 in a hobohemia community (28a). The median rate is 118 and the average rate is 168. It is noted that the high rates are concentrated in communities at and contiguous to the center of the city. In fact the highest-rate communities are the hobo areas, the rooming-house areas, at the center, and the Negro areas, extending southward from the central business district. In general, the high rates start at the center of the city and decline in every direction with few exceptions as one travels toward the periphery. The configuration formed by the rates is not quite as consistent as the configurations for some of the other types of mental disorder, but this is apparently due to the distribution of different ethnic groups in the city population.

In these areas which have high rates for general paralysis, many forms of prostitution flourish, and venereal infections are quickly spread. The high rates for this form of mental disorder are also in the same areas as the high rates for the different venereal diseases.[3] However, it is apparent that

[2] *Mental Patients in State Hospitals, 1928* (Washington, D.C.: U.S. Department of Commerce, Bureau of the Census).

[3] W. C. Reckless, *Vice in Chicago* (Chicago: University of Chicago Press, 1934), pp. 208–13.

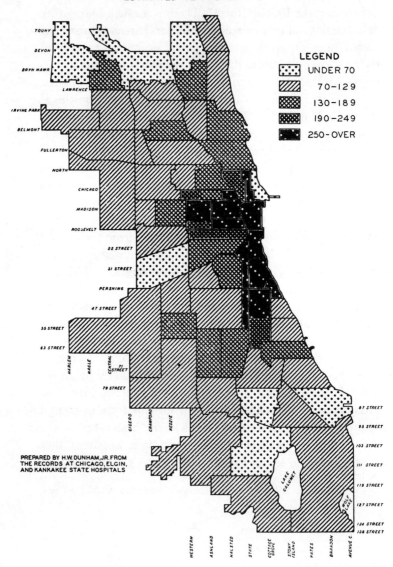

MAP XXV

GENERAL PARALYSIS RATES
IN CHICAGO, 1922−1931
PER 100,000 ADULT POPULATION

ESTIMATED 1927 POPULATION

LEGEND
UNDER 70
70−129
130−189
190−249
250−OVER

PREPARED BY H.W. DUNHAM, JR. FROM
THE RECORDS AT CHICAGO, ELGIN,
AND KANKAKEE STATE HOSPITALS

the presence of vice establishments is not the only factor to account for the high rates. This is especially seen in contrasting the rates in the Italian and Jewish communities. The rates are high in the Italian communities 8c and 28c near the center of the city, while they are fairly low in the Jewish communities 24d and 29. As in the case of the alcoholic psychoses, there is almost a total absence of Jewish paretics.

It is known that the Negroes have a higher rate of syphilis than the whites in the United States. The general paralysis rates for the Negro areas in Chicago, however, vary from near the highest rate to a moderately low rate. The rates in the three Negro communities, 35, 38, and 30, the column extending south of the central business district, are 580, 321, and 205 respectively. Therefore, although the rates in the Negro areas are higher in general than the rates in the white areas, there is still a considerable amount of fluctuation by community. This fact would seem to indicate that the rate for this disorder tends to decrease among Negroes as their cultural and economic level rises and they become more like the whites in their cultural patterns.[4]

Although there are fewer women than men in this group, the female rates show a similar pattern. The correlation between the male and female rates is .73 with a standard error of .05.

The age rates are highest between the ages of thirty-five to sixty-four, with the group forty-five to fifty-four years having the highest rate.[5] The median rental of $39.30 is

[4] Franklin Frazier, *The Negro Family in Chicago* (Chicago: University of Chicago Press, 1932).

[5] See also M. C. Peterson, "Age Incidence of Paresis," *American Journal of Psychiatry*, XII (November, 1932), 521–22.

somewhat higher than that of the schizophrenic series ($33.45) and somewhat below that of manic-depressive state hospital series ($43.44).

In Table 38 are shown the rates for the different nativity and racial classifications in the eleven housing areas of the city. The results correspond closely to the analogous figures for the alcoholic psychoses series. As in this series, it is significant to note the low rate in Area 8, the foreign-born apartment-house district. This area has the third lowest rate in comparison with all the other areas of the city. As might be expected after viewing the distribution map, we find the rooming-house and Negro areas with rates which are very much higher than the rates in any of the other areas of the city. In all the nativity classifications the lowest rates are to be found in the single home and two-flat areas. The rates for the native white of foreign or mixed parentage and the foreign-born white in the foreign-born apartment-house area (8)[6] are exceptions to this generalization, for within these classifications they represent the lowest rates for all the areas of the city. In addition, the rates for the two native white groups within the Negro apartment-house area (9) are the highest for any of the areas of the city. However, the rate within this area (9) for Negroes is very much lower than the rates for Negroes in the other areas of the city. Obviously, other factors are at work to produce these rates besides the proximity to districts of the city, where prostitution flourishes.

Other evidence which tends to support the facts presented in the foregoing table is shown when the rates of general

[6] The population of the foreign-born apartment-house areas in Chicago is predominantly Jewish. As indicated, Jewish communities have low rates for general paralysis.

TABLE 38

AREA RATES FOR GENERAL PARALYSIS BY NATIVITY AND RACE, 1922–34

AREA	NATIVE WHITE OF NATIVE PARENTAGE		NATIVE WHITE OF FOREIGN OR MIXED PARENTAGE		FOREIGN-BORN WHITE		TOTAL WHITE*		NEGRO		OTHER RACES		TOTAL (ALL CLASSES)	
	No.	Rate	No.	Rate	No.	Rate	No.	Rate	No.	Rate	No.	Rate	No.	Rate
1. Single home $50+	49	4.7	82	4.6	102	9.0	263	6.7	8	19.6	....	....	271	6.8
2. Single home $50−	33	8.6	33	4.2	72	9.2	148	7.6	1	7.3	....	....	149	7.5
3. Two-flat $50+	47	7.3	69	6.9	71	9.3	202	8.4	2	54.6	1	95.0	205	8.5
4. Two-flat $50−	132	12.9	200	8.2	224	10.3	593	10.5	18	29.8	3	11.4	614	10.7
5. Apt. (n.-b.)	212	8.9	191	7.9	193	11.2	643	9.9	3	24.2	2	17.6	648	9.9
6. Hotel, etc.	119	11.9	74	11.0	68	14.4	290	13.5	5	25.2	3	29.8	298	13.7
7. Apt.-two-flat	64	10.7	104	7.4	196	12.4	385	10.7	16	44.8	11	13.4	412	11.1
8. Apt. (f.-b.)	14	13.9	21	3.9	73	7.6	123	7.7	1	16.8	2	181.0	126	7.8
9. Apt. (Negro)	96	97.2	43	46.1	53	48.3	235	77.9	625	29.4	5	21.7	865	35.3
10. Tenement	48	16.4	106	17.3	185	23.8	370	22.0	13	32.6	1	2.7	384	21.8
11. Rooming	117	35.2	90	38.7	148	55.4	392	47.1	32	77.1	7	31.7	431	48.1
City total	931	11.8	1,013	8.5	1,385	12.9	3,644	11.9	724	30.1	35	15.0	4,403	13.2

* Includes "White of Unknown Parentage" and this accounts for corrected figures in total cases.

paralysis are correlated with certain indices of community social life. These coefficients of correlation are shown in Table 39.

Perhaps the most significant correlations in the foregoing table are the ones for the foreign-born and Negro communities. The negative correlation figure in the case of the for-

TABLE 39

RELATIONSHIPS BETWEEN THE RATES FOR
GENERAL PARALYSIS AND CERTAIN
SELECTED INDICES BY COMMUNITIES

Rates for General Paralysis with:	Pearson R	Standard Error
Percentage of foreign-born plus Negroes..................	.15	±.11
Percentage of foreign-born....	−.17	±.11
Percentage of lodging-house and hotel residents........	.58	±.08
Percentage of lodging-house and hotel residents plus Negroes.....................	.71	±.06
Percentage of home-ownership.	−.55	±.09
Percentage of single homes....	−.09	±.12

eign-born exclusively, apparently indicates that the foreign-born within their respective immigrant colonies are not likely to develop general paralysis. The strong family ties and primary group relationships apparently protect their members from coming in contact with sexual vice. These ties become weakened in the first generation born in America and, as has been shown, the rate for this group tends to rise. It is to be noted that the addition of Negroes to the foreign-born tends to give a positive correlation although a low one. This fact is more clearly seen in the next set of correlations where the addition of the Negroes to the lodging-house and hotel population tends to raise the correlation figure by almost two points. These correlations with the general paralysis rates indicate the close association of this disease with areas of high mobility. The median negative correlation with home-ownership shows the relative absence of this disease in the well-organized communities.

The close identification of the high rate areas for general paralysis with those areas having high rates for venereal disease and prostitution has been pointed out above. This fact is more definitely demonstrated when the general paralysis rates are correlated with the rates for venereal disease and prostitution in the local communities of the city. The correlation of the general paralysis rate with the venereal disease rate for 1928 gives a coefficient of .87 ± .03. When the general paralysis rates are correlated with the vice-resort rates for 1928, the resulting figure is .72 ± .06. This coefficient of correlation drops slightly, to .66 ± .07, when a correlation is effected between the general paralysis rate and the 1928–30 vice-resort rate.[7] These figures indicate a fairly definite relationship between the incidence of general paralysis and the proximity to houses of prostitution.

While no actual distribution of the rates for the 120 subcommunities is presented here, these rates have been computed on the basis of the case distribution shown in Table 38. The relationships of these rates to certain social in-

[7] The figures which made these correlations possible are taken from Reckless' study of vice in the city of Chicago. See Reckless, *op. cit.*, pp. 180–81 and 210–11. It should be noted, of course, that the venereal disease rate is based upon all types of venereal disease including syphilis. Syphilis in its distribution in the city apparently follows the pattern for the other types of venereal disease. Further, it should be noted that the correlation figures are based upon fifty-five communities instead of the sixty-eight used in this study. This was made necessary because Reckless used a slightly different combination of communities than did the authors of this study.

dices in the population appear to have some significance and aid in interpretation. The relationship between these rates and the percentage of population on relief is .66± .05, and with the sex ratio is .56 ± 06. These relationships tend to show that high general paralysis rates are connected with fairly low-income areas as well as with a disproportion of the sexes. This latter point would indicate that isolation from normal contacts with members of the opposite sex tends to foster a situation conducive to the development of prostitution and consequently to a certain amount of syphilitic infection.

In Table 40 the extent of concentration of the general paralysis cases is shown. The concentration of cases in this series is very similar to the various types of schizophrenia and is quite marked with the bulk of the cases falling in the high-rate communities near the center of the city.

While treatment of this disease is entirely a medical matter, its prevention is primarily a social problem. Certainly, here the mores which restrict knowledge concerning prophylaxis define certain social aspects of the problem. It is significant that only between 5 and 10 per cent of persons infected with syphilis develop general paralysis. Such low percentages no doubt bear some relationship to success in treatment, age of infection, and the death-rate of persons with syphilis. But, unlike the syphilitic cases, the poor prognosis and chronicity of the disease make practically all cases available for study and treatment. The first step in attempting to control this disease is to determine the number and distribution of both syphilitic persons and general paralysis cases in the city. The evidence presented here shows rather definitely that the high incidence of general paralysis is to be found in the rooming-house and hobohemia areas and that a much lower incidence is in the areas of home-ownership. The small percentage of these cases in the private

TABLE 40

PERCENTAGE OF GENERAL PARALYSIS AND THE
PERCENTAGE OF POPULATION IN EACH FOURTH
OF THE SIXTY-EIGHT COMMUNITIES GROUPED
ON THE BASIS OF THE MAGNITUDE OF THE
RATES

Quartile Grouping	Percentage of Cases in Each Quartile	Percentage of Population in Each Quartile
Fourth or upper.............	39.3	17.2
Third.....................	31.0	31.4
Second...................	17.7	26.6
First.....................	12.0	24.8
Total.................	100.0	100.0

hospitals also attest to this point. This has also been shown to be true of the rates for venereal disease. Both types of data have been found of value to the local public health authorities in the present campaign to eradicate syphilis.

CHAPTER VIII

THE CORRELATION OF OLD AGE PSYCHOSES WITH AREAS OF TENANCY

The senile psychoses are similar to the other clinical classifications which have been examined, inasmuch as there are no adequate and objective criteria for distinguishing them. Here, also, the etiological base is still obscure. Some psychiatrists insist that senile psychosis is in reality late schizophrenia; others point to tissue changes of the brain cells as the causative factor while at the same time stressing the part played by heredity. Certain factors, largely social in origin, such as old age dependency, the isolation of the aged, sudden changes in the aged person's routine of life, and the disintegration of families, also tend to make the problem of diagnosis more difficult. Some psychiatrists recognize this fact and warn that mere senility must be distinguished from the symptoms of a real senile psychosis. A study of the distribution of these psychoses[1] should show how these social factors may enter into the diagnostic picture.

THE SENILE PSYCHOSES

Of the 1,118 cases diagnosed as senile psychoses, 491 are male and 627 are female. The ages of this group are much

---

[1] This diagnostic category contains several types which can be distinguished in the clinic but which also often overlap. These types include: simple deterioration, the presbyophrenic, the delirious and confused, the depressed and agitated, the paranoid, and the presenile. However, the small number of cases in each type make it necessary to ignore these subdivisions in the statistical analysis.

higher than for any other form of mental disorder. The rates begin to be high over the age of sixty-five years and are much higher at ages of seventy-five and over.

The community rates (expressed per 1,000 of the 1930 population, sixty-five years of age and older) vary from 0.8 in a two-flat community (44) to 35 in a rooming-house community (33). The median rate is 7.3 and the average rate 9.9. Because of the small number of cases and the low population base the chance variation of rates is great. The pattern of distribution, shown in Map XXVI shows that highest rates are in the Negro and rooming-house areas with the next highest rates in the foreign-born communities at the center of the city.

In Table 41 are shown the rates for senile psychoses by nativity and race for the different housing areas of the city. The rates for the native-born white of foreign parentage and for the foreign-born white within the foreign-born area (8) are the lowest for any of the areas of the city. In turn, the native white of native parentage has next to the highest rate for this area, the highest rate of 143.1 being found in the Negro apartment-house area (9). In fact, for all the white nativity groupings this area (9) has the highest rate in the city with the rooming-house area (11) following next in order. The rate for Negroes within their own area is also one of the highest in the city for this racial grouping. While many of the other areas do have high rates, the low case basis on which these rates are figured raises some question as to their reliability. The fact that both races and all nativity groups have high rates consistently in the Negro and rooming-house areas is in marked contrast to the evidence presented on this point for the alcoholic psychoses and general paralysis.

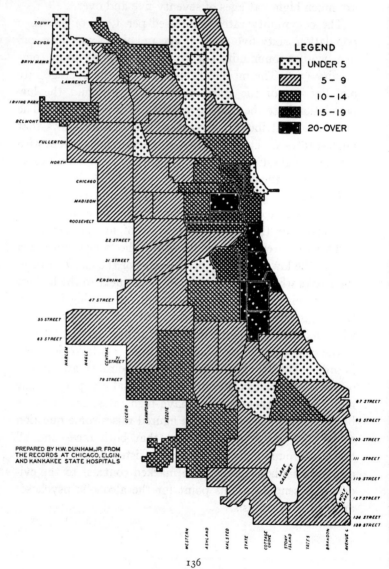

MAP XXVI

SENILE PSYCHOSES RATES
IN CHICAGO, 1922–1931
PER 1,000 POPULATION
65 YEARS OF AGE AND OVER

1930 POPULATION

LEGEND

▨	UNDER 5
▨	5 – 9
▨	10 – 14
▨	15 – 19
■	20 – OVER

PREPARED BY H.W. DUNHAM, JR. FROM
THE RECORDS AT CHICAGO, ELGIN,
AND KANKAKEE STATE HOSPITALS

TABLE 41

AREA RATES FOR SENILE PSYCHOSES ACCORDING TO NATIVITY AND RACE, 1922–34

AREA	NATIVE WHITE OF NATIVE PARENTAGE		NATIVE WHITE OF FOREIGN OR MIXED PARENTAGE		FOREIGN-BORN WHITE		TOTAL WHITE*		NEGRO		OTHER RACES		TOTAL (ALL CLASSES)	
	No.	Rate	No.	Rate	No.	Rate	No.	Rate	No.	Rate	No.	Rate	No.	Rate
1. Single home $50+	40	52.1	24	18.6	92	30.3	161	31.6	7	166.2	1	1923.1	169	32.9
2. Single home $50−	16	57.7	4	9.5	47	29.5	70	30.5	....	....	....	....	70	30.3
3. Two-flat $50+	31	56.9	25	25.5	71	31.8	133	35.4	1	170.9	....	....	134	35.6
4. Two-flat $50−	37	54.3	36	24.9	222	43.0	317	43.5	6	91.2	....	....	323	43.9
5. Apt. (n.-b.)	100	40.5	87	27.2	158	32.9	373	35.6	4	29.8	1	139.9	378	36.0
6. Hotel, etc.	40	32.5	18	16.5	44	42.7	110	32.9	1	74.7	....	....	111	33.0
7. Apt.-two-flat	32	71.5	27	29.7	136	44.0	208	46.7	2	86.9	....	....	210	46.6
8. Apt. (f.-b.)	7	106.6	1	6.5	49	28.4	61	31.4	1	284.9	....	....	62	31.8
9. Apt. (Negro)	24	143.1	15	102.7	40	130.9	99	159.8	121	84.6	....	....	220	106.8
10. Tenement	15	52.5	23	55.2	107	68.6	152	67.2	2	75.8	....	....	154	66.9
11. Rooming	41	84.3	30	64.8	73	122.7	164	106.2	3	58.9	....	....	167	104.3
City total	383	51.6	290	27.6	1,039	41.3	1,848	42.9	148	87.6	2	24.8	1,998	44.5

* Includes "White of Unknown Parentage," and this accounts for corrected figures in total cases.

The extent of concentration shown in Table 42 is not as marked as the concentration found in the general paralysis and the alcoholic psychoses series.

TABLE 42

PERCENTAGE OF SENILE PSYCHOSES AND THE PERCENTAGE OF THE POPULATION IN EACH FOURTH OF THE SIXTY-EIGHT COMMUNITIES GROUPED ON THE BASIS OF THE MAGNITUDE OF THE RATES

Quartile Grouping	Percentage of Cases in Each Quartile	Percentage of Population in Each Quartile
Fourth or upper............	32.2	13.3
Third....................	29.7	26.8
Second..................	22.3	28.0
First....................	15.8	31.9
Total.................	100.0	100.0

TABLE 43

RELATIONSHIPS BETWEEN THE RATES FOR SENILE PSYCHOSES AND CERTAIN SELECTED INDICES BY COMMUNITIES

Rates for Senile Psychoses with:	Pearson R	Standard Error
Percentage of home-ownership.	−.75	±.05
Percentage of lodging-house and hotel residents........	.48	±.09
Percentage of foreign-born plus Negroes.................	.17	±.12

The relationship between three selective indices of social disorganization and the senile psychoses rates are shown in Table 43. The high negative correlation of this series with the percentage of home-ownership indicates that the high rates of this psychosis appear in areas of high mobility. It also indicates that poverty is probably a definite selective factor in this series. While there are high rates in the Negro areas, the low correlation of this series with the foreign-born index is consistent with the other evidence presented and indicates that the foreign-born areas tend to outweigh the Negro areas in this percentage.

PSYCHOSES WITH ARTERIOSCLEROSIS

Of the 3,432 cases of psychoses with arteriosclerosis in the data, 1,882 are male and 1,550 are female. It might be noted that the sex ratio is somewhat the reverse of the senile series. Most of the cases are in the age groups over forty-five years, the peak age group being between sixty-five and seventy-four years.

The subcommunity rates (per 100,000 of the 1930 population, forty-five years of age and over) vary from 2.9 in an apartment-hotel subcommunity (22) to 134.4 in subcommunity 61, the West Side hobohemia. The median rate is 30.2 and the average rate 38.5. The pattern of the distribution of rates, shown in Map XXVII, is very similar to that of the senile psychoses. The high rates are in the Negro districts and rooming-house areas. The correlation of the senile and arteriosclerosis series by the 120 subcommunities gives a coefficient of .85 ± .03.

The percentage concentration of cases and population in each quartile is shown in Table 44. The cases are much more definitely concentrated than those of the senile psychoses series.

The further close identification of these two old age psychoses with poverty can be seen when their combined

MAP XXVII

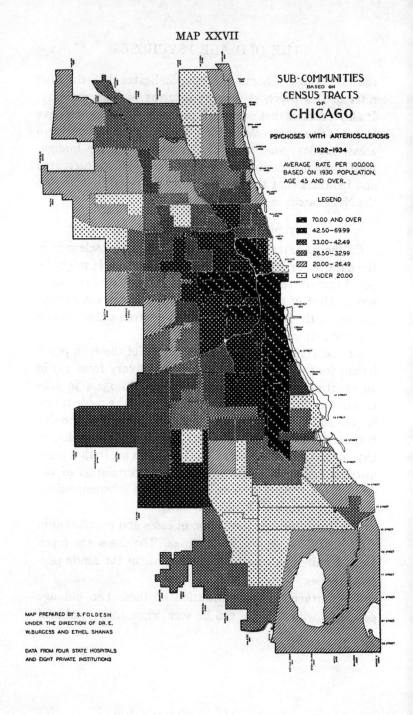

SUB·COMMUNITIES
BASED ON
CENSUS TRACTS
OF
CHICAGO

PSYCHOSES WITH ARTERIOSCLEROSIS

1922–1934

AVERAGE RATE PER 100,000.
BASED ON 1930 POPULATION,
AGE 45 AND OVER.

LEGEND

70.00 AND OVER

42.50–69.99

33.00–42.49

26.50–32.99

20.00–26.49

UNDER 20.00

MAP PREPARED BY S.FOLDESH
UNDER THE DIRECTION OF DR. E.
W.BURGESS AND ETHEL SHANAS

DATA FROM FOUR STATE HOSPITALS
AND EIGHT PRIVATE INSTITUTIONS

rates are correlated for certain social indices by the 120 subcommunities. The combined rates correlate with the percentage of the population on relief .82 ± .03 and with the percentage of the population of native white of native parentage, −.87 ± .03. These figures indicate rather definitely that poverty is a real selective factor for both of these psychoses.

TABLE 44

PERCENTAGE OF PSYCHOSES WITH ARTERIOSCLERO-
SIS AND THE PERCENTAGE OF THE POPULATION
IN EACH FOURTH OF THE 120 SUBCOMMUNITIES
GROUPED ON THE BASIS OF THE MAGNITUDE
OF THE RATES

Quartile Grouping	Percentage of Cases of Each Quartile	Percentage of Population in Each Quartile
Fourth or upper.............	42.6	22.6
Third......................	24.2	24.1
Second....................	18.9	25.4
First......................	14.3	27.9
Total.................	100.0	100.0

The statistical evidence presented for the organic psychoses[2] in this chapter indicates that they do not fit as

[2] It is pertinent to point out here that besides the distribution of these organic psychoses which have been presented, a study of the distribution of another organic disorder, epilepsy, was also made. However, the small number of cases in the epilepsy series in comparison to the probable number of epileptics in the population made it inadvisable to present such distribution data. However, two distributions of epilepsy cases, both with and without psychosis, were made. The first map showed a distribution of 965 cases admitted to the Cook County Psychopathic Hospital, and the latter map showed a distribution of 656 cases admitted to the state hospitals. There proved to be quite a variation in the pattern of the rates when the two maps were compared even though there was a duplication of cases as practically

evenly into the ecological structure of the city as do the schizophrenic rates. While, in general, the high rates are to be found in the central slum and Negro communities, the size of the rates does not always appear to represent a function of the distance traveled from the center of the city. This difference in the pattern of rates of these organic psychoses as contrasted to schizophrenia, the main functional psychosis, gives some additional weight to the hypothesis that the schizophrenic disorder bears some causal relationship to the nature of the social life within the different communities of the city.

---

the same periods of time were covered on both maps. It would seem from these figures that only approximately two-thirds of the epilepsy cases admitted to the psychopathic hospital ever reach a state hospital. The significance of these maps rested also on the fact that neither one of them showed a typical configuration or showed any similarity to any of the schizophrenic distributions. In general, the high rates for epilepsy tended to fall in the foreign-born communities as evidenced by a coefficient of correlation of .53 ± .08.

CHAPTER IX

INSANITY DISTRIBUTIONS IN A SMALLER CITY, PROVIDENCE, RHODE ISLAND[1]

Providence, Rhode Island, differs from Chicago in several respects. The 1930 population was 252,981, which was about one-thirteenth that of the Chicago population at the same time. It is also a much older city, having had about two centuries of existence before Chicago began. The growth of Providence in recent decades has been much slower than that of Chicago—6.5 per cent during the decade 1920–30. The general prosperity and expansion during the 1920's generally missed Providence, so that the city was relatively stable during that period. The streams of immigration of foreign populations and of southern Negroes consequently poured into other cities much more than into Providence. The most numerous foreign nationalities are the Italian and the French Canadian, and both of these groups have been settled long enough to have outlived the most severe disorganization that immigrant peoples experience. The total Negro population in 1936 was only 4,250, and many of these are descendants of families that have lived in Providence for generations. The Negroes do not live in segregated districts and do not exhibit the symptoms of disorganization that are characteristic of the Chicago slums.

In general, then, Providence is smaller, more stable, slower growing, and more orderly than Chicago or most

[1] The material on insanity in Providence is taken from the early stages of a project which will be reported more fully in the future. The study is being made by Robert E. L. Faris, Claire G. Faris, and Thurston Steele.

other large industrial cities of the United States. Such characteristic signs of social disorganization as crime, vice, family disorganization, political corruption, and the like are of less frequency in Providence. The stability is also reflected in such conditions as the general conservatism, the comparative lack of receptivity to fads and fashions, and the general satisfaction of the residents with existing conditions, as compared to the larger cities.

The topography of Providence differs considerably from that of Chicago. The city is located at the head of Narragansett Bay and has an irregular water front, used mostly for shipping and industrial purposes. The pattern of ecological zones is somewhat less apparent than in Chicago, owing to the water front and other features, such as hills, streams, railroads, and parks. The most noticeable variation is that caused by the steep hill directly east of the central business district. Neither business nor industry climbs this hill, consequently there is a desirable residential section within a quarter of a mile of the downtown area. Only on the southern tip, where the hill slopes more gradually, has severe disorganization encroached on the eastern side of the city.

In general, the old sections and the deteriorated section surrounding the business district are also the industrial and slum regions. Map XXVIII,[2] showing the percentage of new houses in each census tract, defines these regions of

[2] Data are from the real-property inventory made in 1933 by the Federal Housing Administration. New houses are residential structures which were less than fifteen years old in 1933. The rates in Providence are computed on the basis of forty-nine census tracts. The boundaries of these tracts, drawn for research purposes by Robert E. L. Faris, inclose areas which are as far as possible homogeneous in population characteristics and of maximum utility for ecological research.

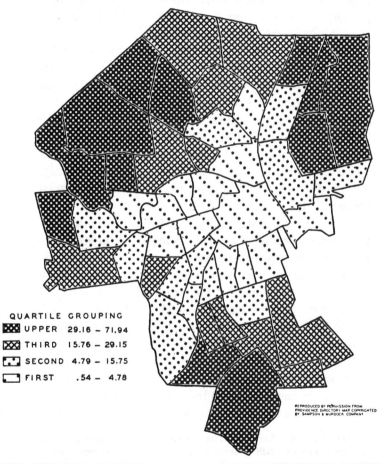

MAP XXVIII
PERCENTAGE OF NEW HOUSES
BY CENSUS TRACTS
IN PROVIDENCE

QUARTILE GROUPING
UPPER 29.16 – 71.94
THIRD 15.76 – 29.15
SECOND 4.79 – 15.75
FIRST .54 – 4.78

REPRODUCED BY PERMISSION FROM
PROVIDENCE DIRECTORY MAP COPYRIGHTED
BY SAMPSON & MURDOCK COMPANY

DATA FROM REAL PROPERTY
INVENTORY, BY FEDERAL
HOUSING ADMINISTRATION
1933

MAP PREPARED BY H.ZACHIA,
UNDER DIRECTION OF R.E.L.FARIS

deterioration fairly accurately. The tracts with the lowest percentages of new houses are the most deteriorated slums. Surrounding these are apartment- and rooming-house areas and areas of workingmen's homes. The three most desirable residential regions are shown in the sections with the largest percentages of new homes. Additional residential areas in the suburbs are not shown on this map.

Unpublished studies of Providence, made by the sociology staff at Brown University, have shown that the characteristics of these areas are generally similar to the corresponding areas in Chicago and other cities. This central region has the lowest rents, the highest poverty rates, the highest delinquency, crime, suicide, and divorce rates. The streams of population flow outwardly from these regions toward the residential and suburban areas. The resemblance to larger cities is close, except for the qualification that the contrasts are less sharp.

The data for the study of the distribution of insanity in Providence were taken from the State Hospital for Mental Diseases. No private hospital cases are included in this study. Inquiry at the only large private hospital in the state revealed that most of the serious cases are eventually transferred to the state hospital, so that little could be gained by including the relatively few cases there.[3]

Because of information that diagnoses made before 1929, the time of a change in the administration of the state hospital, would differ somewhat from those of the following period, only cases of first admissions within the period of 1929–36 were used. The total number of cases from Provi-

---

[3] It is to be noted that this fact has been amply demonstrated by the Chicago data where the addition of private hospital cases was shown to have no effect upon the pattern of rates. See chap. ii.

dence during this period, excluding those of unknown address, those from out of the state, and those not insane, was 1,030.

The average annual rates, computed per 100,000 population of the ages of 15 and over from the census of 1930, are shown in Map XXIX. The median rate is 61 and the average rate is 65. Tract 1, the central business district and industrial, hobo, and rooming-house area, has the highest rate of 194. Most of the very high rates are in adjacent areas. The lowest rates are in the residential areas. With some exceptions, due possibly to chance variation,[4] the pattern resembles that in Chicago.

Although the total number of schizophrenia cases (301) during the period is too small to yield very reliable rates, a distribution was made. The average annual rates in the tracts vary from 0 to 45 per 100,000 population ages fifteen and over and are shown on Map XXX. The median rate is 17 and the average 19. The highest rate is in the central area and the next highest rates are in adjacent areas. The pattern, however, shows somewhat less regularity in the distribution of rates than does the general insanity map. Because of the small numbers, no significance can be attached to single rates, but a general pattern can be seen, with high rates predominating in the central slum areas and low rates in the outlying districts. Since there were insufficient numbers of any other psychoses, no further maps were made. Rates for all other psychoses (excluding schizophrenia), correlate $+.49 \pm .11$ with the schizophrenia rates, indicating possibly some difference in distribution.

[4] The average population of the tracts is about 5,000. In some of them the number of cases is as low as four and the average number is only twenty. Thus the possibility of chance variation is great, and interpretation must be made with some caution and must be based on the general pattern rather than on single areas.

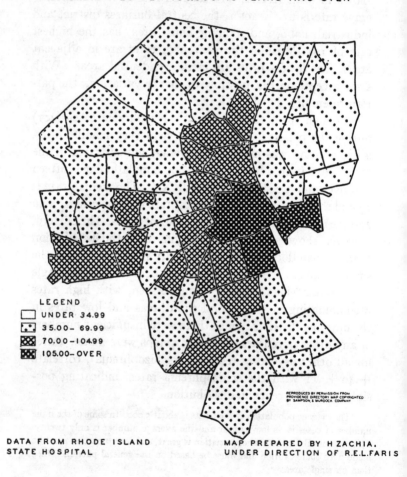

MAP XXIX

INSANITY RATES
BY CENSUS TRACTS IN PROVIDENCE
1929 – 1936
BASED ON 1930 POPULATION
AVERAGE RATES PER 100,000. 15 YEARS AND OVER

LEGEND
☐ UNDER 34.99
▨ 35.00– 69.99
▨ 70.00–10499
▨ 105.00–OVER

REPRODUCED BY PERMISSION FROM
PROVIDENCE DIRECTORY. MAP COPYRIGHTED
BY SAMPSON & MURDOCK COMPANY

DATA FROM RHODE ISLAND   MAP PREPARED BY H ZACHIA.
STATE HOSPITAL   UNDER DIRECTION OF R.E.L.FARIS

148

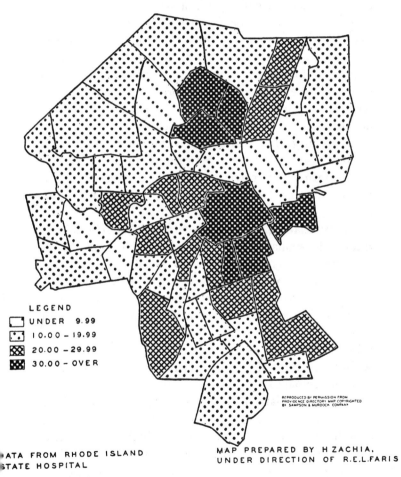

MAP XXX
SCHIZOPHRENIA RATES,
BY CENSUS TRACTS IN PROVIDENCE,
1929 – 1936.
BASED ON 1930 POPULATION.
AVERAGE RATES PER 100,000. 15 YEARS AND OVER

LEGEND
☐ UNDER 9.99
▨ 10.00 – 19.99
▨ 20.00 – 29.99
▨ 30.00 - OVER

REPRODUCED BY PERMISSION FROM
PROVIDENCE DIRECTORY MAP COPYRIGHTED
BY SAMPSON & MURDOCK COMPANY

DATA FROM RHODE ISLAND
STATE HOSPITAL

MAP PREPARED BY H ZACHIA,
UNDER DIRECTION OF R.E.L.FARIS

The percentages of persons of foreign extraction[5] in each tract are not distributed in a pattern similar to those of the various forms of social disorganization. The highest percentages are mostly in the northwestern quarter of the city. The correlation between the percentage of persons of foreign extraction and rates of total insanity for each census tract is $-.01 \pm .14$. Nor is the proportion of foreign-born insanity cases high in those tracts where the proportion of foreign-born population is high. The correlation between the percentages of foreign-born (not foreign extraction in this case) and the percentages of foreign-born in the total insanity series in each area is only $+.28 \pm .13$. There is, however, a definite negative relationship between home-ownership and total insanity. The correlation coefficient is $-.55 \pm .09$. There is also a relationship between total insanity and economic status. The correlation with the average rental paid in each tract is $-.53 \pm .10$ and with the rates for persons on relief, $+.68 \pm .07$.

The correlations of the same data with the schizophrenia rates yield similar results. The relationship with the percentages of foreign extraction is low, $+.15 \pm .14$. As in Chicago, schizophrenia appears to be related to areas of mobility, as measured by home-ownership rates. The correlation between the home-ownership and schizophrenia rates in Providence is $-.64 \pm .08$. There is also a definite relationship between the economic status of communities and schizophrenia rates. The coefficient for average rentals is $-.51 \pm .10$, and for relief rates $+.65 \pm .08$.

So far as the data show, Providence exhibits very similar characteristics to Chicago and other large cities. The small-scale insanity study in Providence, though incomplete, reveals results that agree with those of the Chicago study.

[5] Includes foreign-born and native-born of foreign and mixed parentage.

CHAPTER X

MIND AND SOCIETY

The ancient problem of the nature of the relationships between mind and society is involved in this study of the distribution of insanity rates in the city. Of the many solutions or attempted solutions of this problem, few are relevant in the interpretation of the patterns formed by these rates.

One point of view, somewhat old but still alive, regards the mind as nothing more than a physiological mechanism. The causes of its origin, its individuality, and its abnormalities are all supposed to lie in physiological processes alone. The level of intelligence is thought to be determined by heredity and by modifications and pathologies in the nervous system. Mental diseases are defined as pathological conditions resulting from bodily disturbances, in the same sense that typhoid and tuberculosis result from bodily disturbances.[1] Research methods based on such a point of view consist of attempts to locate physiological defects, and treatment consists of attempts to repair the defects. From this point of view, life history studies showing the relation of experience to the development of behavior are of minor significance at most.

Although much brilliant and distinguished work has been done on this basis and some significant victories won, there are some characteristics of human mentality and behavior that have not so far been successfully explained by this

[1] This notion is expressed by Fred A. Moss and Thelma Hunt, *Foundations of Abnormal Psychology* (New York: Prentice-Hall, Inc., 1932), p. 21.

approach. There has developed a growing realization among students that the complete explanation of mental phenomena will not be found on a physiological level. In some forms of mental abnormality, research repeatedly fails to find physical defects sufficient to explain the trouble. At the same time, a growing body of knowledge on the relation of sociopsychological factors to mentality and behavior has been accumulating and yielding promising results.

That the human mind is built on, and is never independent of, a physiological base cannot be denied. But although this base is an absolutely necessary element, it is not coextensive with the mind itself. The mind, built on a physiological base, is a product of a process of social interaction. Mentality, abilities, behavior, are all achievements of the person, developed in a history of long interaction with his surroundings, both physical and social.[2]

Membership in society is, of course, necessary to life itself. Except for rare and apocryphal cases of "feral men" cared for by animals, no human beings survive without many years of care by other humans. Every human society provides some organized system for taking care of infants and for providing for the development of knowledge and behavior of infants, children, and youths. Moreover, every society bears and transmits a body of ways of acting, thinking, and feeling, which provides a framework in which the mentality and behavior of each new member is developed. In order that persons may act together and co-operate at

[2] This statement has been fully and competently stated by many students, among whom should be mentioned John Dewey, Charles H. Cooley, George H. Mead, William I. Thomas, Ellsworth Faris, Robert E. Park, Ernest W. Burgess, and others. The psychological literature of recent years contains a significant amount of research substantiating this point of view. References can be found in almost any recent textbook of social psychology.

all, it is necessary that such a framework exist to mold the nature of each member. Some system of gestures and language is essential to communication. Folkways are necessary in order that each person will know what to expect of others. Not only does every society possess such an organized system of action patterns, but each also possesses many mechanisms of social control by means of which it is insured that the members of the society will conform to these essential patterns. Both must function to insure the successful development of the person and the perpetuation of the society.

Normal mentality and behavior develops over a long period of successful interaction between the person and these organized agencies of society. Defects in mentality and behavior may result from serious gaps in any part of the process. The failure of society to transmit language, for example, or even partial failure through parental neglect of children results in mental retardation of the children. Among the necessary elements in the process of development of the child are such subtle conditions as intimacy and affection between the child and the members of his primary groups, reasonable consistency of the influences to which he is exposed, and reasonable harmony between the influences in the home and those met in more formal situations outside the home. It is probable that there are many more unrecognized requisites of this sort. A failure in any one of them damages the development of the normal mentality and behavior. For example, in family situations that lack sufficient intimacy and affection, the amount of transmission from parent to child is lessened, with resulting retardation which may be marked. Inconsistency of influences may so discourage the child that he may feel that it is useless to make any effort to understand the world about him and tempt him to fall back on simple traditional formulae of behavior, on magic, or intuition, or on his own illogical whims and impulses. Where there is a lack of harmony between the family and community influences, there is likely to be conflict in the person with resulting confusion, or else he is likely to discount or devalue one or the other source, thereby cutting down the quantity of developing influences.

There is some evidence that even a normal adult mentality is not equipped to continue under its own power, but that it must be supported constantly by a consistent and fairly harmonious stream of primary social contacts. Persons who have been isolated, through physical or cultural barriers, have been observed to undergo a personality deterioration which frequently continues as long as the isolation lasts.[3]

To summarize, the development of normal mentality and normal behavior demands a complicated chain of successfully functioning elements on paths of very different sorts. Among the essentials are: paths of social communication involving both printed and spoken language transmitting influences from the community at large to persons, and from persons to intimate friends; paths of physiological communication, including sense organs, nerve paths connecting with centers, all supported by sufficiently normal function-

[3] A number of cases of physical isolation are described in Maurice Small "On Some Psychical Relations of Society and Solitude," *Pedagogical Seminary* (April, 1900), Vol. VII, No. 2. S. Hobhouse and A. F. Brockway, *English Prisons Today* (London, 1922) contains material on deterioration of prisoners in solitary confinement and under the silence rules. A. F. Tredgold (*Mental Deficiency* [New York, 1912]) describes cases of deterioration due to defects in sense organs. See also Robert E. L. Faris, "Cultural Isolation and the Schizophrenic Personality," *American Journal of Sociology* (September, 1934), XL, 155-69.

ing of many parts of the body, including glands, muscles, etc.; and outgoing activity of the person in responding to others. Breaks occurring at any of these essential points may damage the mentality and affect the behavior. The medical approach has so far been most successful in the study of those breaks in the physiological essentials. Defects of the brain, injuries, physical diseases, disorders due to use of drugs, to biochemical disturbances, and the like, all interfere with normal function and behavior. Breaks in the essentials on the social level, because of the complexities of the processes, are more difficult to study. Progress in this field is also slower because the realization of the significance of social factors is more recent.

Abnormality of behavior and mentality is not easy to define. It is difficult to point out any physical or social acts which in themselves are evidences of insanity. Interpretations of the normality of actions must be made with reference to the cultural setting. Many actions of natives of preliterate societies, normal in their own cultures, would be regarded as evidence of insanity in our society. Actions which are normal in one culture are abnormal in others. This generalization is even true of such variations in culture as may be seen within one large nation. For example, certain types of religious fanaticism are normal in parts of the rural sections of southern states, while the same behavior may be the occasion for commitment to a hospital in a northern city.

The normality of actions may depend on considerations not always obvious to casual observation. Such eccentric behavior as attempting to push a peanut along a sidewalk with the nose may appear insane, until it is discovered that the performer is a college student being hazed or the loser of an election bet. The definition of insanity, then, is not a description of any list of actions, but consists in a lack of fitness between actions and situations. In the summary of a mental examination of a patient, a psychiatrist writes, "The patient evidenced a feeling of happiness and well-being not at all warranted by her surroundings." Showing happiness, of course, is not abnormal, but when entirely uncalled for in the situation, it is regarded as evidence of insanity.

Many of the terms used to describe some of the functional psychoses show this definition of abnormality, namely, that it is only in the relation between action and situation. The concept, delusion, for example, refers not simply to a false belief, but a false belief which a reasonable person would not hold. There are a great many false beliefs held by groups of normal persons. These false beliefs are held because the persons have not had the opportunity to learn better, or because the authority of tradition or of religion is behind them. These have sufficient explanation. They become delusions only when the situation does not offer an explanation.

Mental abnormality, then, must be defined in terms of the relationship between actions and situations. But it is not always easy to say exactly what the actual situation is. Persons do not simply respond to the immediate environment of physical objects. The external world of physical reality is always transformed by the person; he reacts not to the world but to his conceptions of it. The act of perception itself is never independent of much selection and interpretation. The person responds to his axiological world, that is, one which is constructed by himself out of material which is culturally given to him, but always fashioned individually by him and inevitably somewhat differently from all other persons.[4]

The situation to which the action is relative, then, is not the surroundings of physical reality or even the conventional view of it, but the individual's axiological version, which, though ordinarily built on the conventional view, always contains portions entirely individual. No two persons see the same situation, then, even among normal persons, but their situations are sufficiently similar and in accord with conventional patterns to enable them to act in reasonable harmony.

Actions of persons become unintelligible to one another, as we have seen, if they come from very different societies. But even within one culture there may be great separation of minds. Different socioeconomic strata contain divergent conceptions of surroundings. Wall Street is entirely different for the banker and the banana-peddler. The slum dwellers, immigrants, mobile persons, and other such types, all have different conceptions of the world, but not always too different for others to understand. Often, however, uneducated natives of this country believe the foreigner to be slightly queer—perhaps touched with insanity. Children are especially liable to make these judgments of foreigners unless contacts with them are sufficiently frequent to give familiarity.

A series of life-experiences of an unusual character may produce a mental organization in the person which is so different from all others that his actions may be unintelligible to others.[5] Persons who grow up in a harmonious and

[4] This statement is developed fully in the writings of John Dewey, George H. Mead, Ellsworth Faris, and others.

[5] John Dollard, "The Psychotic Person Seen Culturally," *American Journal of Sociology*, XXXIX (March, 1934), 637–48.

consistent culture cannot understand or communicate with disorganized persons who have very different axiological worlds. The actions appear to be senseless, the moods and emotions meaningless, and the words without significance. The disorganized person often senses his failure to communicate and decides that the effort is hopeless. Ordinary words and phrases, limited in what they can describe by conventional usage, are incapable of bearing the meanings felt by him. He may attempt to transmit his meanings by the use of metaphors or he may give up the effort entirely and fall back on his inner life, indifferent to others. Metaphorical speech and allusions can bear communication only if there is sufficient similarity in the axiological worlds of both persons. If this condition is not fulfilled, this form of communication fails even more than simpler speech. The disorganized person appears to be even more senseless than he really is. His actions appear more capricious and unmotivated and inappropriate to his surroundings. Mental disorder, therefore, lies in the great divergence between the person's axiological world, and the standardized cultural view of the world.

Successful transmission of the essential standardized cultural view of the world, and therefore successful production in the person of a sufficiently normal mental organization, requires a normal family life, normal community life, reasonable stability and consistency in the influences and surroundings of the person, all supported on a continuous stream of intimate social communication. In the disorganized areas of the large industrial city many of these necessary conditions are lacking. The slum area populated by heterogeneous foreign-born elements forms a chaotic background of conflicting and shifting cultural standards, against which it is quite difficult for a person to develop a stable mental organization. Disharmony in family life is likely to be frequent in interracial and intercultural marriages. Conflict between family life and neighborhood influences is common. Continuity of tradition and of life-experiences is more rare. In the highly mobile hobo and rooming-house areas there is scarcely sufficient social life of any kind to develop or support a conventional organization of mind.

In these most disorganized sections of the city and, for that matter, of our whole civilization, many persons are unable to derive sufficient mental nourishment from the normal social sources to achieve a satisfactorily conventional organization of their world. The result may be a lack of any organization at all, resulting in a confused, frustrated, and chaotic personality, or it may be a complex but unconventional original organization. In either case there is a serious divergence from the conventional organization which makes communication and understanding impossible and, for that matter, makes any form of co-operation difficult. It is just this type of unintelligible behavior which becomes recognized as mental disorder.

CHAPTER XI

HYPOTHESES AND INTERPRETATIONS OF DISTRIBUTIONS

The establishment of the fact that there are great differences in the patterns of rates for different psychoses in the natural areas of the city is in itself a complicated task. The interpretation of the meaning of these facts is a separate problem; different methods of study are necessary for this part of the research. The distributions of certain psychoses can be fairly successfully explained; others are more difficult and explanations can only be suggested.

It is necessary before discussing the meaning of the configuration of rates for the different psychoses to examine certain possible flaws in the method. It may be possible that insanity is not concentrated, and that it appears to be so only because of some statistical illusion. Several possible explanations for the appearance of concentration are discussed below.

An obvious possibility is that the concentration of cases in certain areas of the city may be due to chance. This suggestion has been made by Professor Frank Alexander Ross,[1] with reference to the computation of rates based on data for a single year. Using a formula to test the chance variation of a rate, he tested whether each rate was significantly different from the rate in an adjacent community. In some cases he found differences were not significant and in other

[1] F. A. Ross, "Ecology and the Statistical Method," *American Journal of Sociology*, XXXVIII (January, 1933), 507–22.

cases they were. By combining two communities and computing a rate he was able to show more definitely that the concentration of rates could not be due to chance alone. The logic of this procedure has been questioned by Charles C. Peters, who pointed out the fact that many rates combined into a pattern greatly increased the statistical significance of the pattern itself, and that the possibility that chance variation alone could produce such a pattern is too small to be considered.[2] Since this preliminary study was made, much larger numbers have been used, further decreasing the possibility that the patterns could be due to chance. It was therefore considered necessary to use the formula for testing chance variation only once—in the study of foreign-born rates of schizophrenia. In those maps which show a clear pattern of distribution, the conclusions are drawn from the pattern and not from differences between adjacent communities. It seems permissible to dismiss the possibility that these patterns are due to chance variation.

A second possibility is that the patterns of rate distribution represent only a concentration of cases of mental disorder which have been institutionalized because of poverty. If the actual incidence of mental disorder is equal in all parts of the city and if those in the higher-income classes are more frequently cared for at home or sent out of the state, the hospitalized cases would show a bias toward the lower-income classes and therefore toward the slum section of the city. An attempt is made to minimize this bias by including in the rates all the cases from the regional private hospitals as well as from public hospitals. Because of the small number of patients in the private hospitals, the rates

[2] Charles C. Peters, "Note on a Misconception of Statistical Significance," *American Journal of Sociology*, XXXIX (September, 1933), 231–36.

were only slightly affected by the addition of these cases. No way has been found to estimate the amount of bias in the rates caused by the practice of caring for some patients in the homes. It is possible that there is an income selection in such cases. But it appears unlikely that such an effect dominates the patterns of distribution, because of the fact that different psychoses show different patterns of distribution. If a poverty concentration were the only, or the principal, factor in producing these patterns, they should be reasonably similar for all psychoses.

Another possibility is that the apparent concentration of cases is due to a statistical error or failure to adjust the rates for transiency. That is, if the cases from an area taken during the period of a year are divided by the population taken as of a single day, the rate may be regarded as too high if the population during the year had turned over enough to make a significantly larger population than was present on the one census enumeration day. Professor Ross made this point in the discussion previously mentioned.[3] No satisfactory method was found to make a direct adjustment for this criticism. It is known, however, that in the hobo and rooming-house areas, which show very high rates for several types of mental disorder, the population is transient enough to turn over, perhaps two or three times or more. Ross made the suggestion that in such cases the rate be reduced to one-half or one-third. To justify this, however, it would be necessary to know where the excess population was the rest of the year and what the chances of hospitalization were wherever the people were. Only if it is true that the other cities and towns in which this transient population spends a part of the year do not take their quota in

[3] Ross, *op. cit.*

their hospitals, should the rate be adjusted. It seems significant, here, to point out that if the rates in the hobohemia communities for all types of mental disorders were divided by three, the resulting rates would still be two of the highest in the distribution of the rates. These considerations appear to be important in the statistical criticism presented by the factor of mobility.

An interpretation frequently made of the concentration in the center of the city of insanity rates, and the schizophrenia rates particularly, is that persons who are mentally abnormal fail in their economic life and consequently drift down into the slum areas because they are not able to compete satisfactorily with others. Such a process is, of course, possible, although the explanation does not appear to be valid in the case of the manic-depressive patterns. Many of the cases of schizophrenia consist of persons who were born in and have always lived in deteriorated areas.[4] These did not drift into the high-rate areas. There are also cases that are hospitalized from high-income areas, persons who developed a mental disorder before their failure had caused them to drift to the slums. It is a question whether this drift process, which undoubtedly contributes something to the apparent concentration of rates, is anything more than an insignificant factor in causing the concentration.[5] No

[4] A separate study of the catatonic in a foreign-born community now being conducted by Dr. H. Blumer and H. W. Dunham indicates that these persons were born in and brought up in the community. The tendency to drift into an area is more marked and has significance, for the most part, in reference to the hobo and rooming-house areas. Certainly the high schizophrenic rates in the typical foreign-born communities cannot be explained adequately by the "drifting" hypothesis.

[5] It is significant to note that the maps showing the distribution of insanity and of schizophrenic rates in Providence, Rhode Island, give results which are similar to those found in the Chicago study.

decisive material on this point was obtained in this study. Some relevant findings should be stated, however.

One method of testing this drift hypothesis is the comparison of the distribution of young and old cases. For this purpose the paranoid and catatonic types of schizophrenia were selected because of the radical difference in both the pattern of the rates and the age distribution. Since those who are first committed at an advanced age have had a longer time in which to fail in their economic life and consequently to drift toward the slums, the distribution of the older cases should show a sharper concentration than the younger cases. Maps XXXI and XXXII show the concentration of the paranoid schizophrenia cases between the ages of fifteen and twenty-nine years and between the ages of thirty and sixty-four years, respectively. The younger cases, mostly too young to have had much time to drift, are concentrated in the central areas in much the same pattern as the older cases.[6] Table 45 shows the measurement of concentration of these cases. Both show roughly the same degree of concentration.

A somewhat similar result emerges from a comparison of young and old catatonic cases. Maps XXXIII and XXXIV show these distributions. Both young and old cases are concentrated, although in this instance there is an indication of some possible drift. The central business district, which has a low rate of younger cases, has a high rate of older cases. The lack of similarity of the patterns is shown

---

[6] The pattern formed by the distribution of the younger cases is not as even or consistent. Again it is necessary to point out the unreliability of the rates because of the small number of cases. The younger cases amount to 607 in number while the older cases amount to 2,213. The correlation between the two sets of rates is .79 ± .05. In the catatonic series, presented below, the younger cases amount to 1,162 and the older cases to 789.

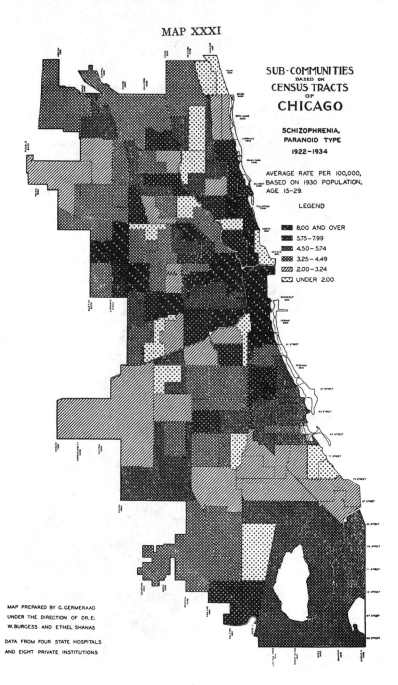

MAP XXXI

SUB-COMMUNITIES
BASED ON
CENSUS TRACTS
OF
CHICAGO

SCHIZOPHRENIA,
PARANOID TYPE
1922-1934

AVERAGE RATE PER 100,000,
BASED ON 1930 POPULATION,
AGE 15-29.

LEGEND

8.00 AND OVER
5.75 - 7.99
4.50 - 5.74
3.25 - 4.49
2.00 - 3.24
UNDER 2.00

MAP PREPARED BY G. GERMERAAD
UNDER THE DIRECTION OF DR. E.
W. BURGESS AND ETHEL SHANAS

DATA FROM FOUR STATE HOSPITALS
AND EIGHT PRIVATE INSTITUTIONS

MAP XXXII

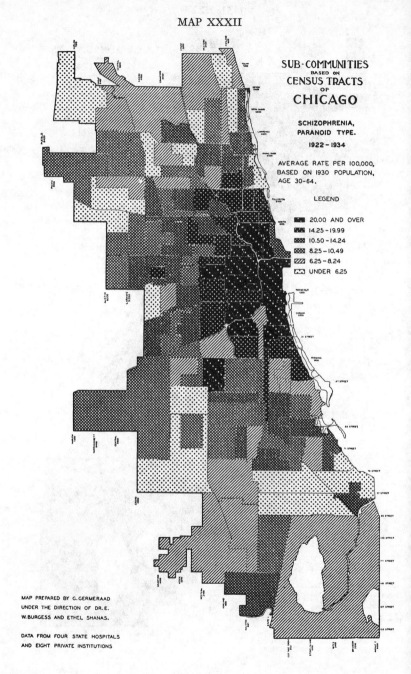

SUB-COMMUNITIES
BASED ON
CENSUS TRACTS
OF
CHICAGO

SCHIZOPHRENIA,
PARANOID TYPE.
1922-1934

AVERAGE RATE PER 100,000,
BASED ON 1930 POPULATION,
AGE 30-64.

LEGEND

20.00 AND OVER
14.25 - 19.99
10.50 - 14.24
8.25 - 10.49
6.25 - 8.24
UNDER 6.25

MAP PREPARED BY G. GERMERAAD
UNDER THE DIRECTION OF DR. E.
W. BURGESS AND ETHEL SHANAS.

DATA FROM FOUR STATE HOSPITALS
AND EIGHT PRIVATE INSTITUTIONS

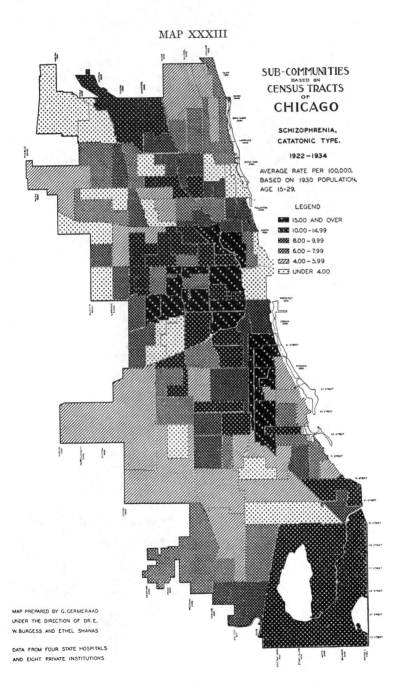

MAP XXXIII

SUB-COMMUNITIES
BASED ON
CENSUS TRACTS
OF
CHICAGO

SCHIZOPHRENIA,
CATATONIC TYPE.

1922-1934

AVERAGE RATE PER 100,000,
BASED ON 1930 POPULATION,
AGE 15-29.

LEGEND

15.00 AND OVER
10.00-14.99
8.00 - 9.99
6.00 - 7.99
4.00 - 5.99
UNDER 4.00

MAP PREPARED BY G.GERMERAAD
UNDER THE DIRECTION OF DR.E.
W.BURGESS AND ETHEL SHANAS

DATA FROM FOUR STATE HOSPITALS
AND EIGHT PRIVATE INSTITUTIONS

MAP XXXIV

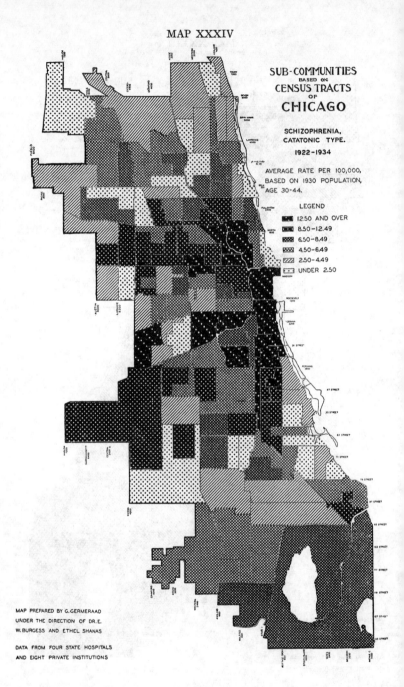

SUB-COMMUNITIES
BASED ON
CENSUS TRACTS
OF
CHICAGO

SCHIZOPHRENIA,
CATATONIC TYPE.

1922-1934

AVERAGE RATE PER 100,000,
BASED ON 1930 POPULATION,
AGE 30-44.

LEGEND

12.50 AND OVER
8.50-12.49
6.50-8.49
4.50-6.49
2.50-4.49
UNDER 2.50

MAP PREPARED BY G. GERMERAAD
UNDER THE DIRECTION OF DR. E.
W. BURGESS AND ETHEL SHANAS

DATA FROM FOUR STATE HOSPITALS
AND EIGHT PRIVATE INSTITUTIONS

by the fairly low coefficient of correlation, .41 ± .07. Except for this, however, the main pattern does not appear to be the product of drift.

A possible interpretation of the concentration of rates in the central areas might be that this measures the racial tendency to mental disorders of the foreign-born popula-

TABLE 45

PERCENTAGE OF PARANOID SCHIZOPHRENIC CASES, 15–29 YEARS, AND 30–64 YEARS, AND THE PERCENTAGE OF THE POPULATION IN EACH ONE-FOURTH OF THE 120 SUBCOMMUNITIES GROUPED ON THE BASIS OF THE MAGNITUDE OF THE RATES

QUARTILE GROUPING	PERCENTAGE OF CASES IN EACH QUARTILE		PERCENTAGE OF POPULATION IN EACH QUARTILE	
	Paranoid 15–29	Paranoid 30–64	Paranoid 15–29	Paranoid 30–64
Fourth or upper......	45.2	41.6	24.9	23.0
Third..............	27.3	26.5	25.7	26.5
Second.............	19.1	19.3	26.1	25.3
First..............	8.4	12.6	23.3	25.2
Total...........	100.0	100.0	100.0	100.0

tions that inhabit these areas. It is pointed out above, however (chap. iii), that rates for foreign-born cases divided by foreign-born populations are distributed similarly to the rates for all cases. Likewise, rates for Negroes show a variation, being high in the central disorganized areas not populated primarily by members of their own race and low in the actual Negro areas. Some factors other than being foreign-born or Negro are necessary to explain these patterns that are the same no matter which race or nationality inhabits the area. Furthermore, not all psychoses are concentrated in foreign-born areas. Although the correlation of several psychoses with percentages of foreign-born and Negro population is high or medium, such as catatonic schizophrenia (0.86), epilepsy (0.53), and alcoholic psychoses (0.48), others such as paranoid schizophrenia (0.11), manic-depressive psychoses (0.14), general paralysis (0.15), and senile psychoses (0.17), show little or no correlation. The supposed tendency to mental disorders of the foreign-born populations, then, does not appear to explain the rate patterns.

The last possibility to be discussed is that the patterns of rates reveal that the nature of the social life and conditions in certain areas of the city is in some way a cause of high rates of mental disorder. If there is any truth in this hypothesis, it will be necessary to find separate explanations for each psychosis, since the distributions of rates differ both to a large and to a small degree for each psychosis.

Although the distributions are not exactly alike, the explanations of the concentration of general paralysis, drug addiction, and alcoholic psychoses rates according to this hypothesis are roughly similar. Different combinations of social factors, however, are no doubt functioning in the case of each of these psychoses. The general paralysis rates are highest in the hobo and rooming-house areas and in the Negro areas. These are the areas in which there is little family life, and in which the sex experience of the men is in large part with casual contacts and with prostitutes, who are relatively numerous in these districts. These conditions make for the spread of syphilitic infection and hence for general paralysis. The dispensing and the use of drugs is very much of an underworld activity and this is reflected by the high rates in the zone of transition. Lack of normal social life may underlie the dissatisfactions which cause the use of drugs to be felt as a release, hence the slight rise in rates in the upper-income hotel and rooming-house districts. Also, for the use of alcohol to become an appealing habit, basic dissatisfactions are often essential. High rates of alcohol consumption and of alcoholic psychoses are in the foreign-born and rooming-house areas and may be caused by such conditions of life as monotony, insecurity, and other problems difficult to solve, from which alcohol may be a temporary relief. The significant variations of rates according to nativity and race in the different housing areas of the city indicate the greater chances for mental breakdown and personality disorganization in relation to these psychoses especially when a person is living in an area not primarily populated by members of his own group. This fact alone would appear to be the beginning for further research in these mental disorders. In the case of the alcoholic psychoses it would seem to indicate the presence of other important factors in addition to the use of alcohol.

Another group of psychoses, namely, senile psychoses, psychoses with arteriosclerosis, and epilepsy, show unusual patterns of distribution and so make interpretation difficult. These psychoses are generally regarded by psychiatrists as having organic bases, and this might account for the absence of the typical ecological pattern. In the case of the psychoses of old age it did appear, however, that poverty was a basic factor in the selection for admission to the state hospitals.

The undiagnosed distribution and the distribution of cases referred to as "without psychoses" are difficult to interpret since the nature of the abnormal behavior is not indicated by the labels. It is suggested, however, that since both distributions resemble that of schizophrenia cases, it is possible that these are disorders of a similar nature.

Perhaps the most provocative finding in this study resulted from a comparison of the distribution of the manic-depressive and schizophrenic rates. The great contrast between these two patterns seems to imply that some valid distinction has been made in classification. The absence of any pattern in the manic-depressive series makes the interpretation of this distribution extremely difficult, although certain leads for further research might be definitely indicated. The absence of any pattern combined with the absence of skewness in the manic-depressive distribution might suggest that social factors are unimportant in relation to this disorder. If such proved to be the case, there would be a certain justification for asserting the priority of the hereditary and constitutional factors. This of course would be in line with the statistical studies of heredity in the functional psychoses which universally show that biological inheritance is more significant in manic-depressive psychoses than in schizophrenia.

While the ecological and statistical evidence does not bring out any relationship between this disorder and the social milieu, it does not follow that there is no such relationship. Manic-depressive psychoses may be connected with a different type of social process than is the case with the schizophrenic disorders. A possible sociological explanation of the manic-depressive pattern might be found in the suggestion that precipitating factors are causal in relation to these psychoses.[7] Such precipitating factors occur in all

---

[7] On this point, see C. A. Bonner, "Psychogenic Factors as Causation Agents in Manic-depressive Psychoses," *Manic-depressive Psychoses—Recent Advances*, reported by the Association for Research in Nervous and Mental

social and economic levels of life and consequently are not so likely to have a definite connection with the community situation but rather with the interplay of personality and psychological factors of family relationships and intimate personal contacts. Such a theory tends to connect the manic-depressive disorder with extremely intimate and intense social contacts. This apparently is just the opposite from the situation of the schizophrenic, where isolation from such contacts appears to be an associated condition.

In contrast the schizophrenic rates are arranged into very definite patterns which follow closely the ecological structure of the city and the concentration of all types is very marked. With the exception of the catatonic type, which differs from the others in several respects, the high rates appear to be related to areas of high mobility and, in somewhat less degree, to foreign-born and Negro areas. In the following paragraphs is suggested a possible explanation of the relation between the social life of these areas and the abnormal behavior of the schizophrenic. The hypothesis is that extended isolation of the person produces the abnormal traits of behavior and mentality.[8]

If the various types of unconventional behavior observed

Disease (New York: Paul B. Hoeber, Inc., 1931), XI, 121–30; M. J. Brew, "Precipitating Factors in Manic-depressive Psychoses," *The Psychiatric Quarterly*, VII (July, 1933), 401–10; and J. H. Travis, "Precipitating Factors in Manic-depressive Psychoses," *ibid.*, pp. 411–18.

[8] It is recognized that much research on the causes of schizophrenia has been carried on from many points of view. At the present time no results are decisive enough to convince all students. Since none of them suggests any reasonable explanation of the facts of distribution shown here, this original explanation is offered. The essentials have previously been published in a paper by Robert E. L. Faris, "Cultural Isolation and the Schizophrenic Personality," *American Journal of Sociology*, XL (September, 1934), 155–69.

in different schizophrenic patients can be said to result from one condition, it appears that extreme seclusiveness may be that condition. The hallucinations, delusions, inappropriate action, silliness, and deterioration may all result from the fact that the seclusive person is completely freed from the social control which enforces normality in other people. For example, such hallucinations as "hearing voices" and "seeing visions" may result not only from sensory disturbances, but also from the inability of the seclusive person to communicate. Some investigations have revealed that patients who claim to "hear voices" may admit on further questioning that it is a "quiet voice" or "not really a voice, nor even a whisper, but a sort of silent whisper."[9] Many such persons have some basis in their experience for such a belief. A patient who had spent a period in jail believed people were calling him "jailbird." A school-girl patient who had been the victim of a rape believed that people were talking about her. For isolated persons who feel that they could not know directly what persons might be whispering, such thoughts are not entirely unreasonable. The powerful feeling of embarrassment, disgrace, and helplessness may give rise to the conviction that other persons are discussing them. The statement that they hear voices may be in the nature of a metaphorical means of expression, used because it is felt that such a means is the only way to communicate the strength of the feeling. Thus, the hallucination of "hearing voices" may be seen as the hopeless attempt of an outcast or disgraced person to communicate his feelings to persons too normal to understand.

Similarly, the statement by a patient that he is Christ

[9] Max Levin, "Auditory Hallucination in Non-psychotic Children," *American Journal of Psychiatry*, Vol. XI (May, 1932).

may mean that he feels himself to be a very special person, as important as Christ. Only the form of statement that he *is* Christ could communicate the strength of his feelings.

Silliness is a sign of abnormality only when it is inappropriate to the social situation. Collective silliness is a common occurrence. The willingness to be silly when others are solemn or indifferent may be merely a sign that the person is seclusive or isolated enough to be indifferent to the opinions of others. Similarly, other traits may be seen to proceed from the one condition of extreme seclusiveness.

If seclusiveness is the key trait of the schizophrenic, the explanation of the disorder lies in the cause of the development of this trait. It is important to determine whether the seclusiveness is due to an innate lack of sociability or to experiences which destroyed the sociability. An examination of one hundred and one consecutive cases of schizophrenia in an eastern state hospital by one of the authors revealed that twenty-seven were definitely reported to have been normally sociable in their childhood. Only twenty-one were reported never to have been sociable. In the remaining fifty-three cases, there was not enough evidence to decide. The cases reported as formerly sociable showed three typical stages in the development of their seclusive personality: (1) sociably inclined, making attempts to get the companionship of others; (2) being excluded by the others, but continuing to make the effort to establish intimate social relationships; (3) accepting defeat, changing the interests, and building up a system of rationalization. After this third stage, a sort of "vicious circle" process begins to operate. The acceptance of failure to mix with others and the development of a certain profile of personality traits makes the person less acceptable to others than before and more than ever liable to exclusion and, in the case of boys especially, more liable to actual persecution. The treatment in turn furthers the development of the schizophrenic traits.[10] Of the one hundred and one cases included in this study forty-eight contained sufficient data to reveal the isolating factors. Twenty-nine of these persons were reported to have been "spoiled children." Many of these became the victims of practical jokes at school, and were subject to a considerable amount of persecution. Four cases were discovered with no evidence of being spoiled but with very strict moral and religious training. Each of these four had a strong sense of guilt because of sex experiences and had delusions referring to them.

In addition, there were four cases which showed hallucinations and delusions due to the isolation brought on by deafness. Other cases showed such isolating factors as the in-

[10] This description of the development of the seclusive personality appears to be essentially true of the paranoid type. The study now being made of both the catatonic and paranoid in relation to their social experience and the development of the personality tends to show that the catatonic is isolated but, unlike the paranoid, he does not attempt to establish social contacts of an intimate nature. However, he does not lack contacts completely but has them only on an extremely formal level. The evidence to date seems to indicate that both the paranoid and the catatonic develop their respective psychotic reactions from the basis of different profiles of personality traits. On this point see especially K. M. Bowman, "A Study of the Pre-psychotic Personalities in Certain Psychoses," *American Journal of Orthopsychiatry*, IV (October, 1934), 473–98; N. J. T. Bigelow, "Pre-psychotic Personality of Catatonic Schizophrenics," *Psychiatric Quarterly*, VI, 642–50; J. Page, C. Landis, and S. Katze, "Schizophrenic Traits in Functional Psychoses and in Normal Individuals," *American Journal of Psychiatry*, XIII (1934), 1213–25; G. S. Amsden, "Mental and Emotional Components of Personality in Schizophrenia," *Schizophrenia—An Investigation of Most Recent Advances*, reported by the Association for Research in Nervous and Mental Diseases (New York: Paul B. Hoeber, Inc., 1928).

ability to speak English, not being allowed by strict parents to play with other children, and sensitivity because of disfiguring physical deformities.

Any factor which interferes with social contacts with other persons produces isolation. The role of an outcast has tremendous effects on the development of the personality. Lack of sufficient self-confidence and the consciousness that others do not desire one's company may act as a serious barrier to intimate social relations. The individual who feels that he is conspicuously ugly, inferior, or in disgrace may be isolated through this conception of himself.

The hypothesis that such forms of isolation are significant factors to account for the high rates of schizophrenia in certain parts of the city is strengthened by the studies which have shown that the conditions producing isolation are much more frequent in the disorganized communities.[11] Especially significant is the connection between the rates of schizophrenia, excepting the catatonic type, and indices of mobility, presented in chapter iv. In addition, the fact that rates for Negro, foreign-born, and native-born are all significantly higher in areas not primarily populated by their own members tends to support this isolation hypothesis. When the harmony of all these facts bearing on the isolation hypothesis is considered, the result is sufficiently impressive to make further pursuit of this lead appear to be worth while.

[11] Much carefully collected evidence on this point is published in Nels Anderson, *The Hobo* (Chicago, 1923); Louis Wirth, *The Ghetto* (Chicago, 1926); Harvey W. Zorbaugh, *The Gold Coast and the Slum* (Chicago, 1927); Ruth S. Cavan, *Suicide* (Chicago, 1928); and E. Franklin Frazier, *The Negro Family in Chicago* (Chicago, 1931).

APPENDIX A

COMMUNITY MAPS BY NUMBER AND HOUSING AREAS

Maps XXXV and XXXVI show the location of the various local communities and subcommunities by number in Chicago. These maps, together with Map I and Charts I and II, are to aid the reader in locating the communities to which reference has often been made in the text. Map XXXVII shows the location of the census tracts by number in Providence, Rhode Island. The eleven housing areas are also included here with the different subcommunities, listed by number, used in constructing each housing area.

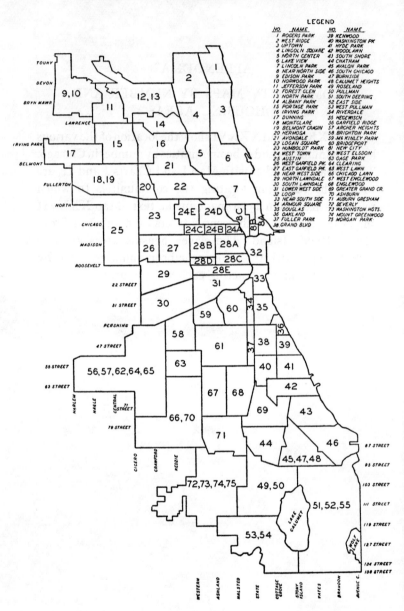

MAP XXXV

COMMUNITY AREAS OF CHICAGO

LEGEND

NO.	NAME	NO.	NAME
1	ROGERS PARK	39	KENWOOD
2	WEST RIDGE	40	WASHINGTON PK
3	UPTOWN	41	HYDE PARK
4	LINCOLN SQUARE	42	WOODLAWN
5	NORTH CENTER	43	SOUTH SHORE
6	LAKE VIEW	44	CHATHAM
7	LINCOLN PARK	45	AVALON PARK
8	NEAR NORTH SIDE	46	SOUTH CHICAGO
9	EDISON PARK	47	BURNSIDE
10	NORWOOD PARK	48	CALUMET HEIGHTS
11	JEFFERSON PARK	49	ROSELAND
12	FOREST GLEN	50	PULLMAN
13	NORTH PARK	51	SOUTH DEERING
14	ALBANY PARK	52	EAST SIDE
15	PORTAGE PARK	53	WEST PULLMAN
16	IRVING PARK	54	RIVERDALE
17	DUNNING	55	HEGEWISCH
18	MONTCLARE	56	GARFIELD RIDGE
19	BELMONT CRAGIN	57	ARCHER HEIGHTS
20	HERMOSA	58	BRIGHTON PARK
21	AVONDALE	59	Mc KINLEY PARK
22	LOGAN SQUARE	60	BRIDGEPORT
23	HUMBOLDT PARK	61	NEW CITY
24	WEST TOWN	62	WEST ELSDON
25	AUSTIN	63	GAGE PARK
26	WEST GARFIELD PK.	64	CLEARING
27	EAST GARFIELD PK.	65	WEST LAWN
28	NEAR WEST SIDE	66	CHICAGO LAWN
29	NORTH LAWNDALE	67	WEST ENGLEWOOD
30	SOUTH LAWNDALE	68	ENGLEWOOD
31	LOWER WEST SIDE	69	GREATER GRAND CR.
32	LOOP	70	ASHBURN
33	NEAR SOUTH SIDE	71	AUBURN GRESHAM
34	ARMOUR SQUARE	72	BEVERLY
35	DOUGLAS	73	WASHINGTON HGTS.
36	OAKLAND	74	MOUNT GREENWOOD
37	FULLER PARK	75	MORGAN PARK
38	GRAND BLVD		

MAP XXXVI

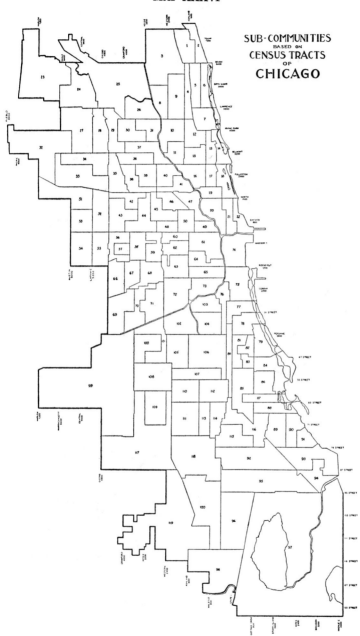

SUB·COMMUNITIES
BASED ON
CENSUS TRACTS
OF
CHICAGO

MAP XXXVII

NUMBERS

OF

CENSUS TRACTS OF PROVIDENCE

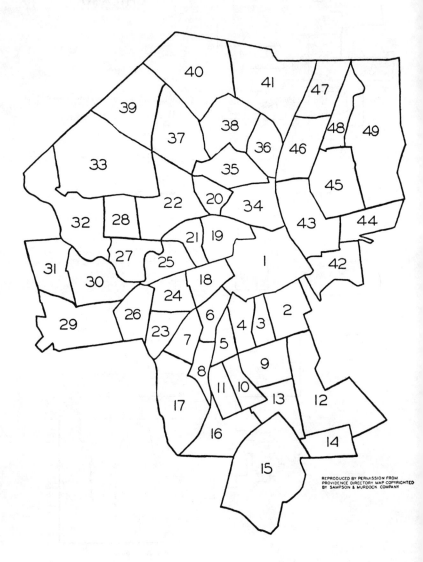

REPRODUCED BY PERMISSION FROM
PROVIDENCE DIRECTORY MAP COPYRIGHTED
BY SAMPSON & MURDOCK COMPANY

URBAN AREAS IN TERMS OF HOUSING WITH SUBCOMMUNITIES BY NUMBER LISTED IN EACH AREA

1. Single home and two-flat area— over $50

23	29	115
24	34	117
25	93	118
27	108	119
28	109	120

2. Single home and two-flat area— under $50

32	97	99
95	98	111
96		

3. Two-flat and single home area— over $50

10	35	52
30	44	53
31	51	116

4. Two-flat and single home area— under $50

11	103	42
40	104	43
48	106	59
69	107	100
70	33	110
71	36	112
101	37	113
102	38	

5. Apartment area (native-born)

1	12	86
2	13	87
3	26	88
4	39	89
5	54	90
8	55	91
9	58	114

6. Hotels and apartment-hotel area

6	14	79
7	22	84
18		

7. Apartment and two-flat area

15	50	76
16	56	92
19	57	94
41	63	105
66	72	

8. Apartment-house area (foreign-born)

45	67	68
46		

9. Apartment-house area (Negro)

60	78	82
65	80	83
77	81	85

10. Tenement-house and rooming area

17	62	73
20	64	47
49		

11. Rooming-house area

21	74	75
61		

APPENDIX B
SUPPLEMENTARY STATISTICAL TABLES

APPENDIX B

TABLE 46

DISTRIBUTION OF ALL CASES OF MENTAL DISORDER ADMITTED TO
PSYCHOPATHIC HOSPITAL WITH POPULATION AND RATES IN
THE LOCAL COMMUNITIES IN CHICAGO, 1930–31

Community	No. of Cases	Adult Population 1930	Rate	Community	No. of Cases	Adult Population 1930	Rate
1	50	42,444	117	31	194	37,044	523
2	37	26,205	141	32	130	7,397	1,757
3	210	96,190	218	33	77	8,227	935
4	77	33,254	231	34	82	12,338	665
5	91	32,880	276	35	275	37,096	751
6	260	85,949	302	36	52	11,510	451
7	250	67,949	368	37	54	8,182	660
8a	30	15,112	198	38	300	64,436	465
8b	199	29,248	680	39	34	21,629	110
8c	114	16,036	710	40	128	32,000	400
9, 10	21	11,917	176	41	64	37,523	170
11	25	11,979	208	42	117	50,725	230
12, 13	18	9,789	163	43	96	57,688	166
14	67	36,606	183	44	45	24,605	186
15	79	40,196	121	45, 47, 48	40	12,395	322
16	80	44,713	178	46	88	32,424	271
17	27	11,014	243	49, 50	80	30,646	261
18, 19	84	40,025	219	51, 52, 55	45	18,064	249
20	39	15,395	253	53, 54	43	16,732	256
21	56	30,498	183	56, 57, 62, 64, 65	46	16,076	301
22	203	72,453	280	59	39	11,989	325
23	159	50,746	311	58	93	25,103	370
24a	50	4,960	1,008	60	127	29,589	429
24b	45	12,420	362	61	159	47,327	336
24c	31	6,462	479	63	60	18,298	327
24d	208	43,401	479	66, 70	52	30,758	168
24e	104	36,382	286	67	120	39,120	306
25	200	91,410	218	68	171	59,725	286
26	102	34,441	299	69	96	40,777	235
27	152	42,665	356	71	64	37,871	169
28a	223	16,979	1,313	72, 73, 74, 75	50	29,617	169
28b	188	27,611	608				
28c	78	19,800	393				
28d	78	13,504	577				
28e	110	18,138	606	City total	7,069	......	.....
29	198	67,542	293				
30	105	46,290	227				

TABLE 47

DISTRIBUTION OF ALL CASES OF MENTAL DISORDER ADMITTED TO STATE HOSPITALS WITH POPULATION AND RATES, IN SUBCOMMUNITIES IN CHICAGO, 1922–34

Sub-community	No. of Cases	Population Age 15 and Over, 1930 ×13	Rate	Sub-community	No. of Cases	Population Age 15 and Over, 1930 ×13	Rate
1	147	304,057	48.35	39	198	350,727	56.45
2	91	304,044	29.93	40	192	228,774	83.93
3	116	377,585	30.72	41	211	220,662	95.62
4	129	238,017	54.20	42	137	191,854	71.41
5	168	345,280	48.66	43	177	261,651	67.65
6	154	345,033	44.63	44	244	327,847	74.42
7	330	438,516	75.25	45	330	443,183	74.46
8	75	194,480	38.56	46	328	329,862	99.44
9	153	289,068	52.93	47	465	305,838	152.04
10	149	273,468	54.49	48	128	104,962	121.95
11	150	213,564	70.24	49	278	135,876	204.60
12	223	348,881	63.92	50	493	359,554	137.11
13	301	340,821	88.32	51	115	259,454	44.32
14	106	274,924	38.56	52	161	245,492	65.58
15	255	272,181	93.69	53	152	254,514	59.72
16	270	262,769	102.75	54	134	335,465	39.94
17	222	242,411	91.58	55	148	250,380	59.11
18	300	298,792	100.40	56	196	300,365	65.25
19	243	201,604	120.53	57	140	215,878	64.85
20	454	250,393	181.31	58	240	338,793	70.84
21	819	403,286	203.08	59	335	303,069	110.54
22	86	204,711	42.01	60	226	127,556	177.18
23	64	178,087	35.94	61	1,289	276,757	465.75
24	95	184,327	51.54	62	537	303,394	177.00
25	128	252,382	50.72	63	364	287,625	126.55
26	213	448,695	47.47	64	390	269,490	144.72
27	184	362,167	50.81	65	375	188,539	198.90
27	126	254,072	49.59	66	125	251,823	49.64
29	102	190,229	53.62	67	270	478,140	56.47
30	114	243,568	46.80	68	320	357,838	89.43
31	117	234,468	49.90	69	168	282,230	59.53
32	126	244,764	51.48	70	121	209,326	57.80
33	167	309,621	53.94	71	176	241,254	72.95
34	92	235,638	39.04	72	399	346,957	115.00
35	137	232,037	59.04	73	388	251,004	154.58
36	160	266,825	59.96	74	427	96,798	441.12
37	119	198,237	60.03	75	396	119,210	332.19
38	211	307,502	68.62	76	199	149,461	133.15

TABLE 47—*Continued*

Sub-community	No. of Cases	Population Age 15 and Over, 1930 X13	Rate	Sub-community	No. of Cases	Population Age 15 and Over, 1930 X13	Rate
77.....	613	196,261	312.34	101.....	177	223,002	79.37
78.....	757	370,084	204.55	102.....	168	192,205	87.41
79.....	305	278,460	109.53	103.....	247	221,312	111.61
80.....	398	200,278	198.72	104.....	295	255,736	115.35
81.....	538	369,967	145.42	105.....	266	223,873	118.82
82.....	443	274,092	161.62	106.....	477	355,797	134.07
83.....	244	215,397	113.28	107.....	216	283,621	76.16
84.....	134	334,178	40.10	108.....	141	289,900	48.64
85.....	619	510,952	121.15	109.....	143	306,956	46.59
86.....	207	351,208	58.94	110.....	229	270,270	84.73
87.....	237	307,398	77.10	111.....	205	333,047	61.55
88.....	222	315,172	70.44	112.....	363	393,666	92.21
89.....	154	376,142	40.94	113.....	146	224,172	65.13
90.....	73	254,657	28.67	114.....	181	278,083	65.09
91.....	59	202,345	29.16	115.....	118	258,765	45.60
92.....	126	374,010	33.69	116.....	227	343,239	66.13
93.....	122	267,111	45.67	117.....	82	157,118	52.19
94.....	219	230,785	91.33	118.....	238	559,728	42.52
95.....	140	198,055	70.69	119.....	161	279,604	57.58
96.....	179	336,102	53.26	120.....	80	211,523	37.82
97.....	259	359,879	71.97				
98.....	177	255,528	69.27	City			
99.....	193	261,898	73.69	total	28,763	33,264,153	86.47
100.....	117	185,471	63.08				

TABLE 48

DISTRIBUTION OF ALL CASES OF MENTAL DISORDER ADMITTED
TO PRIVATE HOSPITALS WITH RATES IN SUBCOMMUNI-
TIES IN CHICAGO, 1922–34*

Sub-community	No. of Cases	Rate	Sub-community	No. of Cases	Rate
1	81	26.64	39	86	24.52
2	119	39.14	40	29	12.68
3	74	19.60	41	19	8.61
4	42	17.65	42	21	10.95
5	124	35.91	43	40	15.29
6	123	35.65	44	81	24.71
7	128	29.19	45	96	21.66
8	49	25.20	46	54	16.37
9	62	21.45	47	22	7.19
10	47	17.19	48	5	4.76
11	36	16.86	49	10	7.36
12	65	18.63	50	32	8.90
13	65	19.07	51	35	13.49
14	123	44.74	52	64	26.07
15	42	15.43	53	53	20.82
16	44	16.74	54	104	31.00
17	45	18.56	55	76	30.35
18	77	25.77	56	74	24.64
19	20	9.92	57	99	45.86
20	27	10.78	58	98	28.93
21	79	19.59	59	44	14.52
22	82	40.06	60	6	4.70
23	21	11.79	61	40	14.45
24	14	7.60	62	45	14.83
25	40	15.85	63	40	13.91
26	145	32.32	64	31	11.50
27	46	12.70	65	20	10.61
28	30	11.81	66	44	17.47
29	33	17.35	67	174	36.39
30	54	22.17	68	130	36.33
31	30	12.99	69	27	9.57
32	15	6.13	70	9	4.30
33	33	10.66	71	11	4.56
34	30	12.73	72	16	4.61
35	30	12.93	73	26	10.36
36	32	11.99	74	56	57.85
37	22	11.10	75	29	24.33
38	41	13.33	76	10	6.69

* The population base for these rates is the same as shown in Table 47.

TABLE 48—*Continued*

Sub-community	No. of Cases	Rate	Sub-community	No. of Cases	Rate
77.........	17	8.66	100.........	14	7.55
78.........	14	3.78	101.........	26	11.66
79.........	55	19.75	102.........	21	10.93
80.........	7	3.50	103.........	26	11.75
81.........	33	8.92	104.........	31	12.12
82.........	11	4.01	105.........	12	5.36
83.........	22	10.21	106.........	43	12.09
84.........	160	47.88	107.........	38	13.40
85.........	80	15.66	108.........	27	9.31
86.........	106	30.18	109.........	52	16.94
87.........	103	33.51	110.........	43	15.91
88.........	73	23.16	111.........	51	15.31
89.........	92	24.46	112.........	82	20.83
90.........	116	45.55	113.........	35	15.61
91.........	40	19.78	114.........	48	17.26
92.........	65	17.38	115.........	65	25.12
93.........	44	16.47	116.........	72	20.98
94.........	15	6.26	117.........	26	16.55
95.........	21	10.60	118.........	121	21.62
96.........	35	10.41	119.........	57	20.39
97.........	16	4.45	120.........	54	11.35
98.........	16	6.26			
99.........	20	7.64	City total	6,101	18.34

TABLE 49

DISTRIBUTION OF ALL CASES OF MENTAL DISORDER ADMITTED
TO STATE AND PRIVATE HOSPITALS WITH RATES IN SUB-
COMMUNITIES IN CHICAGO, 1922–34*

Sub-community	No. of Cases	Rate	Sub-community	No. of Cases	Rate
1........	228	74.99	39........	284	80.97
2........	210	69.07	40........	221	96.60
3........	190	50.32	41........	230	104.23
4........	171	71.84	42........	158	82.35
5........	292	84.57	43........	217	82.93
6........	277	80.28	44........	325	99.13
7........	458	104.44	45........	426	96.12
8........	124	63.75	46........	382	115.81
9........	215	74.38	47........	487	159.23
10........	196	71.67	48........	133	126.71
11........	186	87.09	49........	288	211.96
12........	288	82.55	50........	525	146.01
13........	366	107.39	51........	150	57.81
14........	229	83.30	52........	225	91.65
15........	297	109.12	53........	205	80.55
16........	314	119.50	54........	238	70.95
17........	267	110.14	55........	224	89.46
18........	377	126.17	56........	270	89.89
19........	263	130.45	57........	239	110.71
20........	481	192.10	58........	338	99.77
21........	898	222.67	59........	379	125.05
22........	168	82.07	60........	232	181.88
23........	85	47.73	61........	1,329	480.20
24........	109	59.13	62........	582	191.83
25........	168	66.57	63........	404	140.46
26........	358	79.79	64........	421	156.22
27........	230	63.51	65........	395	209.51
28........	156	61.40	66........	169	67.11
29........	135	70.97	67........	444	92.86
30........	168	68.97	68........	450	125.76
31........	147	62.70	69........	195	69.09
32........	141	57.61	70........	130	62.10
33........	200	64.60	71........	187	77.51
34........	122	51.77	72........	415	119.61
35........	167	71.97	73........	414	164.94
36........	192	71.96	74........	483	498.98
37........	141	71.13	75........	425	356.51
38........	252	81.95	76........	209	139.84

* The population base for these rates is the same as shown in Table 47.

TABLE 49—*Continued*

Sub-community	No. of Cases	Rate	Sub-community	No. of Cases	Rate
77.........	630	321.51	100.........	131	70.63
78.........	771	208.33	101.........	203	91.03
79.........	360	129.28	102.........	189	98.33
80.........	405	202.22	103.........	273	123.36
81.........	571	154.34	104.........	326	126.48
82.........	454	165.64	105.........	278	124.18
83.........	266	123.49	106.........	520	146.15
84.........	294	87.98	107.........	254	89.56
85.........	699	136.80	108.........	168	57.95
86.........	313	89.12	109.........	195	63.53
87.........	340	110.61	110.........	272	100.64
88.........	295	93.60	111.........	256	76.87
89.........	246	65.40	112.........	445	113.04
90.........	189	74.22	113.........	181	80.74
91.........	99	48.93	114.........	229	82.35
92.........	191	51.07	115.........	183	70.72
93.........	166	62.15	116.........	299	87.11
94.........	234	97.59	117.........	108	68.74
95.........	161	81.29	118.........	359	64.14
96.........	214	63.67	119.........	218	77.97
97.........	275	76.41	120.........	104	49.17
98.........	193	75.53			
99.........	213	81.33	City total	34,864	....

TABLE 50

DISTRIBUTION OF SCHIZOPHRENIC CASES WITH POPULATION AND RATES IN LOCAL COMMUNITIES OF CHICAGO, 1922–31

Community	No. of Cases	Estimated Adult Population 1927	Rate	Community	No. of Cases	Estimated Adult Population 1927	Rate
1......	37	33,292	111	31......	252	39,672	635
2......	29	14,913	194	32......	101	8,455	1,195
3......	183	86,594	211	33......	75	10,685	702
4......	50	27,932	179	34......	68	12,937	526
5......	78	31,626	246	35......	250	37,789	662
6......	233	80,202	291	36......	59	11,962	493
7......	287	66,468	432	37......	50	9,153	546
8a.....	16	13,431	119	38......	290	61,685	470
8b.....	202	30,135	670	39......	44	19,997	220
8c.....	99	16,893	586	40......	126	30,752	410
9–10...	12	7,935	151	41......	58	34,445	168
11......	19	8,306	229	42......	135	48,713	277
12–13...	15	6,483	231	43......	77	42,852	180
14......	87	28,859	301	44......	30	15,863	189
15......	75	30,754	244	45–47–48	20	8,686	230
16......	74	37,674	196	46......	105	28,307	371
17......	22	7,135	308	49–50...	80	27,100	295
18–19...	79	24,712	320	51–52–55	70	16,804	417
20......	46	13,173	349	53–54...	51	15,559	328
21......	79	27,654	286	56–57–			
22......	231	70,571	327	62–64–			
23......	140	47,366	296	65....	51	11,866	430
24a.....	40	5,691	703	58......	80	22,236	360
24b.....	99	13,614	727	59......	35	12,227	286
24c.....	35	6,440	543	60......	145	30,658	474
24d.....	268	45,577	588	61......	217	48,690	446
24e.....	180	36,291	496	63......	41	13,515	303
25......	189	75,887	249	66–70...	56	20,625	272
26......	95	32,087	296	67......	115	36,889	312
27......	135	41,848	323	68......	174	58,869	296
28a.....	199	17,681	1,125	69......	79	36,918	214
28b.....	157	28,679	547	71......	48	24,805	194
28c.....	130	21,536	604	72–73–			
28d.....	63	14,562	433	74–75.	60	24,828	242
28e.....	135	19,204	703				
29......	225	64,236	350	City			
30......	168	45,605	368	total	7,253	....	......

TABLE 51

DISTRIBUTION OF MALE SCHIZOPHRENIC CASES WITH POPULATION
AND RATES IN THE LOCAL COMMUNITIES
IN CHICAGO, 1922–31

Community	No. of Cases	Estimated Adult Male Population 1927	Rate	Community	No. of Cases	Estimated Adult Male Population 1927	Rate
1	12	15,137	79	31	148	21,692	682
2	17	7,103	239	32	98	6,922	1,416
3	90	41,133	219	33	45	6,365	707
4	25	13,400	187	34	42	7,503	560
5	42	15,789	266	35	129	19,624	657
6	117	38,939	300	36	23	6,076	379
7	147	34,268	429	37	28	4,796	584
8a	6	5,721	105	38	128	30,458	420
8b	119	18,122	657	39	14	8,776	160
8c	53	9,228	574	40	60	15,137	396
9, 10	5	3,880	129	41	30	15,377	195
11	9	4,218	213	42	76	23,819	319
12, 13	5	3,156	158	43	42	19,937	211
14	43	14,050	306	44	17	8,069	211
15	29	15,431	188	45, 47, 48	7	4,584	153
16	43	18,559	232	46	69	15,898	434
17	5	3,666	136	49, 50	45	14,478	311
18, 19	41	12,782	321	51, 52, 55	37	9,688	382
20	29	6,629	437	53, 54	32	8,533	375
21	38	13,874	274	56, 57,			
22	116	35,521	327	62, 64,			
23	78	24,287	321	65	23	6,408	359
24a	26	3,443	755	58	40	12,076	331
24b	51	7,457	684	59	17	6,373	267
24c	27	3,524	766	60	80	16,534	484
24d	139	24,323	571	61	126	26,684	472
24e	97	18,709	518	63	19	7,061	269
25	88	36,670	240	66, 70	35	10,435	335
26	46	15,836	290	67	56	18,784	298
27	68	21,479	317	68	85	29,475	288
28a	163	13,820	1,179	69	35	18,369	191
28b	90	15,526	580	71	23	12,234	188
28c	82	12,494	656	72, 73,			
28d	35	7,732	453	74, 75	34	11,977	284
28e	79	10,352	763				
29	118	32,869	359	City			
30	95	23,933	397	total	3,916	. . . .	. . . .

TABLE 52

DISTRIBUTION OF FEMALE SCHIZOPHRENIC CASES WITH POPU-
LATION AND RATES IN THE LOCAL COMMUNITIES
IN CHICAGO, 1922–31

Community	No. of Cases	Estimated Adult Female Population 1927	Rate	Community	No. of Cases	Estimated Adult Female Population 1927	Rate
1	25	18,155	138	31	104	17,980	578
2	12	7,810	154	32	3	1,533	196
3	93	45,416	305	33	30	4,320	694
4	25	14,532	172	34	26	5,434	478
5	36	15,837	227	35	121	18,165	666
6	116	41,263	281	36	36	5,886	611
7	140	32,200	435	37	22	4,357	505
8a	10	7,710	130	38	162	31,227	519
8b	83	12,013	691	39	30	11,221	268
8c	46	7,665	600	40	66	15,615	423
9, 10	7	4,055	173	41	28	19,068	147
11	10	4,088	245	42	59	24,894	237
12, 13	10	3,327	301	43	35	22,915	153
14	44	14,809	297	44	13	7,794	167
15	46	15,323	300	45, 47, 48	13	4,102	317
16	31	19,115	162	46	36	12,409	290
17	17	3,469	490	49, 50	35	12,622	277
18, 19	38	11,930	319	51, 52, 55	33	7,116	464
20	17	6,544	260	53, 54	19	7,026	270
21	41	13,780	298	56, 57, 62, 64, 65	28	5,458	513
22	115	35,050	328	58	40	10,160	394
23	62	23,079	269	59	18	5,854	307
24a	14	2,248	623	60	65	14,124	460
24b	48	6,157	780	61	91	22,006	414
24c	8	2,916	274	63	22	6,454	341
24d	129	21,254	607	66, 70	21	10,190	206
24e	83	17,582	472	67	59	18,105	326
25	101	39,217	258	68	89	29,394	303
26	49	16,251	302	69	44	18,549	237
27	67	20,369	329	71	25	12,571	199
28a	36	3,861	932	72, 73, 74, 75	26	12,851	202
28b	67	13,153	509				
28c	48	9,042	531				
28d	28	6,830	410				
28e	56	8,852	633				
29	107	31,367	341	City total	3,337	....	......
30	73	21,672	337				

TABLE 53

DISTRIBUTION OF SCHIZOPHRENIC CASES WITH POPULATION
AND RATES IN THE SUBCOMMUNITIES IN
CHICAGO, 1922–34

Sub-community	No. of Cases	Population Ages 15–64 1930×13	Rate	Sub-community	No. of Cases	Population Ages 15–64 1930×13	Rate
1.....	48	286,988	16.72	39.....	85	326,339	26.04
2.....	44	288,288	15.26	40.....	85	215,631	39.42
3.....	58	358,696	16.16	41.....	82	209,599	39.12
4.....	52	220,740	23.55	42.....	42	178,698	23.50
5.....	60	315,757	19.00	43.....	69	249,444	27.66
6.....	76	328,978	23.10	44.....	120	311,051	38.57
7.....	133	416,858	31.90	45.....	182	424,632	42.86
8.....	28	181,870	15.40	46.....	152	313,625	48.46
9.....	56	270,400	20.71	47.....	149	292,253	50.98
10.....	63	253,097	24.89	48.....	44	100,737	43.67
11.....	67	198,380	33.77	49.....	102	130,390	78.22
12.....	83	323,440	25.66	50.....	190	348,062	54.58
13.....	119	322,140	36.94	51.....	40	247,325	16.17
14.....	42	260,052	16.15	52.....	73	229,853	31.75
15.....	89	251,550	35.38	53.....	79	233,571	33.82
16.....	98	246,935	39.69	54.....	68	314,691	21.60
17.....	92	228,072	40.33	55.....	70	235,742	29.69
18.....	107	283,465	37.74	56.....	92	283,491	32.45
19.....	86	188,344	45.66	57.....	83	201,916	41.11
20.....	148	236,601	62.52	58.....	97	320,255	30.29
21.....	243	382,109	63.59	59.....	100	286,143	34.94
22.....	46	194,454	23.65	60.....	62	122,564	50.59
23.....	25	167,037	14.97	61.....	308	256,867	119.90
24.....	33	176,475	18.69	62.....	141	285,441	49.39
25.....	62	240,643	25.76	63.....	123	275,041	44.72
26.....	116	426,114	27.22	64.....	130	255,996	50.78
27.....	76	346,151	21.96	65.....	125	181,584	68.83
28.....	52	240,864	21.58	66.....	58	241,007	24.06
29.....	31	179,374	17.28	67.....	179	456,612	39.20
30.....	39	228,020	17.10	68.....	171	339,456	50.37
31.....	38	222,131	17.10	69.....	85	269,997	31.48
32.....	45	235,950	19.07	70.....	53	200,512	26.43
33.....	71	299,338	23.71	71.....	77	233,090	33.03
34.....	38	226,070	16.80	72.....	169	334,529	50.52
35.....	65	218,790	29.70	73.....	154	238,927	64.45
36.....	61	252,759	24.13	74.....	132	87,971	150.04
37.....	49	187,356	26.15	75.....	92	112,983	81.43
38.....	80	286,312	27.94	76.....	56	142,688	39.25

TABLE 53—*Continued*

Sub-community	No. of Cases	Population Ages 15–64 1930×13	Rate	Sub-community	No. of Cases	Population Ages 15–64 1930×13	Rate
77.....	162	188,695	85.85	101.....	78	216,151	36.08
78.....	190	360,282	52.73	102.....	56	182,559	30.67
79.....	84	256,685	32.72	103.....	92	209,365	43.94
80.....	111	192,816	57.56	104.....	103	244,673	42.09
81.....	160	362,596	44.12	105.....	102	217,295	46.94
82.....	122	267,007	45.69	106.....	158	339,677	46.51
83.....	69	208,442	33.10	107.....	81	269,529	30.05
84.....	66	306,384	21.54	108.....	58	281,294	20.62
85.....	197	495,183	39.78	109.....	66	294,528	22.41
86.....	85	325,442	26.11	110.....	81	255,320	31.72
87.....	95	284,596	33.38	111.....	83	312,923	26.52
88.....	63	294,255	21.41	112.....	133	365,729	36.37
89.....	63	352,391	17.87	113.....	54	208,988	25.83
90.....	57	240,318	23.71	114.....	58	256,256	22.63
91.....	28	190,957	14.66	115.....	55	240,981	22.82
92.....	51	356,044	14.32	116.....	91	320,294	28.41
93.....	65	255,931	25.39	117.....	24	150,852	15.90
94.....	77	231,218	33.30	118.....	97	528,476	18.35
95.....	46	189,995	24.21	119.....	63	259,818	24.24
96.....	67	317,512	21.10	120.....	38	200,070	18.99
97.....	110	345,306	31.86				
98.....	75	244,413	30.68	City			
99.....	75	254,553	29.46	total	10,575	31,516,303	33.32
100.....	48	181,103	26.50				

TABLE 54

DISTRIBUTION OF UNDIAGNOSED PSYCHOSES CASES AND RATES
IN THE LOCAL COMMUNITIES IN CHICAGO, 1922–31*

Community	No. of Cases	Rate	Community	No. of Cases	Rate
1	5	15	30	7	15
2	2	13	31	28	71
3	14	16	32	9	106
4	8	29	33	19	178
5	3	9	34	16	124
6	22	27	35	45	119
7	22	33	36	7	59
8a	2	15	37	7	76
8b	41	136	38	37	60
8c	19	112	39	7	35
9–10	1	13	40	17	55
11			41	11	32
12–13	2	31	42	20	41
14	4	14	43	3	7
15	4	13	44	2	13
16	6	16	45–47–48	7	81
17	2	28	46	12	42
18–19	3	12	49–50	9	33
20	5	38	51–52–55	8	48
21	5	18	53–54	8	51
22	16	23	56–57–62–64–		
23	12	25	65	10	84
24a	6	105	58	5	22
24b	11	81	59	8	65
24c	3	47	60	17	56
24d	27	59	61	31	64
24e	13	36	63	5	37
25	8	11	66–70	4	19
26	9	28	67	12	33
27	11	26	68	29	49
28a	35	198	69	12	33
28b	21	73	71	6	24
28c	11	51	72–73–74–75	5	20
28d	4	27			
28e	18	94	City total	814	
29	16	25			

* Population base is the same as in Table 50.

TABLE 55

Distribution of "Without Psychoses" Cases and Rates in the Subcommunities in Chicago, 1922–34*

Subcommunity	No. of Cases	Rate	Subcommunity	No. of Cases	Rate
1	14	4.60	40	11	4.81
2	14	4.60	41	12	5.44
3	11	2.91	42	8	4.17
4	11	4.62	43	7	2.68
5	23	6.66	44	9	2.74
6	23	6.66	45	17	3.84
7	30	6.84	46	19	5.76
8	9	4.62	47	22	7.19
9	10	3.46	48	3	2.86
10	7	2.56	49	8	5.88
11	7	3.27	50	20	5.56
12	18	5.16	51	11	4.24
13	17	4.99	52	11	4.48
14	15	5.45	53	7	2.75
15	14	5.14	54	6	1.79
16	17	6.46	55	7	2.79
17	10	4.13	56	12	3.99
18	23	7.70	57	10	4.63
19	10	4.96	58	26	7.67
20	19	7.59	59	21	6.92
21	45	11.16	60	10	7.84
22	23	11.24	61	78	28.18
23	1	0.56	62	32	10.55
24	4	2.17	63	27	9.39
25	7	2.77	64	15	5.57
26	11	2.45	65	17	9.02
27	11	3.03	66	5	1.99
28	8	3.15	67	18	3.76
29	9	4.73	68	18	5.03
30	12	4.93	69	7	2.48
31	2	0.85	70	8	3.82
32	5	2.04	71	6	2.49
33	10	3.23	72	14	4.04
34	6	2.54	73	18	7.17
35	7	3.02	74	38	39.26
36	12	4.49	75	27	22.65
37	5	2.52	76	8	5.35
38	9	2.93	77	20	10.19
39	14	3.99	78	31	8.38

* Population base is the same as in Table 47.

TABLE 55—*Continued*

Subcommunity	No. of Cases	Rate	Subcommunity	No. of Cases	Rate
79............	16	5.75	101...........	11	4.93
80............	14	6.99	102...........	7	3.64
81............	12	3.24	103...........	7	3.16
82............	17	6.20	104...........	18	7.04
83............	10	4.64	105...........	15	6.70
84............	30	8.98	106...........	27	7.59
85............	36	7.05	107...........	23	8.11
86............	19	5.41	108...........	6	2.07
87............	12	3.90	109...........	10	3.26
88............	12	3.81	110...........	15	5.55
89............	26	6.91	111...........	17	5.10
90............	18	7.07	112...........	20	5.08
91............	10	4.94	113...........	5	2.23
92............	11	2.94	114...........	11	3.96
93............	6	2.25	115...........	8	3.09
94............	12	5.00	116...........	7	2.04
95............	5	2.52	117...........	7	4.46
96............	2	0.60	118...........	21	3.75
97............	9	2.50	119...........	12	4.29
98............	8	3.13	120...........	6	2.84
99............	14	5.35			
100...........	7	3.77	City total	1,706	5.12

TABLE 56

DISTRIBUTION OF MANIC-DEPRESSIVE PSYCHOSES CASES, AND
RATES IN THE LOCAL COMMUNITIES IN CHICAGO, 1922–31*

Community	No. of Cases	Rate	Community	No. of Cases	Rate
1	12	36	30	12	26
2	6	40	31	15	38
3	26	30	32	4	47
4	8	29	33	4	37
5	8	25	34	6	46
6	26	32	35	26	69
7	22	33	36	4	33
8a	3	22	37	5	55
8b	19	63	38	20	32
8c	10	59	39	8	40
9–10	2	25	40	7	23
11	3	36	41	7	20
12–13	1	15	42	17	35
14	12	42	43	7	16
15	8	26	44	7	44
16	10	27	45–47–48	5	58
17	1	14	46	9	32
18–19	11	45	49–50	11	41
20	2	15	51–52–55	6	36
21	11	40	53–54	2	13
22	31	44	56–57–62–64–		
23	15	32	65	4	34
24a	3	53	58	8	36
24b	6	44	59	1	8
24c	3	47	60	5	16
24d	25	55	61	19	39
24e	17	47	63	2	15
25	25	33	66–70	5	24
26	14	44	67	15	41
27	15	36	68	21	36
28a	11	62	69	15	41
28b	22	77	71	6	24
28c	18	84	72–73–74–75	5	20
28d	8	55			
28e	5	26	City total	734	....
29	27	42			

* Population base is the same as in Table 50.

TABLE 57

DISTRIBUTION OF MANIC-DEPRESSIVE PSYCHOSES CASES BY SEX AND TOTAL WITH POPULATION AND RATES IN THE SUBCOMMUNITIES IN CHICAGO, 1922–34

SUB-COMMUNITY	MALE			FEMALE			TOTAL		
	No. of Cases	Population Ages 15–64 1930×13	Rate	No. of Cases	Population Ages 15–64 1930×13	Rate	No. of Cases	Population Ages 15–64 1930×13	Rate
1....	9	132,652	6.78	16	154,336	10.37	25	286,988	8.71
2....	14	130,507	10.73	19	157,781	12.04	33	288,288	11.45
3....	9	172,419	5.22	15	186,277	8.05	24	358,696	6.69
4....	7	109,239	6.41	8	111,501	7.17	15	220,740	6.79
5....	13	146,107	8.90	26	169,650	15.33	39	315,757	12.35
6....	6	153,088	3.92	26	175,890	14.78	32	328,978	9.72
7....	10	208,858	4.79	27	208,000	12.98	37	416,858	8.88
8....	6	86,593	6.93	8	95,277	8.40	14	181,870	7.70
9....	13	131,547	9.88	10	138,853	7.20	23	270,400	8.51
10....	4	126,087	3.17	7	127,010	5.51	11	253,097	4.35
11....	4	101,582	3.94	2	96,798	2.07	6	198,380	3.02
12....	12	158,678	7.56	12	164,762	7.28	24	323,440	7.42
13....	8	168,493	4.75	26	153,647	16.92	34	322,140	10.55
14....	11	108,433	10.14	24	151,619	15.83	35	260,052	13.46
15....	5	132,262	3.78	11	119,288	9.22	16	251,550	6.36
16....	7	132,496	5.28	12	114,439	10.49	19	246,935	7.69
17....	5	118,937	4.20	9	109,135	8.25	14	228,072	6.13
18....	8	140,192	5.71	16	143,273	11.17	24	283,465	8.47
19....	6	98,579	6.09	10	89,765	11.14	16	188,344	8.50
20....	11	126,074	8.73	10	110,617	9.04	21	236,691	8.87
21....	19	224,588	8.46	17	157,521	10.79	36	382,109	9.42
22....	6	85,358	7.03	9	109,096	8.25	15	194,454	7.71
23....	4	82,342	4.86	8	84,695	9.45	12	167,037	7.18
24....	6	89,544	6.70	6	86,931	6.90	12	176,475	6.80
25....	7	118,859	5.89	9	121,784	7.39	16	240,643	6.65
26....	20	205,218	9.75	29	220,896	13.13	49	426,114	11.50
27....	8	174,096	4.60	16	172,055	9.30	24	346,151	6.93
28....	2	122,265	1.64	8	118,599	6.75	10	240,864	4.15
29....	6	88,790	6.76	10	90,584	11.04	16	179,374	8.92
30....	3	110,695	2.71	14	117,325	11.93	17	228,020	7.45
31....	3	111,358	2.69	13	110,773	11.74	16	222,131	7.20
32....	2	121,173	1.65	9	114,777	7.84	11	235,950	4.66
33....	12	155,194	7.73	7	144,144	4.86	19	299,338	6.35
34....	4	114,244	3.50	5	111,826	4.47	9	226,070	3.98
35....	4	110,201	3.63	4	108,589	3.68	8	218,790	3.66
36....	1	125,177	0.80	13	127,582	10.19	14	252,759	5.54
37....	4	93,821	4.26	8	93,535	8.55	12	187,356	6.40
38....	6	144,703	4.15	17	141,609	12.00	23	286,312	8.03
39....	7	160,550	4.36	23	165,789	13.87	30	326,339	9.19
40....	2	109,486	1.83	14	106,145	13.19	16	215,631	7.42
41....	4	108,914	3.67	7	100,685	6.95	11	209,599	5.25
42....	5	92,144	5.43	7	86,554	8.09	12	178,698	6.72
43....	5	127,855	3.91	7	121,589	5.76	12	249,444	4.81
44....	14	159,276	8.79	12	151,775	7.91	26	311,051	8.36
45....	12	217,191	5.53	26	207,441	12.53	38	424,632	8.94
46....	7	163,033	4.29	15	150,592	9.96	22	313,625	7.01
47....	4	152,815	2.62	10	139,438	7.17	14	292,253	4.79
48....	1	54,210	1.84	7	46,527	15.05	8	100,737	7.94
49....	3	74,997	4.00	3	55,393	5.42	6	130,390	4.60
50....	9	185,536	4.85	15	162,526	9.23	24	348,062	6.89

TABLE 57—Continued

SUB-COMMUNITY	MALE			FEMALE			TOTAL		
	No. of Cases	Population Ages 15–64 1930×13	Rate	No. of Cases	Population Ages 15–64 1930×13	Rate	No. of Cases	Population Ages 15–64 1930×13	Rate
51....	4	123,188	3.25	9	124,137	7.25	13	247,325	5.26
52....	2	115,869	1.73	22	113,984	19.30	24	229,853	10.44
53....	10	113,841	8.78	7	119,730	5.85	17	233,571	7.28
54....	12	145,938	8.22	21	168,753	12.44	33	314,691	10.49
55....	8	113,269	7.06	13	122,473	10.61	21	235,742	8.91
56....	8	143,143	5.59	25	140,348	17.81	33	283,491	11.64
57....	5	98,917	5.05	22	102,999	21.36	27	201,916	13.37
58....	8	163,241	4.90	20	157,014	12.74	28	320,255	8.74
59....	6	149,747	4.01	15	136,396	11.00	21	286,143	7.34
60....	1	62,335	1.60	8	60,229	13.28	9	122,564	7.34
61....	21	196,144	10.71	10	60,723	16.47	31	256,867	12.07
62....	11	158,743	6.93	20	126,698	15.79	31	285,441	10.86
63....	10	143,897	6.95	9	131,144	6 86	19	275,041	6.91
64....	8	140,569	5.69	17	115,427	14.73	25	255,996	9.77
65....	3	96,330	3.11	3	85,254	3.52	6	181,584	3.30
66....	7	122,564	5.71	8	118,443	6.75	15	241,007	6.22
67....	12	230,165	5.21	29	226,447	12.81	41	456,612	8.97
68....	10	175,019	5.71	29	164,437	17.64	39	339,456	11.49
69....	6	138,502	4.33	4	131,495	3.04	10	269,997	3.70
70....	1	101,751	0.98	2	98,761	2.03	3	200,512	1.50
71....	......	127,881	......	6	105,209	5.70	6	233,090	2.57
72....	6	178,451	3.36	12	156,078	7.69	18	334,529	5.38
73....	5	130,624	3.83	7	108,303	6.46	12	238,927	5.02
74....	8	69,563	11.50	9	18,408	48.89	17	87,971	19.32
75....	6	66,482	9.02	3	46,501	6.45	9	112,983	7.96
76....	2	84,227	2.37	5	58,461	8.55	7	142,688	4.90
77....	6	97,279	6.17	14	91,416	15.31	20	188,695	10.60
78....	16	184,210	8.69	8	176,072	4.54	24	360,282	6.66
79....	7	126,776	5.52	11	129,909	8.47	18	256,685	7.01
80....	1	97,851	1.02	4	94,965	4.21	5	192,816	2.59
81....	6	179,829	3.34	12	182,767	6.57	18	362,596	4.96
82....	5	131,976	3.79	9	135,031	6.67	14	267,007	5.24
83....	6	101,049	5.93	2	107,393	1.86	8	208,442	3.83
84....	18	129,883	13.86	32	176,501	18.13	50	306,384	16.32
85....	4	243,893	1.64	30	251,290	11.94	34	495,183	6.87
86....	10	153,192	6.53	23	172,250	13.35	33	325,442	10.14
87....	12	141,791	8.46	20	142,805	14.01	32	284,596	11.24
88....	12	145,028	8.27	16	149,227	10.72	28	294,255	9.51
89....	10	165,425	6.05	15	186,966	8.02	25	352,391	7.09
90....	14	107,211	13.06	12	133,107	9.02	26	240,318	10.82
91....	5	89,193	5.61	11	101,764	10.81	16	190,957	8.38
92....	12	173,381	6.92	14	182,663	7.66	26	356,044	7.30
93....	2	129,558	1.54	15	126,373	11.87	17	255,931	6.64
94....	4	138,398	2.89	3	92,820	3.23	7	231,218	3.03
95....	4	99,814	4.01	4	90,181	4.44	8	189,995	4.21
96....	5	166,049	3.01	11	151,463	7.26	16	317,512	5.03
97....	12	194,454	6.17	4	150,852	2.65	16	345,306	4.63
98....	2	131,482	1.52	4	112,931	3.54	6	244,413	2.45
99....	3	136,214	2.20	8	118,339	6.76	11	254,553	4.32
100....	4	93,470	4.28	4	87,633	4.56	8	181,103	4.42
101....	5	115,440	4.33	7	100,711	6.95	12	216,151	5.55
102....	2	94,666	2.11	9	87,893	10.24	11	182,559	6.03
103....	6	109,772	5.47	4	99,593	4.02	10	209,365	4.78
104....	2	130,949	1.53	6	113,724	5.28	8	244,673	3.26
105....	2	119,314	1.68	8	97,981	8.16	10	217,295	4.60

TABLE 57—*Continued*

SUB-COM-MUNITY	MALE			FEMALE			TOTAL		
	No. of Cases	Population Ages 15–64 1930×13	Rate	No. of Cases	Population Ages 15–64 1930×13	Rate	No. of Cases	Population Ages 15–64 1930×13	Rate
106....	10	184,990	5.41	13	154,687	8.40	23	339,677	6.77
107....	8	137,878	5.80	8	131,651	6.08	16	269,529	5.93
108....	4	145,730	2.74	8	135,564	5.90	12	281,294	4.27
109....	5	146,588	3.41	9	147,940	6.08	14	294,528	4.75
110....	10	130,338	7.67	14	124,982	11.20	24	255,320	9.40
111....	10	158,015	6.33	13	154,908	8.39	23	312,923	7.35
112....	6	188,773	3.18	22·	176,956	12.43	28	365,729	7.66
113....	2	105,560	1.89	11	103,428	10.64	13	208,988	6.22
114....	8	125,164	6.39	11	131,092	8.39	19	256,256	7.41
115....	9	117,598	7.65	6	123,383	4.86	15	240,981	6.22
116....	9	162,617	5.53	17	157,677	10.78	26	320,294	8.12
117....	1	77,792	1.29	8	73,060	10.95	9	150,852	5.97
118....	12	259,818	4.62	22	268,658	8.19	34	528,476	6.43
119....	6	125,424	4.78	9	134,394	6.70	15	259,818	5.77
120....	4	99,554	4.02	4	100,516	3.98	8	200,070	4.00
City total	839	16,050,242	5.23	1,472	15,466,061	9.52	2,311	31,516,303	7.33

TABLE 58

DISTRIBUTION OF MANIC-DEPRESSIVE PSYCHOSES, MANIC CASES,
AND RATES IN THE SUBCOMMUNITIES IN CHICAGO, 1922–34*

Subcommunity	No. of Cases	Rate	Subcommunity	No. of Cases	Rate
1	6	2.09	40	7	3.25
2	18	6.24	41	4	1.91
3	6	1.67	42	3	1.68
4	4	1.81	43	5	2.00
5	12	3.80	44	6	1.93
6	12	3.65	45	11	2.59
7	18	4.32	46	11	3.51
8	3	1.65	47	4	1.37
9	10	3.70	48	8	7.94
10	5	1.98	49	2	1.53
11	1	0.50	50	10	2.87
12	9	2.78	51	3	1.21
13	13	4.04	52	9	3.92
14	13	5.00	53	7	3.00
15	3	1.19	54	11	3.50
16	6	2.43	55	7	2.97
17	4	1.75	56	10	3.53
18	12	4.23	57	7	3.47
19	4	2.12	58	10	3.12
20	12	5.07	59	8	2.80
21	16	4.19	60	5	4.08
22	5	2.57	61	8	3.11
23	4	2.39	62	16	5.61
24	1	0.57	63	6	2.18
25	4	1.66	64	14	5.47
26	19	4.46	65	3	1.65
27	7	2.02	66	8	3.32
28	3	1.25	67	21	4.60
29	3	1.67	68	14	4.12
30	6	2.63	69	2	0.74
31	5	2.25	70	2	1.00
32	2	0.85	71	4	1.72
33	7	2.34	72	8	2.39
34	4	1.77	73	2	0.84
35	4	1.83	74	9	10.23
36	4	1.58	75	6	5.31
37	5	2.67	76	4	2.80
38	10	3.49	77	14	7.42
39	12	3.68	78	17	4.72

* Population base is the same as in Table 57.

TABLE 58—*Continued*

Subcommunity	No. of Cases	Rate	Subcommunity	No. of Cases	Rate
79	7	2.73	101	5	2.31
80	1	0.52	102	5	2.74
81	11	3.03	103	5	2.39
82	8	3.00	104	1	0.41
83	4	1.92	105	4	1.84
84	16	5.22	106	11	3.24
85	12	2.42	107	8	2.97
86	14	4.30	108	4	1.42
87	10	3.51	109	2	0.68
88	13	4.42	110	9	3.52
89	6	1.70	111	11	3.52
90	8	3.33	112	12	3.28
91	3	1.57	113	5	2.39
92	10	2.81	114	5	1.95
93	9	3.52	115	2	0.83
94	4	1.73	116	12	3.75
95	6	3.16	117	3	1.99
96	5	1.57	118	12	2.27
97	5	1.45	119	6	2.31
98	2	0.82	120	5	2.50
99	11	4.32			
100	2	1.10	City total.	892	....

TABLE 59

DISTRIBUTION OF MANIC-DEPRESSIVE PSYCHOSES, DEPRESSED
CASES, AND RATES IN THE SUBCOMMUNITIES IN
CHICAGO, 1922–34*

Subcommunity	No. of Cases	Rate	Subcommunity	No. of Cases	Rate
1	11	3.83	40	6	2.78
2	14	4.85	41	7	3.34
3	12	3.35	42	7	3.92
4	8	3.62	43	4	1.60
5	18	5.70	44	18	5.79
6	11	3.34	45	15	3.53
7	11	2.64	46	8	2.55
8	10	5.50	47	10	3.42
9	11	4.07	48	....	....
10	5	1.98	49	3	2.30
11	5	2.52	50	12	3.45
12	9	2.78	51	6	2.43
13	17	5.28	52	10	4.35
14	12	4.61	53	9	3.85
15	11	4.37	54	18	5.72
16	10	4.05	55	10	4.24
17	8	3.51	56	20	7.05
18	7	2.47	57	14	6.93
19	10	5.31	58	14	4.37
20	8	3.38	59	10	3.49
21	16	4.19	60	2	1.63
22	7	3.60	61	19	7.40
23	7	4.19	62	9	3.15
24	11	6.23	63	11	4.00
25	9	3.74	64	8	3.13
26	16	3.75	65	3	1.65
27	13	3.76	66	3	1.24
28	5	2.08	67	10	2.19
29	11	6.13	68	13	3.83
30	8	3.51	69	8	2.96
31	7	3.15	70	1	0.50
32	8	3.39	71	2	0.86
33	9	3.01	72	7	2.09
34	5	2.21	73	7	2.93
35	4	1.83	74	6	6.82
36	9	3.56	75	2	1.77
37	7	3.74	76	3	2.10
38	10	3.49	77	2	1.06
39	16	4.90	78	4	1.11

* Population base is the same as in Table 57.

TABLE 59—*Continued*

Subcommunity	No. of Cases	Rate	Subcommunity	No. of Cases	Rate
79...........	8	3.12	101..........	4	1.85
80...........	4	2.07	102..........	6	3.29
81...........	5	1.38	103..........	5	2.39
82...........	5	1.87	104..........	6	2.45
83...........	3	1.44	105..........	6	2.76
84...........	20	6.53	106..........	9	2.65
85...........	17	3.43	107..........	7	2.60
86...........	16	4.92	108..........	7	2.49
87...........	16	5.62	109..........	12	4.07
88...........	14	4.76	110..........	11	4.31
89...........	14	3.97	111..........	9	2.88
90...........	13	5.41	112..........	9	2.46
91...........	12	6.28	113..........	7	3.35
92...........	13	3.65	114..........	13	5.07
93...........	7	2.74	115..........	11	4.56
94...........	1	0.43	116..........	12	3.75
95...........	2	1.05	117..........	4	2.65
96...........	9	2.83	118..........	20	3.78
97...........	9	2.61	119..........	6	2.31
98...........	4	1.64	120..........	2	1.00
99...........	....	....			
100..........	4	2.21	City total.	1,069	....

TABLE 60

DISTRIBUTION OF MANIC-DEPRESSIVE PSYCHOSES CASES ADMITTED
TO STATE HOSPITALS AND RATES IN THE SUBCOMMUNITIES
IN CHICAGO, 1922–34[*]

Subcommunity	No. of Cases	Rate	Subcommunity	No. of Cases	Rate
1............	4	1.39	39............	12	3.68
2............	9	3.12	40............	9	4.17
3............	9	2.51	41............	10	4.77
4............	4	1.81	42............	6	3.36
5............	10	3.17	43............	6	2.41
6............	8	2.43	44............	13	4.18
7............	13	3.12	45............	20	4.71
8............	3	1.65	46............	15	4.78
9............	7	2.59	47............	10	3.42
10............	6	2.37	48............	8	7.94
11............	3	1.51	49............	3	2.30
12............	8	2.47	50............	20	5.75
13............	18	5.59	51............	7	2.83
14............	11	4.23	52............	9	3.92
15............	8	3.18	53............	9	3.85
16............	14	5.67	54............	10	3.18
17............	8	3.51	55............	5	2.12
18............	9	3.17	56............	13	4.59
19............	15	7.96	57............	8	3.96
20............	17	7.18	58............	13	4.06
21............	25	6.54	59............	9	3.15
22............	3	1.54	60............	8	6.53
23............	7	4.19	61............	23	8.95
24............	6	3.40	62............	24	8.41
25............	8	3.32	63............	12	4.36
26............	16	3.75	64............	20	7.81
27............	10	2.89	65............	3	1.65
28............	4	1.66	66............	10	4.15
29............	5	2.79	67............	14	3.07
30............	6	2.63	68............	16	4.71
31............	11	4.95	69............	9	3.33
32............	5	2.12	70............	3	1.50
33............	14	4.68	71............	5	2.15
34............	6	2.65	72............	12	3.59
35............	4	1.83	73............	9	3.77
36............	8	3.17	74............	10	11.37
37............	7	3.74	75............	7	6.20
38............	14	4.89	76............	6	4.20

[*] Population base is the same as in Table 57.

TABLE 60—*Continued*

Subcommunity	No. of Cases	Rate	Subcommunity	No. of Cases	Rate
77	16	8.48	100	7	3.87
78	23	6.38	101	8	3.70
79	10	3.90	102	7	3.83
80	3	1.56	103	5	2.39
81	11	3.03	104	4	1.63
82	9	3.37	105	9	4.14
83	8	3.84	106	16	4.71
84	9	2.94	107	8	2.97
85	16	3.23	108	6	2.13
86	11	3.38	109	7	2.38
87	10	3.51	110	13	5.09
88	14	4.76	111	15	4.79
89	7	1.99	112	13	3.55
90	4	1.66	113	5	2.39
91	6	3.14	114	7	2.73
92	13	3.65	115	6	2.49
93	7	2.74	116	13	4.06
94	5	2.16	117	3	1.99
95	5	2.63	118	10	1.89
96	9	2.83	119	6	2.31
97	13	3.76	120	5	2.50
98	3	1.23	City total.	1,144	3.63
99	10	3.93			

TABLE 61

DISTRIBUTION OF MANIC-DEPRESSIVE PSYCHOSES CASES
ADMITTED TO PRIVATE HOSPITALS AND RATES IN THE
SUBCOMMUNITIES IN CHICAGO, 1922–34*

Subcommunity	No. of Cases	Rate	Subcommunity	No. of Cases	Rate
1	21	7.32	39	18	5.52
2	24	8.33	40	7	3.25
3	15	4.18	41	1	0.48
4	11	4.98	42	6	3.36
5	29	9.18	43	6	2.41
6	24	7.30	44	13	4.18
7	24	5.76	45	18	4.24
8	11	6.05	46	7	2.23
9	16	5.92	47	4	1.37
10	5	1.98	48	....	....
11	3	1.51	49	3	2.30
12	16	4.95	50	4	1.15
13	16	4.97	51	6	2.43
14	24	9.23	52	15	6.53
15	8	3.18	53	8	3.43
16	5	2.02	54	23	7.31
17	6	2.63	55	16	6.79
18	15	5.29	56	20	7.05
19	1	0.53	57	19	9.41
20	4	1.69	58	15	4.68
21	11	2.88	59	12	4.19
22	12	6.17	60	1	0.82
23	5	2.99	61	8	3.11
24	6	3.40	62	7	2.45
25	8	3.32	63	7	2.55
26	33	7.74	64	5	1.95
27	14	4.04	65	3	1.65
28	6	2.49	66	5	2.07
29	11	6.13	67	27	5.91
30	11	4.82	68	23	6.78
31	5	2.25	69	1	0.37
32	6	2.54	70	....	....
33	5	1.67	71	1	0.43
34	3	1.33	72	6	1.79
35	4	1.83	73	3	1.26
36	6	2.37	74	7	7.96
37	5	2.67	75	2	1.77
38	9	3.14	76	1	0.70

* Population base is the same as in Table 57.

TABLE 61—*Continued*

Subcommunity	No. of Cases	Rate	Subcommunity	No. of Cases	Rate
77..........	4	2.12	100.........	1	0.55
78..........	1	0.28	101.........	4	1.85
79..........	8	3.12	102.........	4	2.19
80..........	2	1.04	103.........	5	2.39
81..........	7	1.93	104.........	4	1.63
82..........	5	1.87	105.........	1	0.46
83..........	....	....	106.........	7	2.06
84..........	41	13.38	107.........	8	2.97
85..........	18	3.64	108.........	6	2.13
86..........	22	6.76	109.........	7	2.38
87..........	22	7.73	110.........	11	4.31
88..........	14	4.76	111.........	8	2.56
89..........	18	5.11	112.........	15	4.10
90..........	22	9.15	113.........	8	3.83
91..........	10	5.24	114.........	12	4.68
92..........	13	3.65	115.........	9	3.73
93..........	10	3.91	116.........	13	4.06
94..........	2	0.86	117.........	6	3.98
95..........	3	1.58	118.........	24	4.54
96..........	7	2.20	119.........	9	3.46
97..........	3	0.87	120.........	3	1.50
98..........	3	1.23			
99..........	1	0.39	City total.	1,167	3.70

TABLE 62

DISTRIBUTION OF PARANOID SCHIZOPHRENIC CASES
AND RATES IN THE LOCAL COMMUNITIES IN
CHICAGO, 1922–31*

Community	No. of Cases	Rate	Community	No. of Cases	Rate
1............	17	51	30............	50	101
2............	11	74	31............	69	174
3............	65	75	32............	45	532
4............	19	68	33............	22	206
5............	19	60	34............	14	108
6............	82	102	35............	56	148
7............	101	152	36............	16	134
8a............	3	22	37............	12	131
8b............	90	299	38............	53	86
8c............	24	142	39............	24	120
9, 10.........	2	25	40............	28	91
11............	6	72	41............	20	58
12, 13.........	6	93	42............	49	101
14............	34	118	43............	27	63
15............	28	91	44............	4	25
16............	23	61	45, 47, 48......	4	46
17............	7	98	46............	28	99
18, 19.........	23	93	49, 50.........	24	89
20............	17	129	51, 52, 55.....	13	77
21............	29	105	53, 54.........	15	96
22............	74	105	56, 57, 62, 64,		
23............	37	78	65..........	11	93
24a............	10	176	58............	18	81
24b............	30	220	59............	6	49
24c............	5	78	60............	49	160
24d............	61	134	61............	51	105
24e............	51	141	63............	12	89
25............	66	87	66, 70.........	19	92
26............	35	110	67............	27	73
27............	38	91	68............	43	73
28a............	76	430	69............	26	70
28b............	54	188	71............	15	60
28c............	44	204	72, 73, 74, 75..	18	72
28d............	18	124			
28e............	29	151	City total.	2,154	....
29............	52	81			

* Population base is the same as in Table 50.

TABLE 63

DISTRIBUTION OF HEBEPHRENIC SCHIZOPHRENIC
CASES AND RATES IN THE LOCAL COMMUNITIES
IN CHICAGO, 1922–31*

Community	No. of Cases	Rate	Community	No. of Cases	Rate
1............	12	36	30............	88	193
2............	10	67	31............	116	292
3............	74	86	32............	48	568
4............	19	68	33............	38	356
5............	44	139	34............	41	318
6............	114	142	35............	143	378
7............	127	191	36............	36	300
8a............	10	74	37............	35	382
8b............	93	309	38............	158	256
8c............	43	255	39............	17	85
9, 10........	5	63	40............	50	163
11............	9	108	41............	25	73
12, 13........	5	77	42............	51	105
14............	34	118	43............	28	65
15............	29	94	44............	20	126
16............	26	69	45, 47, 48......	13	150
17............	12	168	46............	54	191
18, 19........	32	129	49, 50........	34	125
20............	19	144	51, 52, 55......	42	250
21............	34	123	53, 54.........	26	167
22............	105	149	56, 57, 62, 64, 65..........	23	194
23............	64	135	58............	41	184
24a............	23	404	59............	24	196
24b............	45	331	60............	62	202
24c............	21	326	61............	114	234
24d............	154	338	63............	19	141
24e............	88	242	66, 70........	23	112
25............	77	101	67............	58	157
26............	32	100	68............	91	155
27............	51	122	69............	38	103
28a............	98	554	71............	20	81
28b............	70	244	72, 73, 74, 75..	25	101
28c............	62	288			
28d............	29	199	City total.	3,447	....
28e............	67	349			
29............	109	170			

* Population base is the same as in Table 50.

TABLE 64

DISTRIBUTION OF CATATONIC SCHIZOPHRENIC CASES
AND RATES IN THE LOCAL COMMUNITIES
IN CHICAGO, 1922–31*

Community	No. of Cases	Rate	Community	No. of Cases	Rate
1	5	15	30	22	48
2	8	54	31	60	151
3	36	42	32	2	24
4	12	43	33	7	66
5	13	41	34	12	93
6	26	32	35	43	114
7	54	81	36	7	59
8a	2	15	37	3	33
8b	12	40	38	65	105
8c	27	160	39	2	10
9, 10	2	25	40	43	140
11	4	48	41	11	32
12, 13	4	62	42	28	57
14	18	62	43	18	42
15	16	52	44	5	31
16	22	58	45, 47, 48	2	23
17	3	42	46	20	71
18, 19	19	77	49, 50	20	74
20	8	61	51, 52, 55	13	77
21	14	51	53, 54	10	64
22	40	57	56, 57, 62, 64, 65	14	118
23	33	70	58	19	85
24a	6	105	59	4	33
24b	21	154	60	32	104
24c	9	140	61	47	97
24d	47	103	63	10	74
24e	36	99	66, 70	11	53
25	33	43	67	25	68
26	25	78	68	33	56
27	35	84	69	12	33
28a	10	57	71	10	40
28b	24	84	72, 73, 74, 75	10	40
28c	16	74			
28d	14	96			
28e	34	177	City total	1,360	....
29	52	81			

* Population base is the same as in Table 50.

TABLE 65

DISTRIBUTION OF ALCOHOLIC PSYCHOSES CASES AND
RATES IN THE LOCAL COMMUNITIES
IN CHICAGO, 1922–31*

Community	No. of Cases	Rate	Community	No. of Cases	Rate
1.............	4	12	30.............	25	55
2.............	2	13	31.............	111	280
3.............	29	34	32.............	29	343
4.............	6	21	33.............	32	299
5.............	20	63	34.............	37	286
6.............	41	51	35.............	72	191
7.............	77	116	36.............	17	142
8a............	4	30	37.............	22	240
8b............	47	156	38.............	64	104
8c............	43	255	39.............	10	50
9–10.........	....	....	40.............	22	72
11.............	5	60	41.............	6	17
12–13.........	1	15	42.............	10	21
14.............	5	17	43.............	8	19
15.............	10	33	44.............	7	44
16.............	15	40	45–47–48......	7	81
17.............	2	28	46.............	46	163
18–19.........	18	73	49–50.........	21	77
20.............	5	38	51–52–55......	19	113
21.............	13	47	53–54.........	19	122
22.............	62	88	56–57–62–64–		
23.............	22	46	65..........	10	84
24a............	23	404	58.............	28	126
24b............	52	382	59.............	25	204
24c............	11	171	60.............	61	199
24d............	113	248	61.............	111	228
24e............	30	83	63.............	6	44
25.............	30	40	66–70.........	12	58
26.............	18	56	67.............	24	65
27.............	29	69	68.............	28	48
28a............	98	554	69.............	10	27
28b............	37	129	71.............	11	44
28c............	52	241	72–73–74–75...	10	40
28d............	14	96			
28e............	55	286	City total.	1,930	....
29.............	17	26			

* Population base is the same as in Table 50.

TABLE 66

DISTRIBUTION OF DRUG ADDICTION (WITHOUT
PSYCHOSES) CASES AND RATES IN THE SUB-
COMMUNITIES IN CHICAGO, 1922–34*

Subcommunity	No. of Cases	Rate	Subcommunity	No. of Cases	Rate
1............	0	0.0	39............	6	1.7
2............	4	1.3	40............	2	0.9
3............	3	0.8	41............	3	1.4
4............	2	0.8	42............	1	0.5
5............	5	1.4	43............	1	0.4
6............	7	2.0	44............	2	0.6
7............	16	3.6	45............	4	0.9
8............	4	2.1	46............	5	1.5
9............	0	0.0	47............	3	1.0
10............	2	0.7	48............	3	2.9
11............	1	0.5	49............	4	2.9
12............	0	0.0	50............	1	0.3
13............	11	3.2	51............	2	0.8
14............	2	0.8	52............	3	1.2
15............	4	1.5	53............	2	0.8
16............	2	0.8	54............	3	0.9
17............	6	2.5	55............	0	0.0
18............	20	6.7	56............	1	0.3
19............	1	0.5	57............	2	0.9
20............	12	4.8	58............	8	2.4
21............	98	24.3	59............	6	2.0
22............	8	3.9	60............	3	2.4
23............	0	0.0	61............	104	37.6
24............	0	0.0	62............	32	10.6
25............	1	0.4	63............	7	2.4
26............	1	0.2	64............	2	0.7
27............	2	0.6	65............	0	0.0
28............	1	0.4	66............	2	0.8
29............	0	0.0	67............	4	0.8
30............	2	0.8	68............	4	1.1
31............	1	0.4	69............	0	0.0
32............	1	0.4	70............	0	0.0
33............	3	1.0	71............	2	0.8
34............	2	0.8	72............	2	0.6
35............	2	0.9	73............	3	1.2
36............	1	0.4	74............	66	68.2
37............	0	0.0	75............	58	48.7
38............	0	0.0	76............	8	5.4

* Population base is the same as in Table 57.

TABLE 66—*Continued*

Subcommunity	No. of Cases	Rate	Subcommunity	No. of Cases	Rate
77............	14	7.1	100..........	0	0.0
78............	7	1.9	101..........	0	0.0
79............	27	9.7	102..........	2	1.0
80............	4	2.0	103..........	4	1.8
81............	11	3.0	104..........	1	0.4
82............	14	5.1	105..........	1	0.4
83............	3	1.4	106..........	4	1.1
84............	4	1.2	107..........	0	0.0
85............	12	2.4	108..........	0	0.0
86............	9	2.6	109..........	2	0.7
87............	3	1.0	110..........	3	1.1
88............	6	1.9	111..........	0	0.0
89............	3	0.8	112..........	7	1.8
90............	4	1.6	113..........	1	0.4
91............	1	0.5	114..........	2	0.7
92............	7	1.9	115..........	4	1.5
93............	2	0.7	116..........	7	2.0
94............	0	0.0	117..........	6	3.8
95............	2	1.0	118..........	3	0.5
96............	2	0.6	119..........	2	0.7
97............	1	0.3	120..........	0	0.0
98............	0	0.0			
99............	3	1.1	City total.	772	....

TABLE 67

DISTRIBUTION OF GENERAL PARALYSIS CASES AND RATES IN THE LOCAL COMMUNITIES IN CHICAGO, 1922–31*

Community	No. of Cases	Rate	Community	No. of Cases	Rate
1	26	78	30	30	66
2	4	27	31	53	134
3	99	114	32	39	461
4	37	132	33	59	552
5	31	98	34	52	402
6	135	168	35	219	580
7	118	178	36	32	268
8a	7	52	37	32	350
8b	109	362	38	198	321
8c	42	249	39	24	120
9–10	3	38	40	63	205
11	11	132	41	26	75
12–13	4	62	42	88	181
14	28	97	43	32	75
15	31	101	44	6	38
16	48	127	45–47–48	10	115
17	7	98	46	19	67
18–19	22	89	49–50	17	63
20	12	91	51–52–55	15	89
21	38	137	53–54	17	109
22	72	102	56–57–62–64–		
23	43	91	65	11	91
24a	21	369	58	23	103
24b	21	154	59	14	115
24c	13	202	60	44	144
24d	73	160	61	52	107
24e	31	85	63	21	155
25	78	103	66–70	19	92
26	39	122	67	49	133
27	79	189	68	84	143
28a	111	628	69	33	89
28b	102	356	71	25	101
28c	62	288	72–73–74–75	23	93
28d	31	213			
28e	37	193	City total	3,106	....
29	52	81			

* Population base is the same as in Table 50.

TABLE 68

DISTRIBUTION OF SENILE PSYCHOSES CASES WITH
POPULATION AND RATES IN THE LOCAL COM-
MUNITIES IN CHICAGO, 1922–31

Community	No. of Cases	Population Age 65 and Over 1930	Rate	Community	No. of Cases	Population Age 65 and Over 1930	Rate
1......	14	2,525	6	31......	17	1,885	9
2......	4	1,453	3	32......	12	679	18
3......	23	6,501	4	33......	17	479	35
4......	9	2,406	4	34......	11	650	17
5......	10	2,735	4	35......	40	1,225	33
6......	44	6,125	7	36......	19	869	22
7......	51	4,520	11	37......	12	559	21
8a....	1	789	1	38......	42	1,822	23
8b.....	27	1,629	17	39......	13	1,807	7
8c.....	16	1,054	15	40......	21	998	21
9, 10...	2	850	2	41......	17	3,215	5
11......	4	604	7	42......	26	3,758	7
12, 13...	5	487	10	43......	13	3,806	3
14......	14	2,153	7	44......	1	1,276	1
15......	17	2,248	8	45, 47, 48	7	635	11
16......	17	2,980	6	46......	11	1,519	7
17......	4	399	10	49, 50...	12	1,926	6
18, 19...	9	1,806	5	51, 52, 55	5	841	6
20......	2	1,019	2	53, 54...	6	903	7
21......	12	1,919	6	56, 57, 62, 64,			
22......	40	5,368	7	65....	5	565	9
23......	20	3,243	6	58......	6	863	7
24a....	5	286	17	59......	3	742	4
24b.....	7	513	14	60......	27	1,770	15
24c.....	4	325	12	61......	24	2,385	10
24d.....	23	2,131	11	63......	4	662	6
24e.....	12	2,098	6	66, 70...	14	1,438	10
25......	32	6,471	5	67......	14	2,698	5
26......	17	2,372	7	68......	45	4,996	9
27......	23	2,728	8	69......	23	3,134	7
28a....	41	1,351	30	71......	11	2,404	5
28b.....	24	1,685	14	72, 73, 74, 75.	23	2,230	10
28c.....	19	1,217	17				
28d.....	10	656	15	City total	1,118	....	....
28e.....	17	927	18				
29......	26	3,902	7				
30......	12	2,247	5				

TABLE 69

DISTRIBUTION OF PSYCHOSES WITH ARTERIOSCLEROSIS CASES WITH POPULATION AND RATES IN THE SUBCOMMUNITIES IN CHICAGO, 1922–34

Subcommunity	No. of Cases	Population Age 45 and Over 1930×13	Rate	Subcommunity	No. of Cases	Population Age 45 and Over 1930×13	Rate
1.....	20	88,426	22.62	38.....	31	90,649	34.20
2.....	18	85,319	21.10	39.....	21	108,069	19.43
3.....	17	101,088	16.82	40.....	23	61,893	37.16
4.....	19	77,129	24.63	41.....	21	54,015	38.88
5.....	36	129,558	27.79	42.....	25	59,111	42.29
6.....	21	92,690	22.66	43.....	24	68,042	35.27
7.....	42	118,677	35.39	44.....	38	88,062	43.15
8.....	12	61,763	19.43	45.....	36	106,535	33.79
9.....	23	90,376	25.45	46.....	38	86,788	43.78
10.....	27	95,966	28.13	47.....	47	79,833	58.87
11.....	25	65,845	37.97	48.....	10	24,050	41.58
12.....	31	116,493	26.61	49.....	23	34,736	66.21
13.....	35	98,033	35.70	50.....	41	78,598	52.16
14.....	19	83,798	22.67	51.....	12	71,526	16.78
15.....	32	84,435	37.90	52.....	23	74,841	30.73
16.....	34	73,567	46.22	53.....	26	90,688	28.67
17.....	29	71,201	40.73	54.....	22	102,297	21.51
18.....	34	87,750	38.75	55.....	20	72,969	27.41
19.....	25	63,843	39.16	56.....	24	87,386	27.46
20.....	56	75,777	73.90	57.....	20	69,108	28.94
21.....	72	130,663	55.10	58.....	28	95,888	29.20
22.....	2	67,860	2.95	59.....	39	89,362	43.64
23.....	12	49,569	24.21	60.....	32	32,539	98.34
24.....	12	44,681	26.86	61.....	154	114,595	134.39
25.....	18	67,639	26.61	62.....	66	93,665	70.46
26.....	27	127,192	21.23	63.....	49	75,686	64.74
27.....	22	97,019	22.68	64.....	41	67,613	60.64
28.....	15	71,656	20.93	65.....	47	41,912	112.14
29.....	19	55,354	34.32	66.....	14	60,450	23.16
30.....	19	74,828	25.39	67.....	29	128,648	22.54
31.....	21	65,325	32.15	68.....	41	99,073	41.38
32.....	14	57,889	24.18	69.....	22	73,125	30.09
33.....	16	66,664	24.00	70.....	12	50,648	23.69
34.....	10	57,460	17.40	71.....	16	50,414	31.74
35.....	19	64,649	29.39	72.....	38	84,422	45.01
36.....	21	66,716	31.48	73.....	32	73,151	43.75
37.....	12	51,298	23.39	74.....	39	47,814	81.57

TABLE 69—*Continued*

Subcommunity	No. of Cases	Population Age 45 and Over 1930×13	Rate	Subcommunity	No. of Cases	Population Age 45 and Over 1930×13	Rate
75.....	41	38,064	107.71	100.....	16	38,142	41.95
76.....	18	39,559	45.50	101.....	14	48,906	28.63
77.....	63	52,013	121.12	102.....	20	48,126	41.56
78.....	84	85,566	98.17	103.....	26	60,138	43.23
79.....	42	98,917	42.46	104.....	29	68,146	42.56
80.....	53	56,875	93.19	105.....	17	47,372	35.89
81.....	54	67,405	80.11	106.....	53	95,719	55.37
82.....	65	56,030	116.01	107.....	22	73,541	29.92
83.....	21	40,430	51.94	108.....	18	66,027	27.26
84.....	21	126,984	16.54	109.....	13	78,143	16.64
85.....	80	108,394	73.80	110.....	32	79,469	40.27
86.....	35	115,531	30.29	111.....	25	99,073	25.23
87.....	39	103,389	37.72	112.....	45	125,515	35.85
88.....	25	105,781	23.63	113.....	14	71,175	19.67
89.....	13	118,300	10.99	114.....	29	98,267	29.51
90.....	8	83,616	9.57	115.....	24	84,773	28.31
91.....	7	60,307	11.61	116.....	33	109,889	30.03
92.....	19	97,149	19.56	117.....	18	40,352	44.61
93.....	15	65,455	22.92	118.....	31	158,613	19.54
94.....	16	55,029	29.08	119.....	27	94,146	28.68
95.....	10	52,039	19.22	120.....	8	54,119	14.78
96.....	18	94,276	19.09				
97.....	19	92,820	20.47	City total	3,432	9,344,647	36.73
98.....	18	67,106	26.82				
99.....	24	57,564	41.69				

TABLE 70

DISTRIBUTION OF PARANOID SCHIZOPHRENIC CASES, AGES 15–29, WITH POPULATION AND RATES IN THE SUB-COMMUNITIES IN CHICAGO, 1922–34

Subcommunity	No. of Cases	Population Ages 15–29 1930×13	Rate	Subcommunity	No. of Cases	Population Ages 15–29 1930×13	Rate
1.....	1	101,426	1.0	39.....	5	130,208	3.8
2.....	......	110,422	......	40.....	1	89,518	1.1
3.....	4	117,559	3.4	41.....	4	89,310	4.5
4.....	4	78,208	5.1	42.....	......	69,238	......
5.....	3	105,742	2.8	43.....	4	104,897	3.8
6.....	3	130,013	2.3	44.....	5	130,572	3.8
7.....	11	166,127	6.6	45.....	9	186,329	4.8
8.....	3	64,480	4.7	46.....	11	135,603	8.1
9.....	1	98,124	1.0	47.....	4	122,512	3.3
10.....	1	88,712	1.1	48.....	3	43,927	6.8
11.....	4	74,802	5.4	49.....	9	52,780	17.1
12.....	6	116,181	5.2	50.....	9	140,920	6.4
13.....	9	117,325	7.7	51.....	3	84,903	3.5
14.....	5	85,605	5.8	52.....	7	85,397	8.2
15.....	3	95,654	3.1	53.....	8	86,840	9.2
16.....	6	101,400	5.9	54.....	5	121,576	4.1
17.....	9	88,426	10.2	55.....	7	93,470	7.5
18.....	6	100,971	5.9	56.....	11	114,595	9.6
19.....	1	73,788	1.4	57.....	7	81,484	8.6
20.....	7	95,407	7.3	58.....	6	133,627	4.5
21.....	18	128,947	14.0	59.....	3	118,027	2.5
22.....	1	63,154	1.6	60.....	2	50,583	4.0
23.....	2	55,107	3.6	61.....	17	64,558	26.3
24.....	3	65,689	4.6	62.....	12	114,621	10.5
25.....	3	85,917	3.5	63.....	7	122,109	5.7
26.....	12	171,119	7.0	64.....	6	115,640	5.2
27.....	4	128,050	3.1	65.....	4	80,054	5.0
28.....	4	95,810	4.2	66.....	6	106,080	5.7
29.....	4	71,799	5.6	67.....	17	218,140	8.0
30.....	3	86,450	3.5	68.....	13	155,155	8.4
31.....	2	85,670	2.3	69.....	5	117,741	4.3
32.....	2	87,009	2.3	70.....	1	86,996	1.2
33.....	5	126,230	4.0	71.....	3	104,754	2.9
34.....	3	84,721	3.5	72.....	10	141,297	7.1
35.....	6	86,021	7.0	73.....	9	91,169	9.9
36.....	5	105,105	4.8	74.....	7	19,162	36.5
37.....	5	78,078	6.4	75.....	5	42,848	11.7
38.....	3	113,373	2.7	76.....	1	57,460	1.7

TABLE 70—*Continued*

Subcommunity	No. of Cases	Population Ages 15–29 1930×13	Rate	Subcommunity	No. of Cases	Population Ages 15–29 1930×13	Rate
77.....	7	69,706	10.0	101.....	5	94,172	5.3
78.....	5	134,485	3.7	102.....	2	77,922	2.6
79.....	4	85,566	4.7	103.....	2	90,090	2.2
80.....	5	68,991	7.3	104.....	6	98,124	6.1
81.....	10	147,173	6.8	105.....	4	91,897	4.4
82.....	7	107,159	6.5	106.....	5	140,218	3.6
83.....	8	90,116	8.9	107.....	4	114,322	3.5
84.....	5	102,635	4.9	108.....	3	118,573	2.5
85.....	10	200,213	5.0	109.....	4	114,790	3.5
86.....	6	123,110	4.9	110.....	6	102,713	5.8
87.....	4	104,234	3.8	111.....	4	122,785	3.3
88.....	6	103,885	5.7	112.....	7	142,992	4.9
89.....	3	123,331	2.4	113.....	3	78,676	3.8
90.....	1	79,729	1.3	114.....	......	97,019	......
91.....	......	70,928	......	115.....	2	83,733	2.4
92.....	4	123,526	3.2	116.....	3	121,199	2.5
93.....	3	106,496	2.8	117.....	3	58,422	5.1
94.....	3	102,440	2.9	118.....	6	194,441	3.1
95.....	4	75,777	5.3	119.....	3	85,410	3.5
96.....	1	129,051	0.8	120.....	3	72,618	4.1
97.....	7	141,336	5.0				
98.....	7	104,130	6.7	City total	607	....	......
99.....	3	104,819	2.9				
100.....	1	79,456	1.3				

TABLE 71

DISTRIBUTION OF PARANOID SCHIZOPHRENIC CASES, AGES 30–64, WITH POPULATION AND RATES IN THE SUB-COMMUNITIES IN CHICAGO, 1922–34

Subcom-munity	No. of Cases	Population Ages 30–64 1930✕13	Rate	Subcom-munity	No. of Cases	Population Ages 30–64 1930✕13	Rate
1.....	11	185,562	5.93	39.....	21	196,131	10.71
2.....	12	177,866	6.75	40.....	24	126,113	19.03
3.....	16	241,137	6.64	41.....	14	120,289	11.64
4.....	9	142,532	6.31	42.....	12	109,460	10.96
5.....	13	210,015	6.19	43.....	12	144,547	8.30
6....	25	198,965	12.57	44.....	19	180,479	10.53
7.....	28	250,731	11.17	45.....	34	238,303	14.27
8....	7	117,390	5.96	46.....	22	178,022	12.36
9....	15	172,276	8.71	47.....	28	169,741	16.50
10....	18	164,385	10.95	48.....	5	56,810	8.80
11....	8	123,578	6.47	49.....	19	77,610	24.48
12.....	23	207,259	11.10	50.....	35	207,142	16.90
13.....	27	204,815	13.18	51.....	7	162,422	4.31
14.....	7	174,447	4.01	52.....	15	144,456	10.38
15....	23	155,896	14.75	53.....	14	146.731	9.54
16....	22	145,535	15.12	54.....	16	193,115	8.29
17.....	26	139,646	18.62	55.....	15	142,272	10.54
18.....	28	182,494	15.34	56.....	18	168,896	10.66
19.....	20	114,556	17.46	57.....	20	120,432	16.61
20.....	34	141,284	24.07	58.....	22	186,628	11.79
21.....	73	253,162	28.84	59.....	15	168,116	8.92
22.....	17	131,300	12.95	60.....	11	71,981	15.28
23.....	2	111,930	1.79	61.....	92	192,309	47.84
24.....	7	110,786	6.32	62.....	38	170,820	22.25
25.....	11	154,726	7.11	63.....	28	152,932	18.31
26.....	28	254,995	10.98	64.....	29	140,348	20.66
27.....	19	218,101	8.71	65.....	18	101,530	17.73
28.....	13	145,054	8.96	66.....	8	134,927	5.93
29.....	6	107,575	5.58	67.....	15	238,472	6.29
30.....	11	141,570	7.77	68.....	20	184,301	10.85
31.....	6	136,461	4.40	69.....	20	152,256	13.14
32.....	14	148,941	9.40	70.....	10	113,516	8.81
33.....	6	173,108	3.47	71.....	15	128,336	11.69
34.....	11	141,349	7.78	72.....	30	193,232	15.53
35.....	17	132,769	12.80	73.....	35	147,758	23.69
36.....	11	147,654	7.45	74.....	49	68,809	71.21
37.....	11	109,278	10.07	75.....	23	70,135	32.79
38.....	17	172,939	9.83	76.....	7	85,228	8.21

TABLE 71—*Continued*

Subcommunity	No. of Cases	Population Ages 30–64 1930 × 13	Rate	Subcommunity	No. of Cases	Population Ages 30–64 1930 × 13	Rate
77.....	27	118,989	22.69	101.....	11	121,979	9.02
78.....	34	225,797	15.06	102.....	8	104,637	7.65
79.....	27	171,119	15.78	103.....	28	119,275	23.48
80.....	19	123,825	15.34	104.....	21	146,549	14.33
81.....	17	215,423	7.89	105.....	27	125,398	21.53
82.....	12	159,848	7.51	106.....	20	199,459	10.03
83.....	9	118,326	7.61	107.....	18	155,207	11.60
84.....	16	203,749	7.85	108.....	10	162,721	6.15
85.....	33	294,970	11.19	109.....	16	179,738	8.90
86.....	19	202,332	9.39	110.....	13	152,607	8.52
87.....	21	180,362	11.64	111.....	17	190,138	8.94
88.....	21	188,370	11.15	112.....	20	222,807	8.98
89.....	15	229,060	6.55	113.....	16	130,312	12.28
90.....	19	160,589	11.83	114.....	13	159,237	8.16
91.....	6	120,029	5.00	115.....	19	157,248	12.08
92.....	9	232,518	3.87	116.....	19	199,095	9.54
93.....	7	149,435	4.68	117.....	5	92,430	5.41
94.....	15	128,778	11.65	118.....	21	334,035	6.29
95.....	5	114,218	4.38	119.....	11	174,408	6.31
96.....	17	188,461	9.02	120.....	10	127,452	7.85
97.....	16	203,970	7.84				
98.....	16	140,283	11.41	City total	2,213	....	......
99.....	15	149,734	10.02				
100.....	8	101,647	7.87				

TABLE 72

DISTRIBUTION OF CATATONIC SCHIZOPHRENIC CASES,
AGES 15–29, AND RATES IN THE SUBCOMMUNITIES
IN CHICAGO, 1922–34*

Subcommunity	No. of Cases	Rate	Subcommunity	No. of Cases	Rate
1	5	4.9	39	6	4.6
2	7	6.3	40	6	6.7
3	5	4.3	41	8	9.0
4	5	6.4	42	3	4.3
5	6	5.7	43	13	12.4
6	9	6.9	44	19	14.6
7	13	7.8	45	23	12.3
8	4	6.2	46	18	13.3
9	6	6.1	47	20	16.3
10	8	9.0	48	3	6.8
11	9	12.0	49	7	13.3
12	1	0.9	50	19	13.5
13	3	2.4	51	2	2.4
14	2	2.3	52	5	5.9
15	8	8.4	53	7	8.1
16	7	6.9	54	4	3.3
17	8	9.1	55	9	9.6
18	10	9.9	56	14	12.2
19	7	9.5	57	12	14.7
20	24	25.2	58	10	7.5
21	9	7.0	59	22	18.6
22	2	3.2	60	12	23.7
23	2	3.6	61	13	20.1
24	2	3.0	62	9	7.9
25	9	10.5	63	23	18.8
26	14	8.2	64	12	10.4
27	8	6.3	65	27	33.7
28	8	8.4	66	9	8.5
29	5	7.0	67	34	15.6
30	3	3.5	68	35	22.6
31	7	8.2	69	10	8.5
32	4	4.6	70	3	3.5
33	9	7.1	71	4	3.8
34	3	3.5	72	15	10.6
35	7	8.1	73	16	17.6
36	5	4.8	74	......	......
37	10	12.8	75	4	9.3
38	2	1.8	76	5	8.7

* Population base is the same as in Table 70.

TABLE 72—*Continued*

Subcommunity	No. of Cases	Rate	Subcommunity	No. of Cases	Rate
77..........	17	24.4	100..........	5	6.3
78..........	25	18.6	101..........	13	13.8
79..........	5	5.8	102..........	5	6.4
80..........	16	23.2	103..........	11	12.2
81..........	28	19.0	104..........	12	12.2
82..........	18	16.8	105..........	5	5.4
83..........	5	5.6	106..........	14	10.0
84..........	5	4.9	107..........	13	11.4
85..........	40	20.0	108..........	8	6.8
86..........	9	7.3	109..........	4	3.5
87..........	12	11.5	110..........	9	8.8
88..........	8	7.6	111..........	11	9.0
89..........	12	9.7	112..........	16	11.2
90..........	5	6.3	113..........	5	6.4
91..........	3	4.2	114..........	4	4.1
92..........	6	4.9	115..........	3	3.6
93..........	14	13.2	116..........	6	5.0
94..........	10	9.8	117..........	3	5.1
95..........	2	2.6	118..........	9	4.6
96..........	8	6.2	119..........	6	7.0
97..........	16	11.3	120..........	4	5.5
98..........	10	9.6			
99..........	5	4.8	City total.	1,162	....

TABLE 73

DISTRIBUTION OF CATATONIC SCHIZOPHRENIC CASES, AGES
30-44, WITH POPULATION AND RATES IN THE SUB-
COMMUNITIES IN CHICAGO, 1922-34

Subcom- munity	No. of Cases	Population Ages 30-44 1930×13	Rate	Subcom- munity	No. of Cases	Population Ages 30-44 1930×13	Rate
1.....	1	114,205	0.88	39.....	7	112,450	6.22
2.....	3	108,303	2.77	40.....	6	77,363	7.76
3.....	6	158,938	3.78	41.....	9	77,337	11.64
4.....	5	82,680	6.05	42.....	3	63,503	4.72
5.....	3	109,980	2.73	43.....	8	88,712	9.02
6.....	5	122,330	4.09	44.....	11	109,213	10.07
7.....	7	153,712	4.55	45.....	13	150,319	8.65
8.....	....	68,237	....	46.....	5	107,471	4.65
9.....	3	100,568	2.98	47.....	14	103,493	13.53
10.....	1	88,790	1.13	48.....	9	36,985	24.33
11.....	6	72,917	8.23	49.....	11	48,360	22.75
12.....	9	116,207	7.74	50.....	14	140,036	10.00
13.....	5	125,463	3.99	51.....	4	103,025	3.88
14.....	2	105,518	1.90	52.....	10	85,254	11.73
15.....	7	92,092	7.60	53.....	7	76,986	9.10
16.....	10	87,802	11.39	54.....	5	111,592	4.48
17.....	5	82,784	6.04	55.....	2	83,941	2.38
18.....	8	110,071	7.27	56.....	11	98,384	11.18
19.....	9	63,973	14.07	57.....	4	65,286	6.13
20.....	10	179,209	12.62	58.....	4	109,278	3.66
21.....	9	143,676	6.26	59.....	8	95,680	8.36
22.....	1	73,697	1.36	60.....	8	44,434	18.00
23.....	1	76,111	1.31	61.....	9	97,604	9.22
24.....	4	73,957	5.41	62.....	5	95,108	5.26
25.....	4	98,826	4.10	63.....	4	89,830	4.45
26.....	7	150,384	4.65	64.....	6	86,229	6.96
27.....	7	137,098	5.11	65.....	4	66,573	6.01
28.....	6	86,606	6.93	66.....	3	85,293	3.52
29.....	3	63,076	4.76	67.....	8	131,322	6.09
30.....	5	82,290	6.08	68.....	6	101,810	5.89
31.....	7	83,473	8.39	69.....	13	91,364	14.23
32.....	4	101,866	3.93	70.....	3	71,682	4.19
33.....	7	116,727	6.00	71.....	2	86,086	2.32
34.....	2	93,457	2.14	72.....	26	121,238	21.45
35.....	1	75,367	1.33	73.....	17	86,684	19.61
36.....	4	95,004	4.21	74.....	4	29,822	13.41
37.....	1	68,861	1.45	75.....	5	38,298	13.06
38.....	11	103,480	10.63	76.....	4	52,442	7.63

TABLE 73—*Continued*

Subcom-munity	No. of Cases	Population Ages 30–44 1930×13	Rate	Subcom-munity	No. of Cases	Population Ages 30–44 1930×13	Rate
77.....	12	74,542	16.10	101.....	4	79,924	5.00
78.....	22	150,033	14.66	102.....	3	66,157	4.53
79.....	3	93,973	3.19	103.....	6	71,084	8.44
80.....	11	74,412	14.78	104.....	12	89,466	13.40
81.....	14	155,389	9.01	105.....	10	84,604	11.82
82.....	15	110,903	13.53	106.....	7	119,860	5.84
83.....	10	84,851	11.79	107.....	6	95,758	6.27
84.....	3	104,559	2.87	108.....	3	105,300	2.85
85.....	21	202,345	10.38	109.....	11	114,023	9.65
86.....	2	112,567	1.78	110.....	6	88,088	6.81
87.....	6	99,775	6.01	111.....	9	111,189	8.09
88.....	1	103,506	0.97	112.....	11	125,231	8.78
89.....	3	134,511	2.23	113.....	......	74,321	......
90.....	4	91,312	4.38	114.....	2	82,797	2.42
91.....	1	71,110	1.41	115.....	6	90,259	6.65
92.....	4	153,335	2.61	116.....	6	112,071	5.35
93.....	6	95,160	6.31	117.....	1	58,344	1.71
94.....	8	82,316	9.72	118.....	6	206,674	2.90
95.....	2	70,239	2.85	119.....	6	100,048	6.00
96.....	6	112,775	5.32	120.....	4	84,786	4.72
97.....	9	125,723	7.16				
98.....	6	84,292	7.12	City total	789	....	......
99.....	12	99,515	12.06				
100.....	8	67,873	11.79				

TABLE 74

PERCENTAGE OF FOREIGN-BORN POPULATION
BY AREAS BASED ON HOUSING

Areas	Percentage of Foreign-born*
Chicago total	20.05
1. Single home and two-flat, $50.00 and over	15.89
2. Single home and two-flat under $50.00	22.59
3. Two-flat and single home, $50.00 and over	19.82
4. Two-flat and single home under $50.00	23.29
5. Apartment-house (native-born)	17.20
6. Hotel and apartment-hotel	14.61
7. Apartment-house and two-flat	25.64
8. Apartment-house (foreign-born)	38.22
9. Apartment-house (Negro)	2.32
10. Tenement and rooming-house	27.44
11. Rooming-house	20.40

* From census data of the city of Chicago—January, 1934.

TABLE 75

PERCENTAGE OF RESTAURANTS BY CITY TELEPHONE DIRECTORY
CLASSIFICATION AND LICENSE DATA OF CHICAGO,
BY AREAS BASED ON HOUSING

		RESTAURANTS			
AREAS	JANUARY 1934 POPULATION	Total	Licensed	Listed in Directory (Not Licensed)	Rate No. Restaurants per 1,000 Population
Chicago total.............	3,258,528	4,176	2,233	1,943	1.28
1. Single home and two-flat, $50.00 and over....	430,692	233	143	90	0.54
2. Single home and two-flat under $50.00.......	220,543	152	61	91	0.69
3. Two-flat and single home, $50.00 and over..	237,879	175	74	101	0.74
4. Two-flat and single home under $50.00.....	588,394	474	241	233	0.81
5. Apartment-house (native-born).............	603,127	640	372	268	1.06
6. Hotel and apartment-hotel................	177,084	345	212	133	1.95
7. Apartment-house and two-flat..............	377,881	438	199	239	1.16
8. Apartment-house (foreign-born)............	152,858	139	76	63	0.91
9. Apartment house (Negro).................	232,298	295	173	122	1.27
10. Tenement and rooming-house...............	170,891	311	152	159	1.82
11. Rooming-house........	66,901	974	530	444	14.56

TABLE 76

MORTALITY RATES BY AREAS BASED ON HOUSING

Areas	Population 1930	Total Deaths 1928–32	Total Infant Deaths 1928–33	Crude Death-Rates 1928–32*	Infant Mortality Rates 1928–33† per 1,000 Live Births
1. Single home and two-flat, $50.00 and over........	419,875	16,897	1,736	8.05	45.82
2. Single home and two-flat under $50.00...........	221,584	9,059	1,192	8.18	54.69
3. Two-flat and single home, $50.00 and over........	241,376	10,683	864	8.85	44.55
4. Two-flat and single home under $50.00...........	613,481	30,189	3,524	9.84	58.13
5. Apartment-house (native-born).................	618,099	27,791	1,777	8.99	38.86
6. Hotel and apartment-hotel.................	188,306	9,010	471	9.57	43.77
7. Apartment-house and two-flat..............	402,113	20,825	2,530	10.36	61.07
8. Apartment-house (foreign-born).............	167,764	6,935	674	8.27	47.83
9. Apartment-house (Negro)	237,301	20,276	2,046	17.09	81.42
10. Tenement and rooming-house.................	188,188	12,135	1,389	12.90	68.67
11. Rooming-house........	77,811	7,655	612	19.68	133.25

* Rates are average deaths per year (1928–32) based on 1930 population.
† Rates are computed for 6-year combination of births and deaths—1928–33 inclusive.

TABLE 77

PERCENTAGE OF SINGLE HOMES BY AREAS BASED ON HOUSING

Areas	Total Dwellings January 1934	Single Dwellings January 1934	Per Cent
Chicago total............	832,291	164,385	19.75
1. Single home and two-flat, $50.00 and over................	108,733	51,380	47.25
2. Single home and two-flat under $50.00................	51,396	28,872	56.18
3. Two-flat and single home, $50.00 and over................	63,107	14,807	23.46
4. Two-flat and single home under $50.00................	143,419	27,847	19.42
5. Apartment-house (native-born) ...	174,434	17,747	10.17
6. Hotel and apartment-hotel........	58,460	2,935	5.02
7. Apartment-house and two-flat....	92,753	10,746	11.59
8. Apartment-house (foreign-born)....	34,376	1,823	5.30
9. Apartment-house (Negro).........	52,874	4,410	8.34
10. Tenement and rooming-house.....	42,332	3,156	7.46
11. Rooming-house................	10,407	662	6.36

TABLE 78

PERCENTAGE OF HOMES OWNED BY AREAS BASED ON HOUSING

Areas	Total Dwellings January 1934	Homes Owned January 1934	Per Cent
Chicago total...............	831,221*	242,713	29.20
1. Single home and two-flat, $50.00 and over........................	108,640	53,769	49.49
2. Single home and two-flat under $50.00........................	51,352	27,275	53.11
3. Two-flat and single home, $50.00 and over........................	63,023	23,711	37.62
4. Two-flat and single home under $50.00........................	143,300	53,527	37.35
5. Apartment-house (native-born)....	174,186	33,527	19.25
6. Hotel and apartment-hotel........	52,765	3,822	6.55
7. Apartment-house and two-flat.....	92,634	24,541	26.49
8. Apartment-house (foreign-born)....	34,363	7,577	22.05
9. Apartment-house (Negro).........	52,765	5,909	11.20
10. Tenement and rooming-house.....	42,258	8,268	19.57
11. Rooming-house.................	10,350	787	7.60

* This total does not include 1,070 dwellings, ownership status unknown.

TABLE 79

EDUCATIONAL RATES BY AREAS BASED ON HOUSING

AREAS	GRAND TOTAL	TOTAL WITH UNKNOWN DEDUCTED	GRADE COMPLETED									
			None and 1-4		5-8		9-12		13 and over		Unknown	
			Number	Per Cent	Number	Per Cent	Number	Per Cent	Number	Per Cent	Number	Per Cent
Chicago total	2,364,478	2,344,775	272,303	11.61	1,161,772	49.55	705,515	30.09	205,185	8.75	19,703	0.83
1. Single home and two-flat, $50.00 and over	302,539	300,470	18,694	6.22	154,121	51.29	102,600	34.15	25,055	8.34	2,069	0.68
2. Single home and two-flat under $50.00	144,836	144,457	19,076	13.21	80,774	55.92	38,742	26.82	5,865	4.06	379	0.26
3. Two-flat and single home, $50.00 and over	174,789	173,813	9,923	5.71	92,224	53.06	58,339	33.56	13,327	7.67	976	0.56
4. Two-flat and single home under $50.00	401,889	397,044	56,718	14.29	238,316	60.02	88,664	22.33	13,346	3.36	4,845	1.21
5. Apartment-house (native-born)	471,285	466,988	18,820	4.03	184,762	39.56	190,107	40.71	73,299	15.70	4,297	0.91

TABLE 79—*Continued*

AREAS	GRAND TOTAL	TOTAL WITH UNKNOWN DEDUCTED	GRADE COMPLETED									
			None and 1-4		5-8		9-12		13 and over		Unknown	
			Number	Per Cent	Number	Per Cent	Number	Per Cent	Number	Per Cent	Number	Per Cent
6. Hotel and apartment-hotel	153,508	151,316	2,715	1.79	47,298	31.26	67,092	44.34	34,211	22.61	2,192	1.43
7. Apartment-house and two-flat	256,309	255,039	50,372	19.75	135,086	52.97	56,773	22.26	12,808	5.02	1,270	0.50
8. Apartment-house (foreign-born)	106,980	106,642	30,075	28.20	43,256	40.56	26,659	25.00	6,652	6.24	338	0.32
9. Apartment-house (Negro)	175,143	174,037	28,560	16.41	92,882	53.37	43,150	24.79	9,445	5.43	1,106	0.63
10. Tenement and rooming-house	117,697	116,991	28,911	24.71	63,170	54.00	19,458	16.63	5,452	4.66	706	0.60
11. Rooming-house	59,503	57,978	8,439	14.56	29,883	51.54	13,931	24.03	5,725	9.87	1,525	2.56

TABLE 80

PERCENTAGE OF CHICAGO FAMILIES OWNING RADIOS
BY AREAS BASED ON HOUSING

AREAS	ALL FAMILIES	FAMILIES OWNING RADIO SETS	
		Number	Per Cent
Chicago total.....................	842,578	532,731	63
1. Single home and two-flat, $50.00 and over.........................	105,755	81,926	77
2. Single home and two-flat under $50.00.........................	50,922	32,754	64
3. Two-flat and single home, $50.00 and over.........................	64,001	48,170	75
4. Two-flat and single home under $50.00.........................	148,227	86,290	58
5. Apartment-house (native-born)....	174,046	132,044	76
6. Hotel and apartment-hotel........	52,797	35,856	68
7. Apartment-house and two-flat.....	97,197	50,536	52
8. Apartment-house (foreign-born)....	36,876	20,048	54
9. Apartment-house (Negro).........	55,771	24,235	43
10. Tenement and rooming-house......	44,958	16,874	38
11. Rooming-house.................	12,028	3,998	33

TABLE 81

SIGNIFICANCE OF DIFFERENCE BETWEEN FOREIGN-BORN
SCHIZOPHRENIC RATES FOR HOUSING AREAS
IN CHICAGO

Housing Areas	1	2	3	4	5	6	7	8	9	10
2	S									
3	N	N								
4	S	N	N							
5	N	S	N	S						
6	S	N	N	S	N					
7	S	S	S	S	S	S				
8	S	N	S	N	S	N	N			
9	S	S	S	S	S	S	S	S		
10	S	S	S	S	S	S	S	S	S	
11	S	S	S	S	S	S	S	S	N	S
Housing areas.	1	2	3	4	5	6	7	8	9	10

TABLE 82

SIGNIFICANCE OF DIFFERENCE BETWEEN MALE FOREIGN-BORN
SCHIZOPHRENIC RATES FOR HOUSING AREAS IN CHICAGO

Housing Areas	1	2	3	4	5	6	7	8	9	10
2	S									
3	N	N								
4	S	N	S							
5	N	S	N	S						
6	S	N	N	S	S					
7	S	S	S	S	S	N				
8	S	S	S	N	S	N	N			
9	S	S	S	S	S	S	S	S		
10	S	S	S	S	S	S	S	S	S	
11	S	S	S	S	S	S	S	S	N	S
Housing areas.	1	2	3	4	5	6	7	8	9	10

TABLE 83

SIGNIFICANCE OF DIFFERENCE BETWEEN FEMALE FOREIGN-BORN
SCHIZOPHRENIC RATES FOR HOUSING AREAS IN CHICAGO

Housing Areas										
2........	N									
3........	N	N								
4........	S	N	N							
5........	N	N	N	N						
6........	N	N	N	N	N					
7........	S	N	N	N	S	S				
8........	N	N	N	N	N	N	N			
9........	S	S	S	S	S	S	S	S		
10........	S	S	S	S	N	S	S	S	S	
11........	S	S	S	S	S	S	S	S	N	S
Housing areas.	1	2	3	4	5	6	7	8	9	10

TABLE 84

PERCENTAGE DISTRIBUTION OF MANIC-DEPRESSIVE PSYCHOSES BY
SEX ACCORDING TO MARITAL CONDITION, WITH COMPARA-
BLE DATA FROM THE CHICAGO POPULATION IN 1930

MARITAL CONDITION	MANIC-DEPRESSIVE PSYCHOSES						POPULATION 1930		
	Male		Female		Total		Male	Female	Total
	No.	Per Cent	No.	Per Cent	No.	Per Cent	Per Cent	Per Cent	Per Cent
Single..........	246	29.3	305	20.7	551	23.8	36.5	27.9	32.3
Married..........	377	44.9	645	43.9	1,022	44.2	58.0	59.2	58.6
Widowed.........	30	3.6	93	6.3	123	5.3	4.0	11.0	7.4
Divorced.........	24	2.7	30	2.0	54	2.4	1.3	1.8	1.6
Unknown........	162	19.3	399	27.1	561	24.3	0.2	0.1	0.1
Total........	839	100.0	1,472	100.0	2,311	100.0	100.0	100.0	100.0

TABLE 85

PERCENTAGE DISTRIBUTION OF SCHIZOPHRENICS BY TYPE
AND BY SEX, ACCORDING TO MARITAL
CONDITION, 1922–34

MARITAL CONDITION	PARANOID						HEBEPHRENIC					
	Male		Female		Total		Male		Female		Total	
	No.	Per Cent	No.	Per Cent	No.	Per Cent	No.	Per Cent	No.	Per Cent	No.	Per Cent
Single........	874	56.9	382	29.7	1,256	44.5	1,793	73.6	835	37.9	2,628	56.6
Married......	400	26.1	562	43.7	962	34.1	424	17.4	992	45.0	1,416	30.5
Widowed.....	35	2.3	98	7.6	133	4.7	42	1.7	107	4.9	149	3.2
Divorced.....	57	3.7	73	5.7	130	4.6	51	2.1	78	3.5	129	2.7
Unknown.....	169	11.0	170	13.3	339	12.1	125	5.2	193	8.7	318	7.0
Total....	1,535	100.0	1,285	100.0	2,820	100.0	2,435	100.0	2,205	100.0	4,640	100.0

	Catatonic						Simple, Other, and Unclassified					
Single........	593	68.2	358	33.1	951	48.8	361	60.7	157	27.6	518	44.5
Married......	188	21.6	531	49.1	719	36.9	61	10.3	133	23.4	194	16.7
Widowed.....	11	1.3	45	4.2	56	2.9	7	1.1	18	3.1	25	2.2
Divorced.....	10	1.2	15	1.4	25	1.3	10	1.7	8	1.4	18	1.5
Unknown.....	67	7.7	132	12.2	200	10.1	156	26.2	253	44.5	409	35.1
Total....	869	100.0	1,081	100.0	1,951	100.0	595	100.0	569	100.0	1,164	100.0

	Total					
Single........	3,621	66.6	1,732	33.7	5,353	50.6
Married......	1,073	19.7	2,218	43.2	3,291	31.1
Widowed.....	95	1.7	268	5.2	363	3.4
Divorced.....	128	2.4	174	3.4	302	2.9
Unknown.....	518	9.6	748	14.5	1,266	12.0
Total....	5,435	100.0	5,140	100.0	10,575	100.0

TABLE 86

RANK ORDER OF MEDIAN RENTALS FOR
MAJOR PSYCHOSES

Psychosis*	Median Rental†
All Types of Mental Disorder (P.H.)	$75.30
Manic-Depressive, Manic (P.H.)	75.00
Manic-Depressive, All Types (P.H.)	74.43
Manic-Depressive, Depressed (P.H.)	71.73
Psychoneuroses (A.)	68.25
Manic-Depressive, All Types (A.)	61.68
Manic-Depressive, Depressed (A.)	60.74
Manic-Depressive, Manic (A.)	60.31
Manic-Depressive, Manic (S.H.)	50.52
Manic-Depressive, All Types (S.H.)	43.44
General Paralysis (A.)	39.30
All Types of Mental Disorder (A.)	37.76
Schizophrenia, Paranoid (A.)	37.25
Manic-Depressive, Depressed (S.H.)	36.14
Epilepsy (A.)	36.02
Senile Psychoses and Arteriosclerosis (A.)	35.71
Schizophrenia, All Types (A.)	33.45
All Types of Mental Disorder (S.H.)	30.45
Schizophrenia, Hebephrenic (A.)	29.80
Schizophrenia, Catatonic (A.)	29.40
Alcoholic Psychoses (A.)	23.41

* S.H.—State Hospital Cases Only.

P.H.—Private Hospital Cases Only.

A.—Total cases from both state and private hospitals.

† The figure following each psychotic series indicates that one-half of the cases are in subcommunities where the rents are above this figure and one-half the cases are in subcommunities where the rents are below this figure.

TABLE 87

PERCENTAGE DISTRIBUTION OF 814 UNDIAGNOSED PSYCHOSES
BY SEX ACCORDING TO AGE AT COMMITMENT

Age	Male		Female		Total	
	No.	Per Cent	No.	Per Cent	No.	Per Cent
15–19.........	15	3.2	13	3.8	28	3.5
20–24.........	25	5.3	18	5.2	43	5.3
25–29.........	30	6.4	28	8.2	58	7.1
30–34.........	54	11.5	41	11.9	95	11.7
35–39.........	65	13.8	49	13.3	114	14.0
40–44.........	74	15.7	53	15.4	127	15.6
45–49.........	69	14.7	43	12.5	112	13.8
50–54.........	56	11.9	44	12.8	100	12.2
55–59.........	37	7.9	28	8.1	65	8.0
Over 60........	45	9.6	27	7.8	72	8.8
Total.......	470	100.0	344	100.0	814	100.0

TABLE 88

RATES FOR PARANOID AND HEBEPHRENIC TYPES OF SCHIZO-
PHRENIA BY NATIVITY AND RACE FOR CERTAIN
YEAR PERIODS

NATIVITY AND RACE	MALE			FEMALE			TOTAL		
	Cases	Population	Rate	Cases	Population	Rate	Cases	Population	Rate
Native white, native parentage									
1924	249	238,926	20.84	196	235,004	16.68	445	473,930	18.78
1929	244	283,353	21.52	262	278,928	23.48	506	562,281	22.50
1933	171	344,845	12.40	256	357,140	17.92	427	701,985	15.21
Native white, foreign or mixed parentage									
1924	518	364,904	28.39	392	394,911	19.85	910	759,814	23.95
1929	456	418,380	27.25	362	448,728	20.17	818	867,108	23.58
1933	276	432,448	15.96	281	451,937	15.55	557	884,385	15.75
Total native white									
1924	767	603,829	25.40	588	629,915	18.67	1,355	1,233,744	21.96
1929	700	701,733	24.94	624	727,656	21.44	1,324	1,429,389	23.16
1933	447	777,293	14.38	537	809,078	16.59	984	1,586,371	15.51
Foreign-born white									
1924	697	396,173	35.19	481	334,683	28.74	1,178	730,856	32.24
1929	520	401,606	32.37	485	338,956	35.77	1,005	740,562	33.93
1933	291	329,018	22.11	326	285,970	28.50	617	614,988	25.08
Total white*									
1924	1,532	1,000,002	30.64	1,117	964,598	23.16	2,649	1,964,600	26.97
1929	1,251	1,103,339	28.35	1,135	1,066,612	26.61	2,386	2,169,951	27.49
1933	760	1,106,311	17.17	895	1,095,048	20.44	1,655	2,201,359	18.80
Negro									
1924	140	64,875	43.16	111	63,338	35.05	251	128,213	39.15
1929	120	84,473	35.52	103	84,896	30.33	223	169,369	32.92
1933	85	87,774	24.21	108	91,735	29.43	193	179,509	26.88
Other races									
1924	22	7,170	61.37	5	2,048	48.83	27	9,218	58.58
1929	39	11,982	81.37	8	3,964	50.46	47	15,946	73.69
1933	21	9,308	56.40	8	3,648	54.83	29	12,956	55.96
Corrected total									
1924	1,694	1,072,048	31.60	1,233	1,029,984	23.94	2,927	2,102,032	27.85
1929	1,410	1,199,794	29.38	1,246	1,155,473	26.96	2,656	2,355,267	28.19
1933	866	1,203,393	17.99	1,011	1,190,431	21.23	1,877	2,393,824	19.60

* Includes "white of unknown parentage" and this accounts for corrected total figures.

TABLE 89

PERCENTAGE OF MANIC-DEPRESSIVE PSYCHOSES, MANIC TYPE,
PERCENTAGE OF MANIC-DEPRESSIVE PSYCHOSES, DEPRESSED
TYPE, AND PERCENTAGE OF THE POPULATION IN EACH FOURTH
OF THE 120 SUBCOMMUNITIES GROUPED ON THE BASIS OF THE
MAGNITUDE OF THE RATES

QUARTILE GROUPING	PERCENTAGE OF CASES IN EACH QUARTILE		PERCENTAGE OF POPULATION IN EACH QUARTILE	
	Manic-Depressive Manic	Manic-Depressive Depressed	Manic-Depressive Manic	Manic-Depressive Depressed
Fourth or upper..	26.8	29.1	25.5	25.5
Third...........	22.5	26.0	23.8	23.8
Second..........	30.1	23.7	25.5	25.5
First...........	20.6	21.2	25.2	25.2
Total.......	100.0	100.0	100.0	100.0

TABLE 90

PERCENTAGE OF MANIC-DEPRESSIVE PSYCHOSES, STATE HOSPITAL CASES, PERCENTAGE OF MANIC-DEPRESSIVE PSYCHOSES, PRIVATE HOSPITAL CASES, AND PERCENTAGE OF THE POPULATION IN EACH FOURTH OF THE 120 SUBCOMMUNITIES GROUPED ON THE BASIS OF THE MAGNITUDE OF THE RATES

QUARTILE GROUPING	PERCENTAGE OF CASES IN EACH QUARTILE		PERCENTAGE OF POPULATION IN EACH QUARTILE	
	State Hospital	Private Hospital	State Hospital	Private Hospital
Fourth or upper..	40.9	47.0	26.1	23.9
Third...........	29.4	32.2	29.1	30.6
Second.........	18.9	15.1	24.3	24.2
First...........	10.8	5.7	20.5	21.3
Total......	100.0	100.0	100.0	100.0

TABLE 91

PERCENTAGE OF CATATONIC SCHIZOPHRENICS, 15–29 YEARS AND 30–44 YEARS, AND PERCENTAGE OF THE POPULATION IN EACH FOURTH OF THE 120 SUBCOMMUNITIES GROUPED ON THE BASIS OF THE MAGNITUDE OF THE RATES

QUARTILE GROUPING	PERCENTAGE OF CASES IN EACH QUARTILE		PERCENTAGE OF POPULATION IN EACH QUARTILE	
	Catatonic 15–29	Catatonic 30–44	Catatonic 15–29	Catatonic 30–44
Fourth or upper..	48.6	44.8	27.1	23.1
Third...........	25.5	27.9	25.5	25.4
Second.........	16.6	18.8	23.9	25.8
First...........	9.3	8.5	23.5	25.7
Total........	100.0	100.0	100.0	100.0

TABLE 92

PERCENTAGE DISTRIBUTION OF MANIC-DEPRESSIVE PSYCHOSES BY SEX ACCORDING TO NATIVITY AND RACE WITHIN EACH TYPE, 1922–34

NATIVITY AND RACE

TYPE	Native White of Native Parentage						Native White of Foreign or Mixed Parentage						Foreign-born White					
	Male		Female		Total		Male		Female		Total		Male		Female		Total	
	No.	Per Cent	No.	Per Cent	No.	Per Cent	No.	Per Cent	No.	Per Cent	No.	Per Cent	No.	Per Cent	No.	Per Cent	No.	Per Cent
Manic...........	91	27.9	171	30.2	262	29.4	102	31.3	164	29.0	266	29.8	84	25.8	167	29.5	251	28.1
Depressed.......	88	21.9	184	27.6	272	25.4	118	29.4	216	32.4	334	31.2	158	39.3	215	32.2	373	34.9
Mixed..........	9	36.0	39	55.7	48	50.5	1	4.0	12	17.1	13	13.7	11	44.0	18	25.7	29	30.5
Other..........	31	36.1	61	36.1	92	36.1	1	1.2	18	10.7	19	7.5	17	19.8	41	24.3	58	22.8
Total........	219	26.1	455	30.9	674	29.2	222	26.5	410	27.9	632	27.4	270	32.2	441	30.0	711	30.8

TABLE 92—*Continued*

NATIVITY AND RACE

TYPE	Negro						Other Races						Unknown					
	Male		Female		Total		Male		Female		Total		Male		Female		Total	
	No.	Per Cent	No.	Per Cent	No.	Per Cent	No.	Per Cent	No.	Per Cent	No.	Per Cent	No.	Per Cent	No.	Per Cent	No.	Per Cent
Manic	22	6.8	30	5.3	52	5.8	2	0.6	...	...	2	0.2	25	7.7	34	6.0	59	6.6
Depressed	10	2.5	8	1.2	18	1.7	1	0.3	1	0.2	2	0.2	27	6.7	43	6.5	70	6.6
Mixed	2	8.0	1	1.4	3	3.2	2	8.0	...	...	2	2.1	...	...	...	...	...	...
Other	2	2.3	1	0.6	3	1.2	1	1.2	1	0.6	2	0.8	34	39.5	47	27.8	81	31.8
Total	36	4.3	40	2.7	76	3.3	6	0.7	2	0.1	8	0.4	86	10.3	124	8.4	210	9.1

Total (All Classes)

TYPE	Male		Female		Total	
	No.	Per Cent	No.	Per Cent	No.	Per Cent
Manic	326	100.0	566	100.0	892	100.0
Depressed	402	100.0	667	100.0	1,069	100.0
Mixed	25	100.0	70	100.0	95	100.0
Other	86	100.0	169	100.0	255	100.0
Total	839	100.0	1,472	100.0	2,311	100.0

TABLE 93

DISTRIBUTION OF PERCENTAGES OF NEW HOUSES
IN CENSUS TRACTS IN PROVIDENCE,
RHODE ISLAND

Census Tract	Percentage of New Houses	Census Tract	Percentage of New Houses
1	0.73	26	12.59
2	0.54	27	2.10
3	2.58	28	30.72
4	3.73	29	18.90
5	8.20	30	15.60
6	8.18	31	29.41
7	8.55	32	36.23
8	7.03	33	71.94
9	10.65	34	3.00
10	21.46	35	5.85
11	25.58	36	0.65
12	27.93	37	60.61
13	20.08	38	28.90
14	21.19	39	68.97
15	40.65	40	16.67
16	47.85	41	21.83
17	14.60	42	0.58
18	2.51	43	6.61
19	1.54	44	14.01
20	15.92	45	34.36
21	1.09	46	12.63
22	27.93	47	54.05
23	20.04	48	67.57
24	2.12	49	57.47
25	3.40		

TABLE 94

DISTRIBUTION OF ALL CASES OF MENTAL DISORDER WITH POPULATION
AND RATES IN CENSUS TRACTS IN PROVIDENCE,
RHODE ISLAND, 1929–36

Census Tract	No. of Cases	Population 15 Yrs. and Over	Rate	Census Tract	No. of Cases	Population 15 Yrs. and Over	Rate
1........	130	8,370	193.7	27.......	36	4,921	91.5
2........	26	2,609	124.6	28.......	9	3,286	34.3
3........	35	4,680	93.5	29.......	34	5,750	73.9
4........	32	5,615	71.2	30.......	15	3,138	59.8
5........	17	2,763	76.9	31.......	4	1,050	47.6
6........	27	3,659	92.2	32.......	16	3,841	52.1
7........	23	3,640	79.0	33.......	16	3,295	60.8
8........	7	2,012	43.5	34.......	24	3,452	86.9
9........	37	6,623	71.8	35.......	32	5,354	74.7
10........	11	3,233	42.5	36.......	21	2,652	99.0
11........	5	2,530	24.8	37.......	15	4,347	43.1
12........	11	2,012	68.4	38.......	13	2,591	62.8
13........	16	3,608	55.4	39.......	4	2,039	24.5
14........	12	2,606	57.5	40.......	17	3,864	55.0
15........	11	2,852	48.2	41.......	13	3,263	49.8
16........	14	1,872	93.5	42.......	47	5,530	106.2
17........	16	3,068	65.2	43.......	19	5,415	43.9
18........	36	5,226	86.1	44.......	7	2,262	33.4
19........	31	4,464	86.8	45.......	4	3,604	13.9
20........	16	2,854	70.1	46.......	33	6,604	62.5
21........	17	3,639	58.4	47.......	12	3,026	49.6
22........	20	5,782	43.3	48.......	5	1,795	34.9
23........	16	3,674	54.4	49.......	7	2,832	30.9
24........	27	5,307	63.6				
25........	15	5,075	37.0				
26........	19	3,200	74.2	City total	1,030	......	......

TABLE 95

DISTRIBUTION OF SCHIZOPHRENIC CASES AND RATES IN
CENSUS TRACTS IN PROVIDENCE, RHODE
ISLAND, 1929–36*

Census Tract	No. of Cases	Rate	Census Tract	No. of Cases	Rate
1	30	44.8	27	11	28.0
2	9	43.2	28	3	11.4
3	14	37.4	29	8	17.4
4	9	20.0	30	2	8.0
5	3	13.6	31	1	11.9
6	8	27.3	32	5	16.3
7	5	17.1	33	3	11.4
8	2	12.4	34	5	18.1
9	12	22.6	35	13	30.4
10	3	11.6	36	7	32.3
11	3	14.9	37	3	8.6
12	4	24.5	38	7	33.9
13	5	17.4	39	2	12.3
14	3	14.4	40	5	16.1
15	4	17.5	41	5	19.1
16	2	13.4	42	15	34.1
17	5	20.4	43	4	9.3
18	7	16.8	44	1	5.5
19	10	28.0	45	2	6.9
20	3	13.1	46	12	22.8
21	8	27.5	47	5	20.6
22	5	10.8	48	0	0.0
23	3	10.3	49	4	17.6
24	12	28.3			
25	7	17.3			
26	2	7.9	City total	301	....

* Population base is the same as in Table 94.

APPENDIX C

SECOND SET OF CATATONIC SCHIZOPHRENIC RATES

TABLE 96*

DISTRIBUTION OF CATATONIC SCHIZOPHRENIC CASES WITH
POPULATION AND RATES IN THE LOCAL COMMUNI-
TIES IN CHICAGO, 1922–31

Community	No. of Cases	Population Ages 15–44 1930	Rate	Community	No. of Cases	Population Ages 15–44 1930	Rate
1	5	33,412	15	29	52	61,510	85
2	8	21,269	38	30	22	42,971	51
3	36	72,984	49	31	60	33,876	177
4	12	25,493	47	32	2	3,768	53
5	13	25,017	52	33	7	6,242	112
6	26	65,696	40	34	12	10,636	113
7	54	54,555	99	35	43	31,014	139
8a	2	10,527	19	36	7	8,234	85
8b	12	20,971	57	37	3	6,977	43
8c	27	13,432	201	38	65	57,351	113
9–10	2	9,886	20	39	2	15,346	13
11	4	10,742	37	40	43	28,165	153
12–13	4	8,343	48	41	11	26,725	41
14	18	30,599	59	42	28	37,635	74
15	16	34,428	46	43	18	43,917	41
16	22	36,366	60	44	5	20,315	25
17	3	9,986	30	45–47–48	2	10,737	19
18–19	19	36,784	52	46	20	29,724	67
20	8	12,876	62	49–50	20	26,200	76
21	14	26,696	52	51–52–55	13	16,447	79
22	40	61,003	66	53–54	10	15,177	66
23	33	43,549	76	56–57–62–64–65	14	15,718	89
24a	6	4,384	137	58	19	24,725	77
24b	21	12,232	172	59	4	11,083	36
24c	9	6,224	145	60	32	26,828	119
24d	47	41,236	114	61	47	44,192	106
24e	36	33,519	107	63	10	17,221	58
25	33	71,768	46	66–70	11	26,583	41
26	25	27,673	90	67	25	32,675	77
27	35	35,124	100	68	33	46,228	71
28a	10	10,067	99	69	12	31,419	38
28b	24	22,054	109	71	10	30,855	32
28c	16	17,936	89	72–73–74–75	10	23,666	42
28d	14	12,691	110				
28e	34	16,279	209				

* This table contains the second set of catatonic rates refined on the basis of the age distribution in the catatonic series. The coefficient of correlation between the first and second set of catatonic rates is .94 ± .01.

INDEX

INDEX

PHOENIX BOOKS
in Sociology

PHOENIX BOOKS
Education and Psychology

PHOENIX BOOKS
Reference

PHOENIX BOOKS
in Science

PHOENIX SCIENCE SERIES